ABOUT THE AUTHOR

Gerda van de Windt has a lifetime of art making experience and graduated with a Ph.D. in arts education and philosophy from Simon Fraser University in 2008. Her paintings and sculpture have been exhibited throughout Canada, the United States and Europe. Today, she combines both loves; art and philosophy, with authoring a series of historical novels based on the legends of Mary Magdalene and the Black Madonna that linger along the Mediterranean, especially in the south of France where she lived for a time.

ART

AND

PHILOSOPHY

GERDA
VAN DE WINDT

LIMITED EDITION PUBLISHING

Mission   British Columbia   Canada

Art and Philosophy   Gerda van de Windt

LIMITED EDITION PUBLISHING

Mission, BC, Canada

Gerda van de Windt, 1949 -

Art and Philosophy is a philosophical enquiry into the theory of the imagination and the nature of artistic creativity from a painter's perspective.

ISBN 978-1-927741-03-0

Philosophy
Art education
Psychology
Art history

CONTENT

ART

AND

PHILOSOPHY

INTRODUCTION

Artistic creativity is the basis of all learning. It requires releasing the imagination to make inner feelings that hide in the shadows of body memory visible in aesthetic form. Once these thought forms are made visible for all to see, they can be contemplated upon, and understood. Aesthetic form contains valuable information, both personal and cultural, knowledge not accessible in any other way.

However, this inner wisdom has been negated in the west for millennia. As early as the philosophy of Plato and Aristotle, the intellect has been favoured over intuition, yet today we know that both ways of knowing are necessary for holistic thinking. Over the centuries, this unnatural imbalance was perpetuated and came to full bloom with Descartes during the 17th century. The Cartesian mind-body split has haunted western thinking for millennia but imaginative engagement with aesthetic form can reconcile this mental split.

Sharing and enjoying a work of art reveals that despite many differences, there is a distinct universality to aesthetic experience. Art that expresses innerness makes the ineffable visible. By revealing inner sensibilities, aesthetic form preserves these ideas and brings them into the public domain. According to the philosopher Ludwig Wittgenstein, what cannot be spoken of in words must be left in silence. Yet I believe that aesthetic form goes far beyond mere words to express inner sensibility. Art across time and place has articulated inner wisdom in aesthetically pleasing form since anyone can remember.

Understanding meaningful artistic form has both personal and social relevance because art can articulate certain complex ideas that are difficult to express in words alone. However, aesthetic understanding requires activating the imagination to unify two distinctly different types of knowing so they can work better together. Kant's tried to rectify the Cartesian mind body split with an imaginative synthesis between inner sensibilities and the intellect. the mind requires the active imagination to unify intuitions under an intellectual concept. Kant, the first Western philosopher who grasped the complexity of the human mind, understood that aesthetic judgment requires the synthetic power of the imagination to bring harmonious unity between sensible intuition and the intellect.

For Kant, human rationality requires activating the imagination to bring intuitions under a general intellectual concept. He articulates a new understanding that was developed during modernity when artistic creativity increasingly became a form of visual thinking. Rather than realistic depictions of objects and people, during modernity artists began to look within for inspiration. Artistic creativity became a personal quest for greater self consciousness. During the Renaissance, some painters in Europe expressed how they perceived the world and art took on a new aesthetic language.

These paintings reveal a collective truth that far exceeds personal and cultural expression. The author, herself a painter looks at artists as diverse as Rembrandt, van Gogh, Kollwitz, and Kiefer and others who made art that transcend the sorrows of the human condition. In doing so, their work reveals a greater truth of *Being* and being human that opens up the possibility of authentic lived experience. Free by the invention of photography, painters increasingly searched within to find appropriate aesthetic form.

One after another, Impressionism, Expressionism, Cubism and other art movements challenge traditional Western art norms and values with paintings that capture the light in the fleeting moment. In brilliant landscapes, these artists tried to express the essence of their time before it was gone. As the Industrial Revolution devoured the land and wreaked havoc with people's lives, people left the security of family in search of jobs in the city. Some artists were inspired by the sorrow and solitude of the human condition and depict the urban poor in moving images that continue to fascinate to this day. But they were the exception.

With the advent of capitalism, European painting increasingly shows the wealthy new merchant class in exquisitely beautiful works of art still treasured today. Portraits of lusciously dressed people and paintings of the natural beauty of the land were in great demand by people who had money. No longer working as anonymous entities like before, artists could express their individuality. At the same time, art-making became a solitary endeavour, which led to the myth of the tragic artist.

Michelangelo, Rembrandt and van Gogh personified this cultural myth as the tragic hero, and their fascination with the disenfranchised became legendary. Their love for humanity shines through the painted surface with a mysterious sense of *Being* exposed. Authentic self expression in how they saw the world. That quality honestly and genuinely expressed. Emotions informed by lived experience that the artistic process manifests. Authenticity is recognized, not only with the rational mind, but also in the emotions we may experience when engaged with a work of art.

It is the function of art to give unique personal expression to this inner truth. For example, the painting *Run to the Light* (1988) shows emotions informed by inner wisdom that speaks silently of things I needed at the time. These subtle forms, revealed in the beauty of the paint, are an authentic expression of the ineffable.

This painting speaks of personal as well as universal ideas that underlie our cultural conditioning.

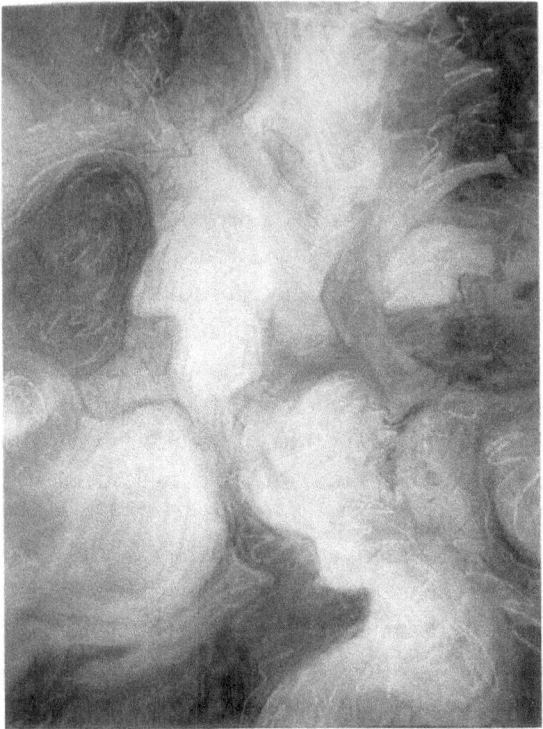

Run to the Light (1988)

Although aesthetic expression is often diverse across cultures, the truth that everyone has feelings and emotions is the common denominator among all living beings. This is universal, emotional truth that the artist strives to bring into being. It is *Being* exposed, yet by revealing one's innermost being, its truth is at the same time universal truth.

This particular painting was inspired by events in my own life and on a larger scale, the misery we hear about in other parts of the world. When the painting was finished, it seemed to suggest that although the times were often difficult, there was light at the end of the tunnel. This expression of inner sorrow inspired a quest for knowledge, artistic as well as intellectual, in the search for beauty and truth. Revelation of an inner wisdom that this painting gently speaks of was the affirmation so desperately needed at the time.

Looking at this painting, as well as many others so many years later, I remember exactly what I was feeling when this image came through me. The artwork has become the artefact for these feelings and holds them secure in time and space, for all to see. It speaks of inner sensibilities that most everyone is able to understand. This is the source of all original works of art, and each will be unique and different from any other work of art. Each work adds a new utterance to a new aesthetic language.

Some philosophers, such as Derrida and Lyotard, began to deconstruct the very essence of aesthetic language and the artist's search for self-consciousness. But some artists use their art making as a means to reach beyond the modernist search for the self to find a collective consciousness. These works of art are meant to be interpreted on many levels. In my own work, aesthetic form carries intuitive insight that provides knowledge I didn't previously have. Often the image displays a sense of humour that gently comes through that develops during the creative process.

As with the painting *Facing the Goddess Within (1988)*. This image makes reference to ancient goddess worship, yet the face is a painter's palette. At the time it was painted, I was steeped in Jungian psychology and search for who I am in relation to others. In a sense, the painter's palette reveals that this may be a self portrait of who I was then. For me, this inner knowing can only be found through the creative act of painting. Artistic creativity then becomes a dialogue with the medium. Colour and paint can illuminate the dark shadows that emerge in colour and form.

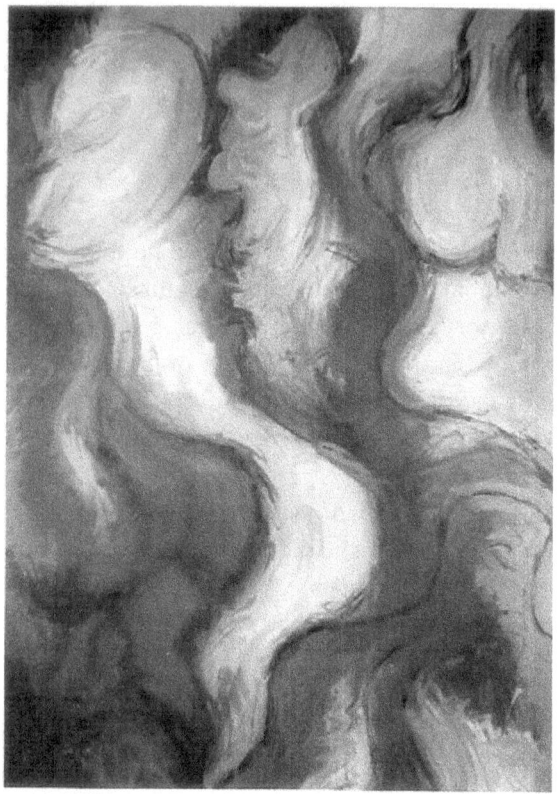

Facing the Goddess Within (1988)

By making innerness visible and open to interpretation, art does the work of exposing truth of being with a subtle and profound wisdom. Other artists such as Anselm Kiefer, Judy Chicago and Tracy Emin also make art to express who they are in relation to the world. Both personal and social concerns are expressed in a new aesthetic language. This 'subtler' language articulates important aesthetic ideas that link ethics and morality to artist creativity. But to understand the meaning behind a work of art requires tolerance, and an enlightened eye. With eyes that look with respect at what the artist has tried to communicate. To make an honest effort to grasp what a work of art truly means.

A work of art eloquently shows a personal view about social issues in a form that draws from the shadow of inner memories. Aesthetic form seems to suggest that there may be new possibilities for a better future for humanity but to understand these subtler ideas requires activating the imagination. When the imagination is free to play between intuition and the intellect, both artist and viewers discover that aesthetic form often contains profound levels of meaning. When the imagination is able to connect sensuous intuition under a concept, archetypal images seem to appear of their own accord in the mind.

It has been my experience that aesthetic form spontaneously appears during the creative process that often makes reference to mythology. This should come as no surprise. Art is the foundation for all knowledge. Since time began, a work of art has expressed who people really were as individuals. But a work of art also holds up a mirror to the culture. Therefore, aesthetic experience is a universal shared phenomenon, invaluable for fostering greater understanding of others and our place in the world.

ARTISTIC CREATIVITY AND INNERNESS

A work of art makes the ineffable visible, transforming sorrow into beauty and truth. Aesthetic form that makes inner feelings public invites viewers to share in the artist's search for self-discovery. This requires thoughtful and emotional participation, which is aided by the actively engaging the imagination. Then tragedy changes into truth. Both artist and viewer experience aesthetic delight. Wonder and awe when this essence is revealed in a great work of art.

Some artists throughout the ages have always made art that transcends the sorrows of the human condition. Rembrandt, van Gogh for example. These artists knew that making visible aesthetic truth opens up new creative possibilities. The words of Albert Hofstadlter, in his introduction to Martin Heidegger's *Poetry, Language, Thought,* are thoughtful and very moving. He writes that a work of "art bids all that is, world and things, earth and sky, divinities and mortals, to join in the simple one-foldedness of their intimate belonging; as beings living together, even with all our differences."

Artists as well as some philosophers know that aesthetic experience reconciles what is commonly known as the Cartesian mind-body split. Therefore, in my view participation with art is a human necessity. Participating emotionally to a work of art shows the value of difference as well as universality of self expression. The arts across time in most cultures shared this timeless idea of the unity of consciousness. Seeing beauty and form in a work of art develops empathy and respect, both for ourselves as well as for others.

The painting *Driving out the Demons (1988)* seems to communicate, in colour and line, the urgency of the inner search for aesthetic form. As this image shows, there is always a sense of fear as one approaches the shadow world of inner knowing that must be overcome.

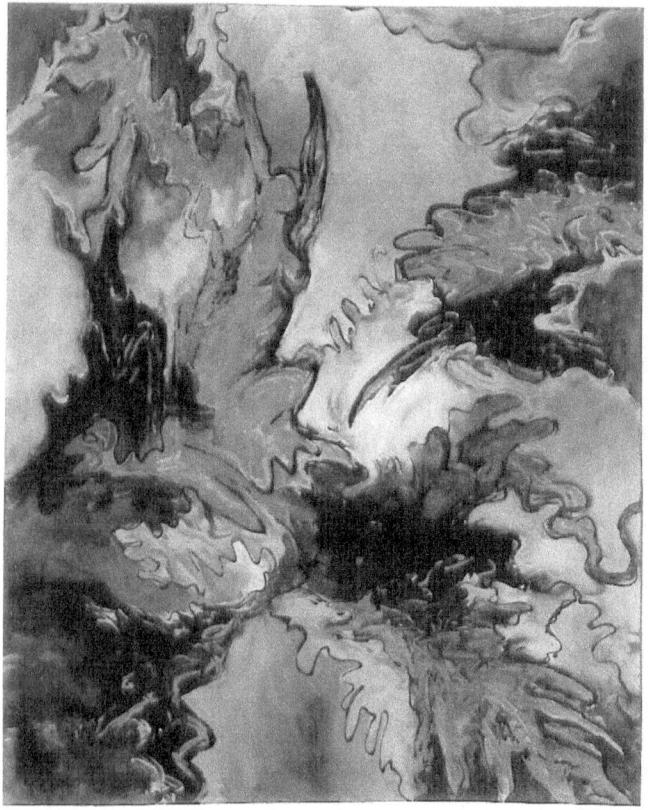

Driving out the Demons (1988)

This painting expresses the power of hidden archetypes that, when faced, become allies and no longer demonic forces. Aesthetic form speaks of truth that sorrow can be transformed by making innerness public. By exposing the shadows that hide within, they become the source of inner transformation. By making inner thoughts and feelings visible, artistic creativity is the means to transform painful memories into a beautiful work of art. Beauty, as in the pleasure of aesthetic experience the image gives both the artist and viewer.

A deep sense of satisfaction, as they engage in the experience of inner truth revealed. By 'truth' I mean honest and sincere recognition of being in harmony with the collective experience of *Being* and being human. Searching for inner truth often exposes subconscious archetypal images that have emotional and philosophic value for the artist as well as for viewers. In my experience, these forms often have a mythic origin. It seems the imagination is able to connect to a collective consciousness that is capable of transcending individual and cultural differences.

Imaginative engagement with a work of art reveals a subtler knowing that seems to come from within. This innerness guides aesthetic experience, if only we stop to listen to our inner voice. For the expressive painter, these archetypal images that emerge in the medium may suggest a myth or a story. These forms appear spontaneously from inner thoughts and feelings as the artist works. They tell a story not readily accessible to the intellect alone. These forms are intuitively grasped as inherent knowledge. Yet it may take time to fully comprehend them, as multiple layers of meaning unfold. I may be reading something years later that triggers a painting that was made twenty years ago. It always makes me smile when yet another bit of wisdom is revealed.

The work of the postmodern artist Anselm Kiefer was also heavily influenced by ancient mythology as well as Germanic folklore. Kiefer uses Greek mythology as a metaphor for the creative process. Prometheus, the hero who stole fire from the gods and gave it to humanity is like the postmodern painter. For Kiefer, fire is symbolic of the light of spirit, which becomes manifest during the creative process. The painting *Chilkat*

Dancers (1989) shows that this essence embodies aesthetic form, no matter which story inspired it.

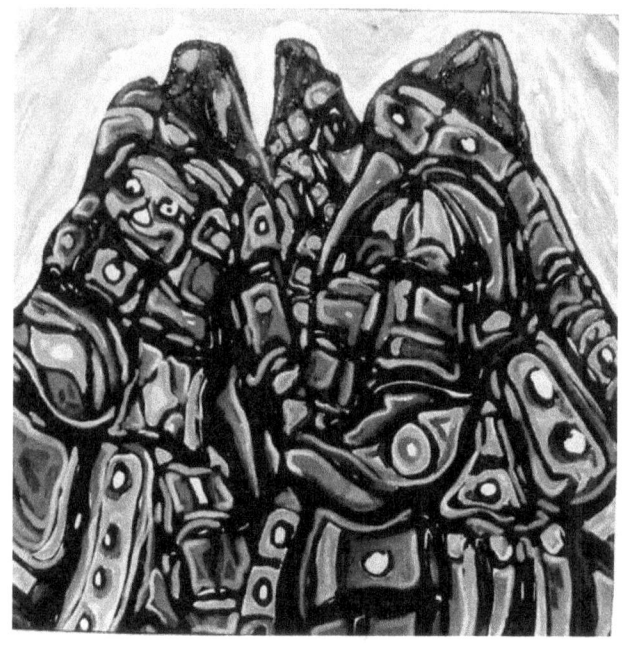

Chilkat Dancers (1989)

Heidegger said in *Being and Time* that a work of art reveals the 'truth of unveiled presence'. Unveiled presence, as innerness or knowing that transcends the body. Exposing unveiled presence goes beyond the senses, into a deeper stratum of consciousness. This innate wisdom seems connected to ancient primordial knowledge, in the sense of prehistoric awareness, suppressed and almost forgotten. Yet this inner wisdom has guided humanity for millennia, linking people securely to the natural world. People danced to celebrate the seasons with songs and stories throughout the year.

Chilkat Dancers makes reference to this innate connection between body and world that is often expressed in a dance or a song. Unveiling the intrinsic knowledge of emotional connection to our inner nature and environment in which we live. To some extent, primitive oral societies still retain the ability to connect innerness with ego intellect by imaginatively participating in their culture's rituals. Through the emotional participation in the arts, everyone knew their mythology by heart. In contemporary society however, western mythologies have all but vanished and the link between body and mind mostly lost.

So where did this split between intuition and intellect originate? That is difficult to discern but it seems to be related to the demise of indigenous oral cultures about twenty-five hundred years ago with the advent of the written word. It appears Greco-Roman philosophers were the precursors of the Cartesian mind-body split. Plato in *The Republic* argues that it is more important to educate using written facts rather than develop the intuitive wisdom of the body. Although developing logical thinking was probably a good thing, in the long run humanity may have lost more than it gained.

Descartes' philosophy echoes Plato's, for whom the world of ideas was a place apart from nature. Widely known as the 'father of modernism', Descartes famously declared, 'I think, therefore I am'. However, Cartesian dualism separated the material body from an immaterial mind, thereby effectively splitting the corporeal from the world of ideas. This discursive view held up a mirror to the culture in which he lived. With the advent of the industrial revolution, the connection between nature and intuitive inner wisdom was increasingly suppressed.

As people lost their affinity for nature and the land that sustained them, innerness became a distinctly different type of knowledge from the intellect. Over time, the artists became the keepers of this hidden knowledge and made it visible in aesthetic form. Perhaps Plato banished artists from his ideal Republic because he feared that unveiled presence of *Being*, would override the rationality of the intellect. Although his fears were unjustified, there is a kernel of truth in his fears.

For example, a painter may intentionally try to loosen intellectual control during the creative process. It seems necessary in order to override the rational need to judge and edit form as it appears. Authentic artistic creativity requires simply interacting with the medium and engaging in a reciprocal dialogue. This mental interaction exposes aesthetic form that connects to unveiled presence. Artistic creativity is a type of meditation that transcends the body. But it can be difficult to stop the nattering ego mind from interfering in the creative process.

Only later, when aesthetic form has been revealed, is the intellect invited to edit and interpret the meaning or message. These subtle ideas are often surprisingly accurate and express not only the artist's feelings but its meaning can also be grasped to some extent by others. Unfortunately, western culture has for the most part negated the inner wisdom, favouring the rational intellect. But that is just one part of consciousness, as many First Nations people still understand. The painting *Kwakuitl Sneezer Mask (1989)* illustrates. This painting is my interpretation of a sacred Kwakuitl mask, used by First Nations people during a ceremony to bring back the moon.

The image still amuses me because the face looks so ferocious until you read the title. A sneezer mask somehow doesn't seem as threatening. We can all relate, as our body reacts in the same way when we sneeze.

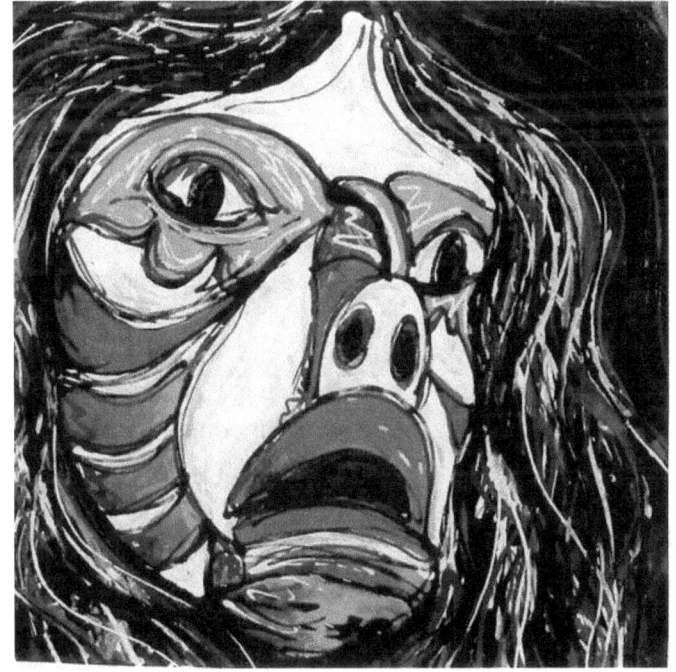

Kwakuitl Sneezer Mask (1989)

But there's more to this image. This mask represents part of Kwakuitl mythology. This mask was used to restore the moon. In a ceremony during the eclipse, Kwakuitl people danced around a smoking camp fire in an effort to make a sky creature who had swallowed the moon sneeze. They believed that by sneezing, the creature would disgorge it. And it worked, because the moon would always slowly return.

Aesthetic experience is awesome. One is filled with wonder at mythic images that are intuitively recognized and understood. We grasp the sincerity of what has been revealed on an affective as well as intellectual level. Bringing long forgotten memories into form goes beyond the pain long suppressed in body memory. As invisible and often troubling thoughts become public, feelings these aesthetic ideas bring up can be reflected upon and understood.

Genuine truth shines forth from the artwork itself. A work of art speaks a subtle yet powerful language that is, at least partially, understood by others. Time and again, archetypal images arise out of innerness. They seem to originate deep within the emotional shadows of body memory. Thoughts and feelings these archetypes evoke can be grasped, but only intuitively. One must be flexible and imagine a playful dialogue with form that appeared in the medium while also maintaining a strong base in reality.

An imaginative interaction between innerness and the intellect often throws valuable information out that is not available in any other way. The imagination naturally knows what needs to be expressed and will guide the creative process if given a chance. When one can relinquish ego control for a time, it becomes possible to access a deeply rooted source of inner wisdom that lies beneath consciousness.

The expressive artist soon discovers that there is an immense oceanic intelligence that waits patiently to be heard. As they search for self-expression and personal truth a vast and much larger truth is also revealed. This sense of profound inter-connectedness to everything in the world is a collective certainty that shows itself through shaping artistic form. This is universal truth that appears to have its roots in an ancient strata of the mind' a type of mythological knowledge that links the body to our ancestors as well as to all living beings on the planet. The painting *Of Gods and Men (1990)* is a good example of what I mean.

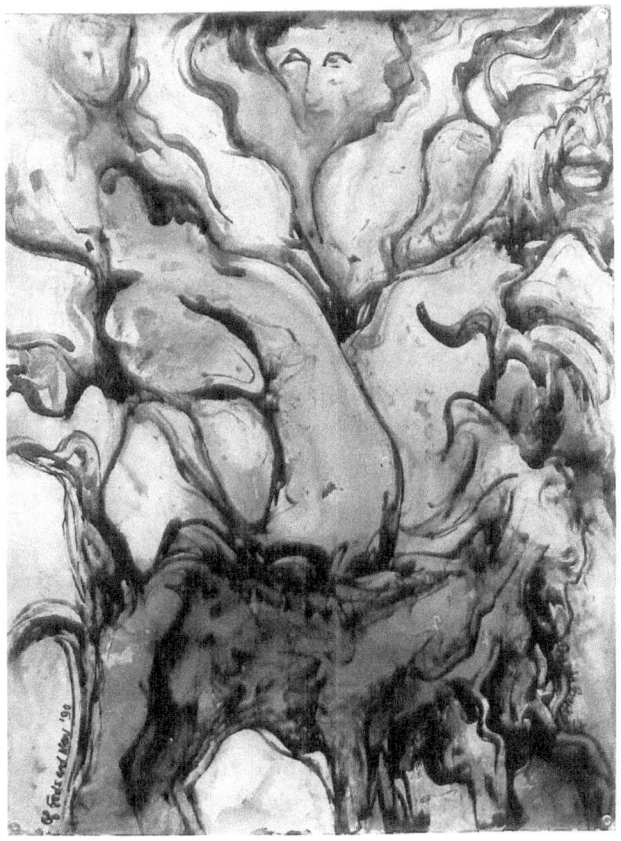

Of Gods and Men (1990)

Not only is this meta-awareness interconnective, but it is also outside time and space, enveloping past and future into the present moment. In my own work, mythical images come into being that I might not understand right away. Often titles that come to mind during the creative process hint at the meaning of form in a painting or sculpture.

Although one always has a sense of knowing what has been revealed, aesthetic form may have multiple meanings that only become more apparent over time. This painting is part of a series that explores the idea of creating out of chaos to reach inner emotional truth. The title came, like the most of the other paintings, before it was finished but at the time I didn't fully understand the meaning. Only a few days ago, twenty odd years later, did the title become clearer.

I was reading Plato's *Republic* where the phrase "of gods and heroes' occurs several times on the same page. Ironically, it's where Plato speaks of education, favouring intellectual rationality over intuitive wisdom of the body. It seems that the truth of *Being* and being in being in the world is still unfolding, and I like the layering of different connotations that the image brings to mind and to the heart. For me, a work of art richer is richer it can be understood on many different levels of experience. The images seem to be both archetypal and mythological yet they represent a very contemporary interpretation of innate and shared humanness.

As form becomes visible, art in whatever form it is, gives tremendous satisfaction that can heal the artist as well as the culture. In prehistoric times, artistic creativity was seen as sympathetic magic, to bring something that carried special emotional appeal into existence. By evoking archetypal, mythological symbols inside caves like Lascaux. Animals were painted on walls in the belief that these representations of the animal would allow them to be killed by the one who had given it form. Aesthetic form may vary from culture to culture, but not the inherent meaning of its symbolic language. Meaning, although culturally determined, exposes the truth of *Being*, shared by all human beings.

This profound sense of unity reveals itself in the artwork itself. In aesthetic form, the language of human emotion shared by everyone. Wittgenstein understood that art, ethics and moral principles were intimately entwined. He concludes that all philosophical problems arose from confusing the logic of language. It's telling that the last words of the *Tractatus* are: 'ethics and aesthetics are one and the same'. Great works of art have a genuine quality, unique to a specific person.

Aesthetic form is a sincere expression of their inner being. There is an acute sense of satisfaction when one discovers inner wisdom emerging out of beauty, be it stone, paint or the words of a poem. But there is always a price to pay. It is true that many artists have lived abysmal lives. Hardship seems to almost be a prerequisite for obtaining an enlightened eye. The consolation is that artists know that the drudge of daily existence can be transformed into a beautiful work of art. Art informed by a compassionate eye expresses a sublime beauty that provides tremendous and often timeless pleasure.

It takes courage to risk exposing one's inner sensibilities, but expressing it in aesthetic form is well rewarded. The act of creating aesthetic form involves revealing the archetypal memories that lie hidden in the shadows, patiently waiting to be brought into manifestation. The illumination of what was previously concealed in the dark and mysterious recesses of body memory, demands that ego mind steps aside. As form emerges from the medium; its message often has a transformative power both for the artist and the community as a whole.

Take for example, the painting *Epona (1992)*, which expresses the experience of freedom by depicting a nude female on the back of a great horse. Epona is the ancient Celtic warrior goddess who was worshipped for her fearlessness in battle. She is a metaphor of the struggle to be free. She represents the artist's need to escape into the creative process in order to discover hidden mythic and archetypal images that contain a message, for me and for others.

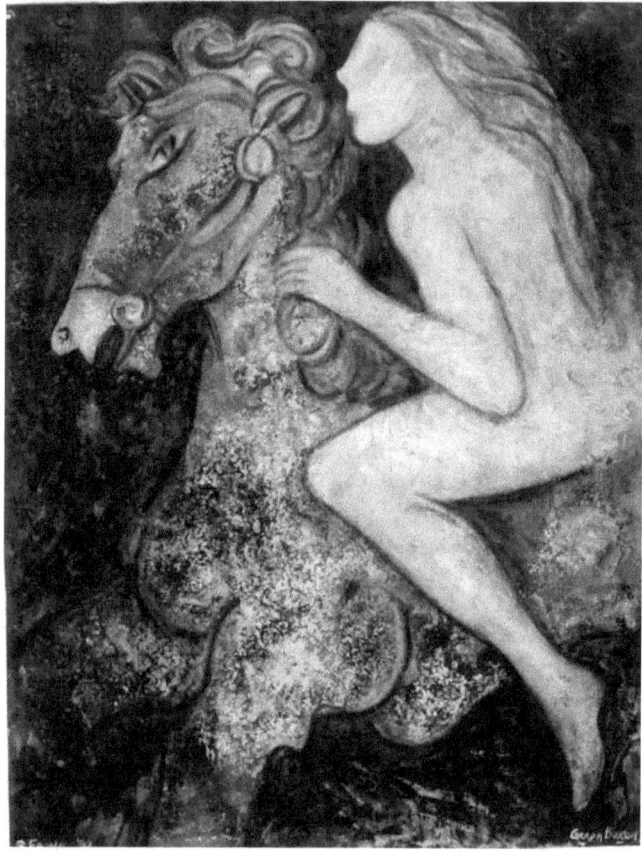

Epona (1992)

Epona is an example of a timeless symbol that gave me courage to go on, in an often mundane existence, to persevere in the face of all obstacles and live life to the fullest. Although not intended as a self-portrait, this image looks back at who I was then and shows that a battle had been won within myself.

This woman, sitting naked and proud on her warhorse, inspires me today. I like the sense of celebration this image now represents. She is a manifestation of a sometimes difficult journey through life, and the trials that must be faced and overcome by us all. By making innerness public, art reconciles the illusion that all life is sorrowful, as Schopenhauer puts it. Aesthetic form dispels the impression of separateness that is the sorrow of the human condition. Bringing forth aesthetic form requires that the artist responds naturally and intuitively to the quiet promptings of fleeting thoughts and emotions that resonate from within their being.

Disclosure of artistic innerness reveals *Being* and how that relates to being human. This disclosure of something greater than our selves is made visible. This knowledge is preserved in the artwork preserved for future generations. As one explores the subtle promptings of innerness that arise in the medium, intuitive responses resonate from within. Kiefer describes this process as perceiving as precisely as possible that which goes through the body and mind as a general template for what goes through others.

Art making has an 'opening of myself to me' sensation that is exhilarating. The art itself is but an imperfect artefact of this elevated and intensely connected meta-awareness that comes from the creative act. The sense of overwhelming joy that this aesthetic experience brings is a gift that speaks directly to the heart. Only later does the intellect get a chance to judge and perhaps edit the image to some extent but the concept must not be altered. Take the painting *Modern Ancients II (1988)* for example.

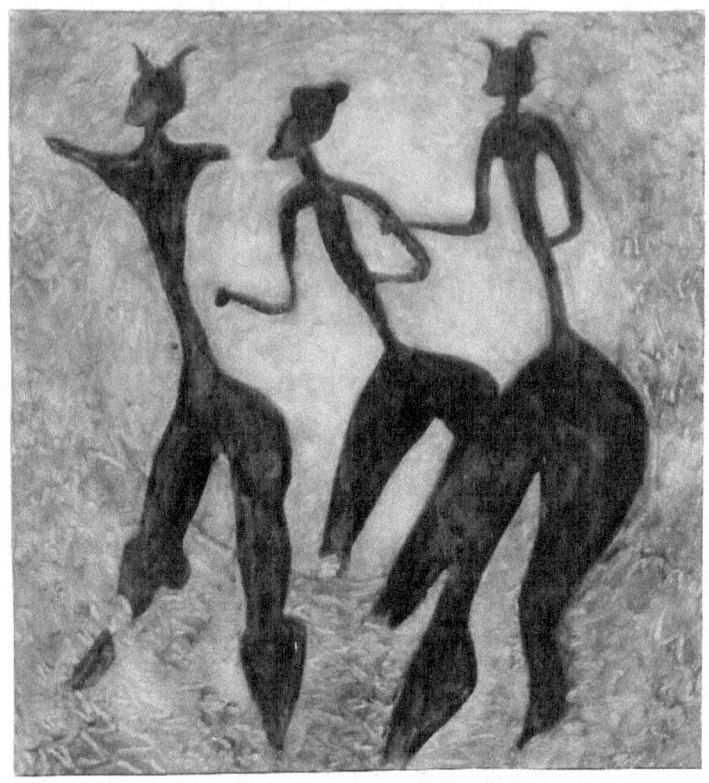

Modern Ancients II (1988)

This image was inspired by prehistoric rock painting in the Middle East. It depicts three female figures that seem somehow very modern. The figures are illuminated by a giant sun-like shape that speaks of the essential nature of the cosmos and our place in it. The women are masked, engaged in some sort of ritual play that animates them. The image presents a sense of lightness and fun. My paintings sometimes incorporate prehistoric archetypal form that holds special meaning for me, yet at the same time seem universal.

To change the essence of inner truth would negate the wisdom of body. Inner truth revealed may not always be pleasant, but seeing it expressed in a work of art is balm to the soul. Its power to heal can be almost overwhelming. Archetypal images brought to consciousness that initiate delight and wonder at what has been revealed often have value for others. If one stays true to what has been revealed, aesthetic form has a recognizable quality. Aesthetic sincerity speaks to the intellect as well as the heart. Then the aesthetic experience is reciprocal. Awe and wonder will be in harmony with the integral message that the artwork articulates.

These truths have been known for millennium. As these images emerge into consciousness, a strong sense of recognition was experienced. This sensibility indicates that I was on the right track as patterns and form shifted into ever deeper levels of meaning. Aesthetic form discloses that this seemingly finite and limited world is but an illusion. We are all part of the rhythms of life; and recurring theme of birth, death and rebirth. A genuine attempt to create art from inner sorrow requires solitude for inner reflection. The quest of seeking self revelation through the creative process requires silence because in quiet contemplation, greater truth is often found.

Silencing the discursive mind allows creativity to flow freely through the body and mind and into the particular artistic medium. Heidegger understood that the artist has to step over a threshold; a stillness that hovers beyond consciousness. The silence of being, in the world but not of it, inner truth is often found. Silent meditation reveals that we are all part of creation and natural cycles of birth, death and regeneration since time began. The painter, Vincent van Gogh's celebrates these eternal rhythms in nature in his paintings.

Intensely personal statements concerning the seasonal cycles and fluctuations of moods he recognized in the landscape as well as within himself. Without having to say a word, these paintings illustrate the powerful connection between inner feelings and the changing whims of nature. In a letter to his brother Vincent describes these powerful eternal rhythms as symphonic and the dramatic music of nature. For van Gogh, the act of painting transformed these natural rhythms and overwhelming emotions into a triumphant hymn to colour an allegro movement of line and aesthetic form.

Inspired by the suffering he saw in others as well as within himself, he discovered infinity and preserves this revelation in the paintings he left behind. Van Gogh believed that he owed the world something in return for his short and often difficult life. His paintings are his legacy to future generations. These paintings show that this planet is still a beautiful place, even when all too often it seems full of suffering. Vincent's paintings are a unique expression of authentic lived experience that celebrates nature and regeneration of the earth and its people.

By living an authentic life, this artist modelled for others how to live as the Eye-I of the World, as Schopenhauer put it. Heidegger refers to it as *Dasein*, to be present or to exist. He goes on to described *Dasein* as laying bare the horizon of being in order to understand *Being* in general. Being present in the world, for Heidegger, was a matter of carrying on an imaginative dialogue between *Being*, the infinite potential of whom we really are, and *being*, as in the temporal body, that which we appear to be. We recognize this truth on an ancient Greek vase or in a contemporary painting such as *Drawing Down the Moon (1989)*, which was inspired by an image on an ancient Greek vase.

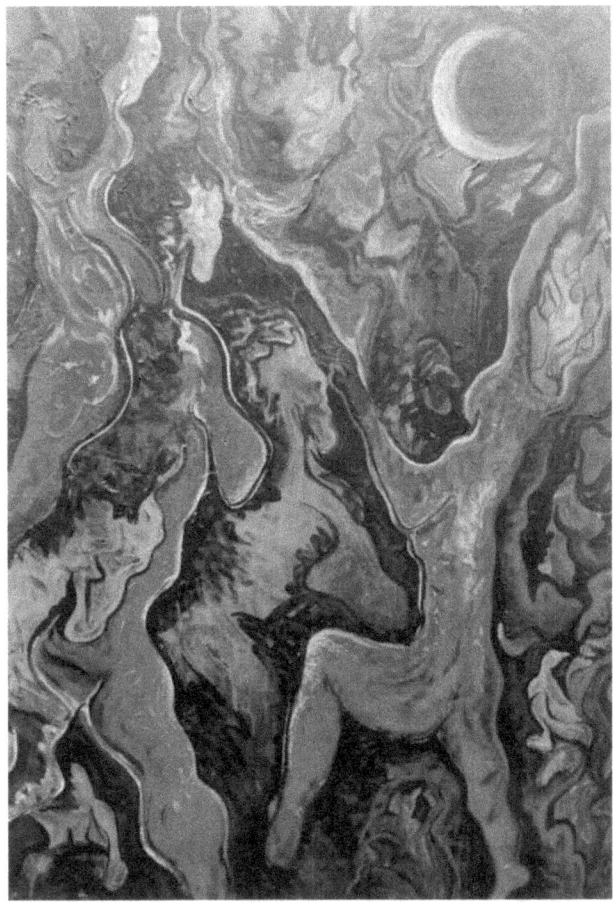

Drawing Down the Moon (1989)

A group of women dance in a circle, reaching for Diana, the moon goddess to draw her power down. As they move to the rhythms of the dance they unite both with her and the goddess within. As *Being* is revealed, they feel her empowerment. Drawing down the moon transforms the sorrows of the world into knowledge of infinity. There is an insurmountable tension between the finite and infinite that the imagination is able to bridge. But it is important to remember that people encounter and interact with each other and the world through being *in* body.

The body is both autonomous and a collective entity. As individuals we are unique from others yet at the same time we are but a part of all creation. In the body, each person is a unique eye on the world and their creative expressions of inwardness cannot be duplicated. Everyone is unique. There never was and never will be another quite like you or I. The simple yet profound fact is that each person has a unique vision that is their life's purpose to express. Finding that spark, that genius within is often difficult in today's fast paced society. Respect for the diversity and spark of genius that resides in us all must be fostered for it to flower.

But drawing down magic requires genius. Genius as the ancient Greeks thought of it; as the innate spark of divinity that is everyone's birthright. Genius resides within us all. It's that flicker of a larger sense of *Being* that guides us through corporeal existence. People intuitively recognize genius when they encounter it, often in a beautiful work of art. Our innermost being resonates to the truth of *Being* that lies exposed in a painting or the haunting refrains of a Gregorian chant. It is the artist's function to bring these aesthetic ideas into artistic form as best as they can, be it a dance, stone or painting.

To give a unique expression to *Being* and truth of being human that most will understand. And it's not an easy task. But I have found that if I start with absolute chaos as a starting point, aesthetic ideas come into form. This process can be compared to ink blot tests used to heal psychological wounds. The images do seem to have a transformative and healing effect. Aesthetic form seems to come from a collective consciousness that underlies everyday reality.

Although rich with meaning, bringing aesthetic form into consciousness involves vulnerability and risking exposure. Self revelation makes the ineffable visible. Showing the mystery of *Being* and essence of being human gives art its authenticity. When innerness has been brought into form, its authenticity is immediately recognized, not only by the intellect but more so by the emotional response to the artwork itself. Artistic form that takes shape from innerness speaks clearly of things that are needed at the time the artwork was made.

Aesthetic form manifests itself as secret knowledge. Inner wisdom comes out of the shadows of body memory and manifests during the creative process. Authentic self expression of the invisible speaks of personal as well as collective knowledge that underlies all cultural conditioning. Manifesting itself as hidden knowledge, aesthetic form develops during a reciprocal dialogue with the medium. Although the expression of innerness may differ across cultures, aesthetic experience reveals that everyone thinks, and has feelings and emotions very similar to our own.

Genuine self expression is a common denominator among all living beings. It is this all encompassing, emotional truth that artists strive to bring into form. It is *Being* exposed, yet by revealing one's innermost being, this truth at the same time, becomes universal truth. Many great artists have been inspired by inner emotions and suffering in their lives and on a larger scale, the misery they hear about in other parts of the world. But their art shows that although times may be difficult, there is always a light at the end of the tunnel. Bringing inner emotions into aesthetic form is the source of authentic art making. Each artistic expression of innerness will be unique and different from any other work of art.

Giving form to the invisible in a work of art makes innerness public and open to evaluation. Heidegger, in his eloquent engagement with van Gogh's painting of peasant shoes, observed that once art is in the public domain, aesthetic form must stand on its own and speaks for itself. He thought the artist was inconsequential compared to the art work itself, an idea ahead of his time. The idea that a work of art speaks an aesthetic language would become the anthem of postmodern philosophers such as Derrida and Lyotard.

Although it may be partially true, these philosophers negate the fact that a art is born from the heart and mind of a particular person. Aesthetic form would not exist if the artist had not brought their unique innerness into form. For the artist, the artwork remains as an imperfect souvenir of a sublime experience that penetrates the often sorrowful human condition. And in the process, aesthetic form reveals inner wisdom that cannot be discovered in any other way.

THAT 'SOMETHING ELSE'

If an artist was successful in projecting and disclosing their inner truth of *Being* into their work, it is instantly recognized as genius, that 'something else'. It shines forth from behind the work itself, no matter what medium the artist chooses. Arthur Koestler in *The Act of Creation* referred to this essence of art, in this case a painting, as being more than a pattern of pigment on canvas. The painting is a singular expression of 'something else' that is not just the canvas and a collection of colourful pigment. Art is much more than that.

True art does not imitate or copy, either from nature or from itself. For one thing, each art work will have its own individual style. And furthermore, a work of art is an invitation to partially share in another person's aesthetic experience by imaginatively seeing through their eyes. Aesthetic form invites viewers to participate in silence as the original manifestation of *Being* and being human unfolds. Self-disclosure of truth goes far beyond what is known. The person that the artist is lies open to view in its authenticity and as an invitation to share their unique vision.

This requires emotional involvement, a viewer who quietly experiences the exposure of *Being* and inner being in the art work itself. This spark of recognition at genuine self-expression can only be appreciated in silence. Aesthetic form speaks of the unspeakable. Heidegger visualized this silence as the rift or threshold both artist and viewer must step over to fully experience *Being* embedded in a work of art. It is in only silence and emotional engagement with the artwork that an opening of the rift between the world and the earth happens.

This happening of truth is where valuable insight into the human condition is often found. Underlying the daily sorrows of life is a profound inner peace. Knowing that the human condition is but an illusion does not mean an artist can ignore human suffering. Often in my own work, social and political statements seem to be embedded in the image, such as in the painting *The Longing* (1989).

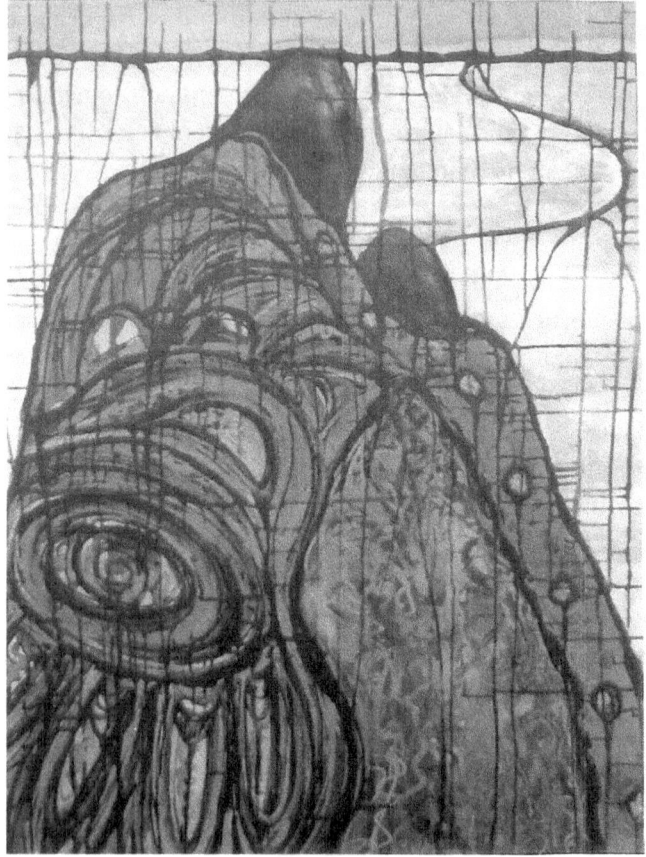

The Longing (1989)

This painting expresses a deep concern with land ownership issue of the indigenous First Nations in Canada. As colonization encroached on their land and their lives, the foundations of their culture were ripped out from beneath their feet. Often these people were separated from the lands of their ancestors. The ensuing social problems created much sorrow in their lives. Yet these people create great works of art that hold profound meaning both for the artist and culture. Aesthetic form transforms their despair and makes the underlying foundation of *Being* visible as a reference to the happening of truth.

Great art reveals the interconnected harmony of the universe. This revelation of truth transforms the sorrow of alienation into gratitude and joy. Vincent van Gogh observed that while he was painting the objects in nature, he was in touch with God. For Vincent, artistic creativity was the link between nature and the divine. He painted in order to console himself and humanity. This connective sense of our divine nature or *Dasein,* as Heidegger called the essence inner being, is facilitated by the connectivity of the imagination.

Kant proposed that activating the imagination is a cognitive necessity. For Kant, human reason requires an imaginative synthesis between inner sensibility and the intellect. As the arbitrator between oppositional ways of knowing, the imagination brings harmony to the mind. Imaginative synthesis is emotional engagement and a non-judgmental opening up, particularly to the meaning of aesthetic form. Totally abandoning to the artwork itself can facilitate the aesthetic experience that takes viewers out of everyday life and into a world that belongs to the imagination.

For example, to fully appreciate Rembrandt's portraits of his fellow citizens requires a conscious effort to see past the canvas to grasp the sentiment made visible in the texture and piercing beauty of the painted surface. The paintings speak silently of things that cannot be said in words. This exposure of *Being* and being human in art has an infinite quality, as past and future melt into the ever present moment. This meta-knowledge of being present in the moment is what Heidegger calls *Dasein*. For Heidegger, the infinity of *Being* and a human being's temporality did not lie beyond the horizons of ordinary time.

Dasein or the experience of *Being* happens in the body, here and now, being alive and aware in a particular time and place. He felt that the concealment of this earth's mystery could never be fully articulated because past and future are either slipping away into memory or projected somewhere else. But for Heidegger, a great work of art somehow can partially reveal the essence of *Being* and being human in a corporeal world. What Heidegger referred to as *Dasein*, Schopenhauer describes as the Ego-Eye, and Carl Jung calls the Self.

A transcendental part of being that he sees as the collective unconscious. For Jung, the Self is the collective, non-personal, transcendent part of human nature. The Self constitutes the single world-eye. This single world-eye or Ego-Eye holds the universe in its endless field of vision, and is limited only by the unseeing eye itself. This transcendental part of human nature resides in the shadows of inner sensibility. The sensuous and emotional body and can only be found by intuition and listening to our inner voice.

Although this elusive collective memory resides in the mists of innermost body awareness, artists may access this innate wisdom during the creative act. Through a reciprocal dialogue with the medium as it is worked, forms emerge, bringing long forgotten thoughts and feelings into manifestation. Inner truth of a collective consciousness becomes visible in the artwork itself. As images become visible in my own work, they often contain timeless references. *Music of the Spheres* (1989) expresses imaginary and cosmic innerness that makes reference to prehistoric, primordial origins of the universe.

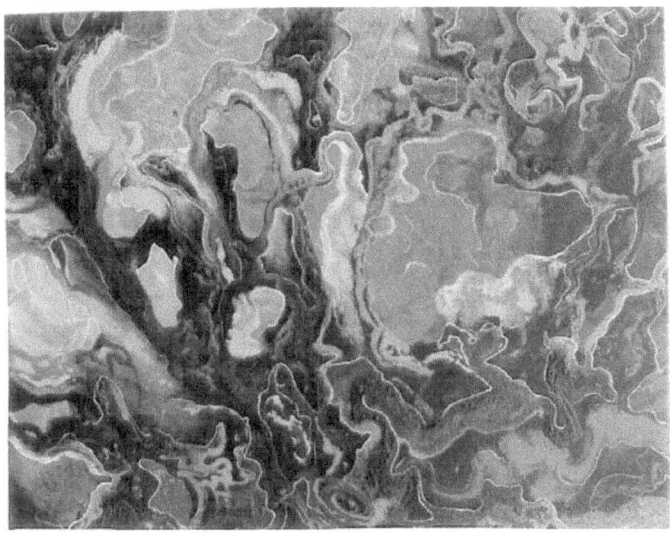

Music of the Spheres (1989)

Aesthetic form makes it possible to experience and render what being in the body, here and now really entails. As authentic innerness is revealed, its essence is intuitively understood by the artist and viewers alike. This revelation of truth confirms the existence of a monumental matrix of a shared reality that informs and underlies our mundane existence. It reveals that life is timeless and eternal, a half forgotten memory of our divine origins.

A greater sense of self lies hidden in the shadows of our inner being. For me, it is through the act of painting that this sense of interconnectedness of all that is can be discovered. Sometimes it is much later that a title can be verified. In literature or mythology and the meaning of what has been revealed in the artwork becomes clearer. For instance, the title *Harmony of the spheres (1989)* refers to precession. The cosmological cycle of

25,290 years it takes the earth to travel around the sun. For the Greeks, Apollo, the sun god was the god of music and truth. Pythagoras and Plato both taught that precession creates harmonics in the universe.

The Pythagorean theory of music and colour recognized that there was a relationship between beauty and harmony, both in art and in nature. The earth is beautiful in its own nature and good as it was created by god. Therefore good is harmonious with beauty and manifests itself in aesthetic form. This revelation transcends the sorrowful sense of separateness that many people experience. When they engage with their inner voice, they can share in this remembered inner wisdom. Like Friedrich Nietzsche's Dionysian, who saw the world with all its cruelties as merely benign entertainment.

If we are present in the moment, in the body, it is possible to experience the world as if anew; to really see what surrounds us with childlike wonder and awe. Perceiving the serenity that underlies the tragic-comedy of life gives people the courage to joyfully participate in the sorrows of the world. Then they understand that the illusion of separateness, from others as well as from nature, can be overcome. There is a rhythm to existence that imitates nature as people, things and events ebb and flow in and out of life.

Vincent van Gogh also believed in the cyclical nature of existence. He believed that instead of life being a flat and linear distance from birth to death, it was more probable that it was spherical and much more extensive and capacious than the hemisphere of life we know at present. Life would not be if there is no death, as the cycles of nature should have taught us long ago. To everything there is a season. Death follows birth, generation after generation. Our beingness is eternal as sure as the sun will come up tomorrow. This has always been so.

We see this truth in the paintings of Rembrandt that reflect his quest for the mystery of *Being* and the meaning of being human. Rendering innerness with a compassionate eye, he strove to depict the inner spirit of the people he painted, both in his religious paintings as well as in insightful self-portraits that trace the marks of time on his skin. In one of his rare surviving letters, he wrote that his overriding concern as a painter was to express the greatest inward emotion of the human soul. His portraits reveal the artist's calm and wise penetration to the essential character of the sitter.

The paintings are authentic expressions of *Being* and human nature that are still capable of stirring us today. The portraits in particular are powerfully sensitive character analyses of inner sensibility that has been given visible form. These images reveal what it meant to be living in Rembrandt's world at that particular time in history. They seem to be rooted in an ancient memory that taps into a collective consciousness. As artists search for self knowledge, a larger and more universal vision of humanity is often found that shows the infinity of *Being* and being human.

The postmodern German artist Anselm Kiefer also strove to understand the process of making intuitive sensibility, both personal and cultural, visible in his work, By going deep into inner awareness, his paintings and sculpture are a call to memory. Kathe Kollwitz, another German artist who survived two world wars, was also inspired by collective memories that hide in the recesses of body memory. The painting *A Ride with Raphael (1991-1992)*, is an expression of this inner spirit that guided me though a difficult time in my life.

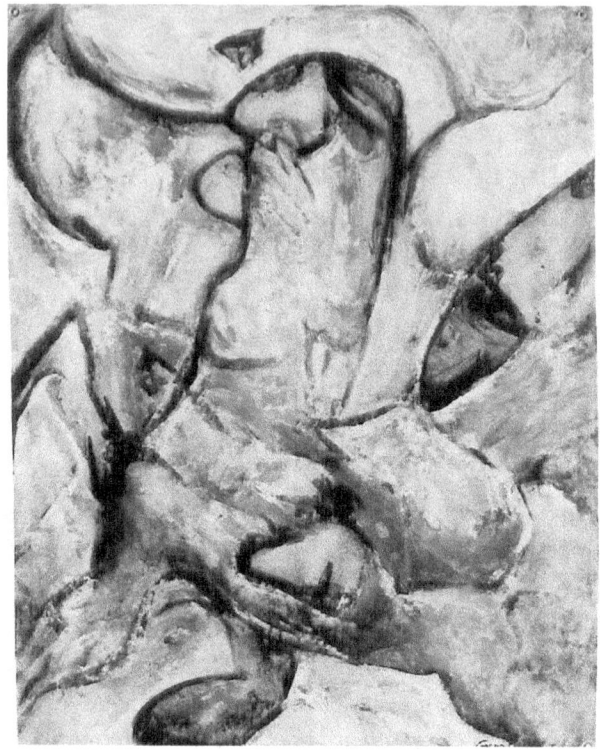

A Ride with Raphael (1991-1992)

Later, when I painted this image, I intuitively recognized its symbolic meaning in the forms that appeared. Distilling innerness to its simplest form, it gives outward expression to intensely emotional content for which there are no adequate words. The simplicity of the figures speaks eloquently of the a profound journey, which was intuitively understood. I saw myself being transported on a great white horse in the protective arms of the archangel Raphael.

This image was an aesthetic response to a transformative journey through the American south-west while my work was on exhibit in Phoenix Arizona. My marriage was in trouble and I had decided to take this time for some serious thinking about the future. It was a momentous time of self discovery and it seemed as if a guiding spirit was always there and could be relied upon during these troubled times. This painting still speaks to me of that time with great eloquence of the frightened woman I was then. It reminds me that we are not alone, but are part of all existence, even when we are far away from the people we love.

I also enjoy its Picasso-like fragmentation but the obvious reference to the female body is uniquely my own. As a postmodern artist, I believe strongly that women are equal and the female body is not just a titillating object of desire. This image echoes the ancient Greek dictum 'Know thyself' with all the courage that such a seemingly simple injunction demands. Often, the images found during the creative process carry multifaceted, intuitive information that offers greater insight into situations or thoughts that were lost to consciousness.

Often, a benevolent sense of amusement gently comes through, as form develops during the creative process. It's as if a greater Self guides our thoughts and feelings into a gentler place, reminding us not to take life too seriously. The hidden shadows and fears that may haunt us are but a benign illusion. By making inwardness open to appraisal and interpretation, aesthetic form does the work of exposing the truth of our inner being to ourselves. Sometimes it reveals innerness with a chuckle but always with subtle and profound wisdom.

In *Poetry, Language, Thought,* Heidegger used van Gogh's painting of peasant shoes to illustrate the idea of and being a particular human and how this concept has been embedded in a great work of art. In its simplicity, this powerful painting depicts a pair of shoes that silently articulates emotional content of the life of the peasant who had worn them. Vincent's sensitive treatment and careful observation of every nuance of these worn-out shoes is equalled only by Heidegger's poetic treatise.

Heidegger gives the reader a sense of being a peasant in the nineteenth century. His emotional visualization seems informed by a timeless collective memory, which is intuitively understood. Aesthetic form shows the reality of living in a peasant's world, in that time and place. The truth of *Being* and this human being's possible existence lies embedded in this painting. The painter has silently described the quality of her life, the truth of which can be intuitively understood by a reflective viewer.

With great insight, the philosopher describes the daily struggle of peasant life with all the suffering and hardship that was involved. But he also took note of small joys inherent in the beauty of nature and seasons of people's lives. The greater part of what it means to be human silently shines forth from beneath the painted surface as truth is revealed in a subtle yet unmistakable language that everyone understands. An aesthetic articulation informed by a meditative spirituality that touches the hearts of all who open their eyes to a deeper mystery.

An inner wisdom linked to metaphor and ancient mythology appears appear as if by itself in symbolic form that are intuitively recognized. Sometimes, these images may be interpreted as a timely warning such as the painting *Icarus* (1990) that metaphorically expresses the danger of flying too close to the sun.

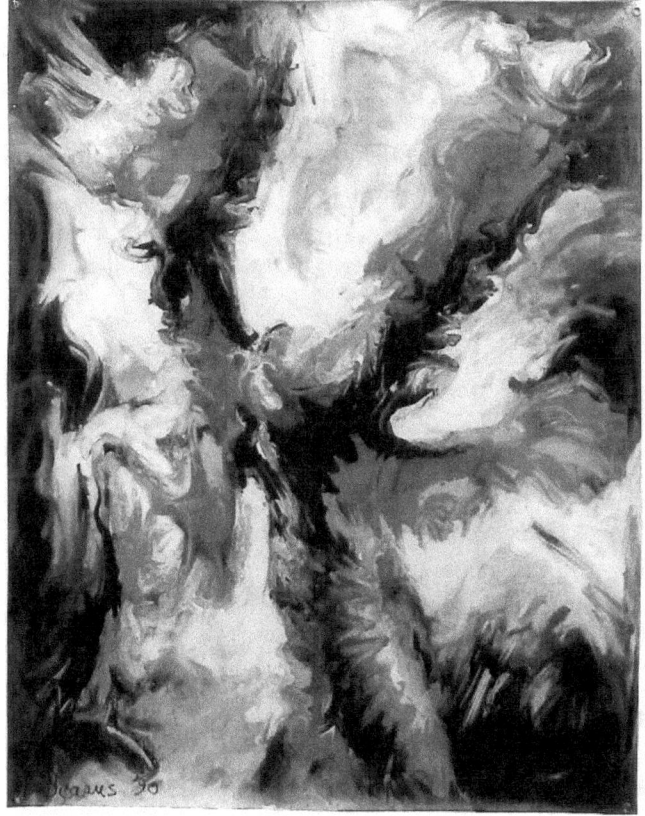

Icarus (1990)

Perhaps this image is symbolic of my own inner search that can become overwhelming and even dangerous if heart and mind are not in balance. This image seems to warn that searching for hidden truth has its perils and requires faith to continue the journey to the Self. The mythology behind this image was not familiar to me at the time it was painted but as often happens, the title popped into my head spontaneously when it was almost finished. Only later did I realize the significance of its message.

This image speaks in silence and warns of danger yet is full of cheerful energy. This painting seems to celebrate the inner shadows, transformed these memories into beauty, colour and gesture. Aesthetic form that brings to light an ancient truth that holds true today. Only later did I learn Kiefer around the same time it was painted also painted a powerful image of Icarus. It seems to me that these ideas come out a collective consciousness, which become accessible by going inward where hidden wisdom lies waiting to be tapped.

An expressive work of art speaks an aesthetic language that most people readily grasp as true. This subtle language has no a name but it strives to look inward with empathy while expressing a mysterious current that has a sublime quality of 'other' worldliness. This secretive and subtle language speaks of human dignity and the need to remember and listen to the inner wisdom of the body. Aesthetic form expresses this innate wisdom that reminds people of the privilege of their existence on this earth. But with that privilege come obligations to at least pay attention to the beauty that surrounds us all.

Authentic self- expression conceals and yet discloses the tangible and intangible in a synthesis of inner and outer worlds. Facilitated by the imagination, the artist's search for self-revelation and Being is made tangible by engaging with archetypal memories and emotions that are embedded within the subconscious part of the human mind. No matter what medium is used, artistic creativity may be viewed as a process of self discovery. The search for aesthetic form unearths hidden analogies or likenesses of sometimes ancient and long forgotten memories that rise to the surface of consciousness.

This process of discovery requires seeing through the subconscious mind's eye of the imagination. The imagination is subconscious in the sense that there is no clear differentiation between sensibility and the intellect but that a third field of vision is required to unite these two cognitive opposites. Through the process of creating a work of art, a cognitive synthesis is made possible between interlocking explorations of inner sensibility and conscious awareness, which is both verbal and visual.

This change of perceptual frame allows the creative artist to discover similarities and differences between forms that beg to be revealed. And this cognitive and affective process of self discovery often leads to a recognition of valuable knowledge. Grasping the infinite truth of *Being* may be accompanied by an 'aha' moment felt deep within the body. This moment of revelation can be described as a profound connection to the inner wisdom of the body. This sense of connectivity has a sense of oceanic wonder, which seems to transcend the self. This transcendental feeling of awe and wonder is at the root of the artist's quest for the ultimate reality of aesthetic experience.

While creatively inspired, and concern is focused entirely on the medium; be it colour, rhythm, or stone, the artist is led by the imagination on a personal quest for the sublime light of 'something else'. All that is required is the willingness to follow where the process leads and trust that the aesthetic illuminations that are found will be unique and the spark of *Being* will reveal itself. The scientist Albert Einstein spoke of the sensuous enchantment of this oceanic feeling when all the cognitive pieces suddenly fell into place. Einstein thought people were half dead if left unmoved by their capacity to wonder, calling this amazing sense of awesome wonder the emotional bond and common human denominator. The painting *Epiphany (1990)* articulates the experience of a sudden and striking realization.

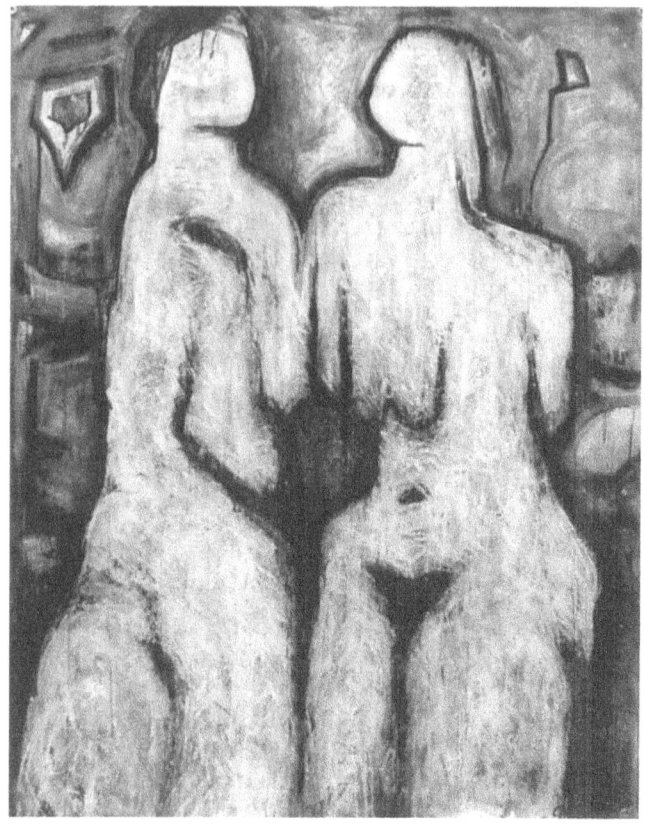

Epiphany (1991)

Although the term epiphany is often used to describe a scientific, or religious or philosophical breakthrough, it can also be applied to enlightenment or a deeper perspective. An epiphany occurs spontaneously, triggered by new information that fits with a priori knowledge. Often, it is experienced as a leap of understanding that transcends all what was known before. For the ancient Greeks, epiphany referred to a manifestation of the divine. It is still thought of today as a supernatural concept. Discovery comes suddenly, seemingly from outside, often sparking a reversal or change of heart. In pre-modern cultures where the audience understood the symbolic language, the arts and religious mystery rites served as vehicles for an epiphany.

But today it is a rare occurrence, usually experienced during the creative process after a long incubation period. And not every epiphany leads to a successful conclusion. Both scientists and artists must be willing to risk failure and it helps to approach the creative process with a playful and open mind, where elements of chance are seen as opportunities for inner discovery. This imaginative attitude seems to allow the unconscious processing of perceptions and buried memories to come into visual play.

This meta-awareness is similar to the dream state, which comes naturally to children and primitive people. But all too often, this state of attentiveness has been largely subdued in favour of intellectual rationality. But with inspiration as their guide, expressive artists temporarily disengage from time and everyday existence to commune creatively with their chosen medium. During this process of self-discovery, the artist searches for something that is at once familiar and yet unknown. That 'something else' that people intuitively recognize when they make the connections and the pieces find their place to display a larger story.

Many years later, van Gogh recognized that the fire of love is in every source of light, be it the stars in the heavens or sunlight reflecting on the foliage of a tree. His search for the spiritual light in people as well as nature gave the world magnificent paintings that continue to glow with the sublime light of *Being*. His paintings reveal his profound spiritual devotion as aesthetic form speaks of his love for humanity.

Kiefer on the other hand, found his inspiration in the sagas and Germanic mythology, especially the Nibelungen Ring that also inspired the great music of Wagner. But while Wagner celebrates the nationalistic mythologies of Germany, Kiefer aims at confronting the shame of German history and the atrocities that were committed during two world wars. Kiefer's encounter with his culture's mythology can be viewed as an act of personal and collective atonement as he courageously confronts the horrors of the Nazi past.

Kiefer's more recent paintings are inspired by the celestial light that shines in the primordial darkness. One of these massive paintings depicts a lonely stick-man who is lying beneath a myriad of stars that are sprinkled across the heavenly sphere. Kiefer paints the stars and natural cycles that unfold in a predestined pattern much like van Gogh did a century earlier. His poignant depiction of the illusion of man' isolation offers both artist and viewers the opportunity to be one with the universe as the imagination takes them on an inner journey of aesthetic remembering.

It was the plight of women and the urban poor that inspired Kathe Kollwitz to create images that celebrate the dignity of the people that came through her husband's infirmary. Empathy for the difficult life of women and children in Germany during the wars shows in their faces and bodily gestures. Kollwitz conveys a deep pathos, which is as poignant today as the day these images were created. These figures of emaciated humanity continue to inspire contemporary viewers to reconsider the consequences of war and poverty. In my work, aesthetic form may hold up a reproachful image that brings tears to my eyes. As in the painting *Ode to Gaia* (1990).

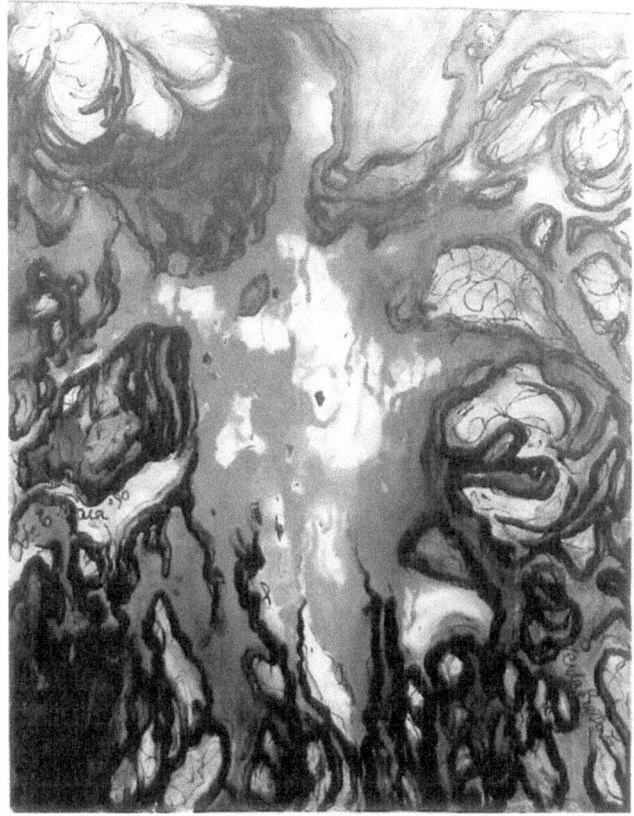

Ode to Gaia (1990)

This painting shows my affinity and emotional sympathy with the earth that sustains us. The damage that has been inflicted on our collective home; be it through war or globalization, has almost destroyed the atmosphere and is unprecedented in the known history of the world. The earth is represented as a combination of a woman's body and a tree that branches out across the canvas. The image expresses a profound concern with the future of our planet, yet celebrates the fecundity of the regeneration of nature, given half a chance. As Kiefer did a generation later, Kollwitz also makes art as an act of redemption. The light of *Being* shines bright from the figures in her art, speaking of things that cannot be said in words.

An expressive visual image is able to communicate the urgency of the artist's search for inner truth. But there is always a sense of fear as one approaches the shadow world of innerness, which must be overcome. There is a power behind these hidden archetypes that when faced, can becomes our allies and no longer will they be seen as demonic forces. Aesthetic form speak truthfully that sorrow can be transformed by making innerness public. By exposing the shadows within, these fleeting images become the source of transformational power. But it requires a childlike faith to believe that the creative process offers the possibility that expressing the sorrows of the world in a visual image contains aesthetic truth.

Yet the search for aesthetic form is the overriding objective of the artistic pursuit. Artistic creativity is an act of love that transcends the everyday world and leaves behind a work of art that others may enjoy and intuitive understand. As we face our inner demons, they are magically transformed and salvation is found. Salvation, not only for the artist but also for viewers who are able to respond to the spirit of *Being* in a work of art. This requires a self-reflective, analytical perspective and willingness to be open to seeing aesthetic truth as it materializes during the creative process.

As in the painting *Woman Waiting* (1991), which is symbolic of the renewal of our culture expressed in the female who is patiently waiting to be heard.

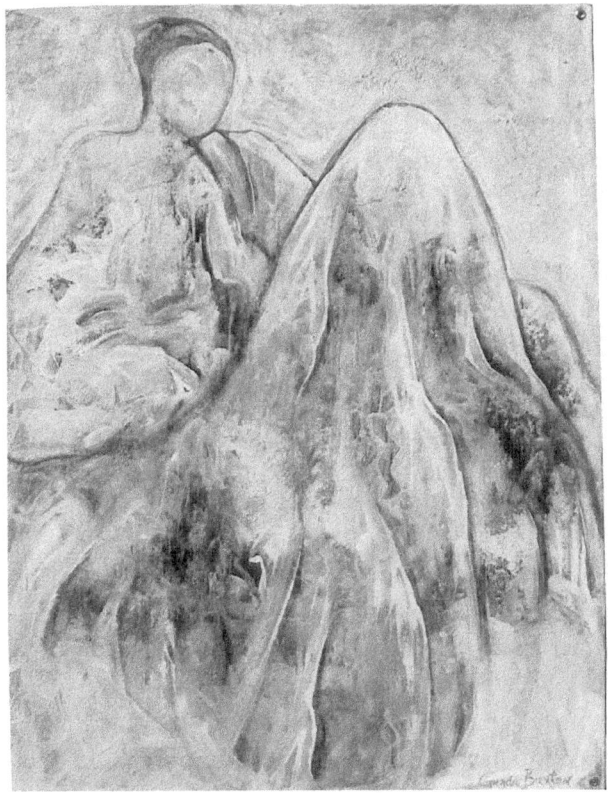

Woman Waiting (1991)

This figure represents the wisdom of nature and the emotional body that informs us that what we do to one we do to the whole. She waits for the recognition of our connection to all living things. But we can only begin to change society if we are willing to begin the change within ourselves. It is only a matter of time, the image seems to suggest, before we come to our senses. On a more personal level, this painting represents my mother who had been struck down by a massive stroke, and lay dying in a hospital far away. Her wisdom over the years has taught me to respect nature and family, and this image is a small tribute to my love for her.

This painting still speaks to me of the emotions of that difficult time of loss with bitter sweet beauty. Like the other paintings, this work transcends the sorrow of our mortal existence and leaves only a sublime beauty that goes beyond paint and canvas. Aesthetic form speaks of a collective consciousness that resides within us all. This universal consciousness is the mythic-poetic part of the human mind that children and primitive cultures intuitively remember. This collective awareness has informed all art-making from the beginning of time. Artists recognize this creative force when it courses through their veins and leaves behind yet another artefact that however imperfectly, has embedded within the medium, that 'something else' of *Being* and being human in the world.

The artist who uses art as an instrument of discovery and reflects on these hidden emotions, more often than not brings forth that 'something else', which has a healing effect, both for the individual as well as for the culture. Once these mysterious images have been revealed, they can be meditated upon, connecting intellectual rationality with emotional inner wisdom. An imaginative synthesis between intellect and innerness unites the mind-body opposition and consciousness is no longer split. The imagination then can freely play between innerness and the intellect and make the necessary cognitive connections for new and valuable ideas to form in the mind.

These imaginative reflections may be rewarded with fresh insight that expands our perception, which has a transformational effect. As such, aesthetic form put the artist in touch with an ancient source of knowledge that appears to be embedded in a greater consciousness that underlies our everyday existence. Many artists are aware of the transformative power of aesthetic form and toyed with the notion of transcending the tragedy of the world in their work. For example, in the painting *Father, Son,*

Holy Ghost, Kiefer uses three wooden chairs as a symbol for religious and ethical values.

These familiar props serve as a reminder that these spiritual values are vulnerable and must be protected. His preoccupation with faith and goodness in this painting offers the viewer hope of transcending the evil that he sees in the world. In his artistic quest, Kiefer is also drawn to ancient alchemical practices and used fire and molten lead as a simulation of the alchemical process. The ancient alchemists were concerned with transforming lead into gold, which can also be understood as a metaphor for the inner search for the Self. As he explored the relationship between modern and ancient technology,

Kiefer attempts to understand many questions left unresolved in modernism but are still relevant to the postmodern world. By making these complex and emotionally charged questions visible, he confronts these lingering philosophical issues and attempts to shed light on the sorrow embedded within body memory. Kiefer uses the personal and collective shadow as raw material to create the great art of tomorrow. The ability to confront the suffering that exists in the world is a courageous act that informs both the individual artist, and the larger society in which they live.

True wisdom can only be learned by accepting the indisputable fact that *this is how it is*. Aesthetic form speak of inner light and the human spirit, much like the painting, *Moon Dance (1991)*.

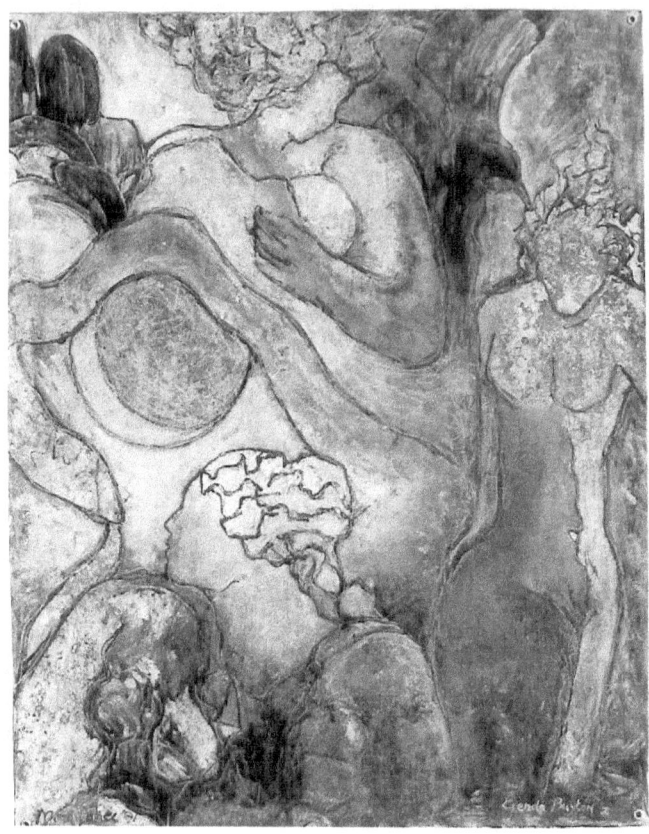

Moon Dance (1991)

This image illustrates the stages of a woman's life; maiden, mother, crone. Symbolized by the cycles of the moon and shedding of a snake's skin, both metaphors for the cyclical nature of life and regeneration. As death waits in the background, a raven flies over the mother and child as a reminder of the passage of time. This painting speaks of the universality of the human condition wherein birth follows death, but also rebirth. In an eternal dance of *Being*, these natural cycles are understood by all, especially women. No matter who you are, this timeless image of a fundamental truth may be intuitively comprehended within the emotional body. It shares our connectedness to each other beyond the diversity of culture.

Heidegger came to the conclusion that sorrow and joy are but two sides of the same coin. People cannot have one without the other and both are part of being in the world. The tragedy, despair, and pathos that people encounter in their everyday existence can be perceived as lessons to learn from, rather than annoying inconveniences. It is a fact that life on earth ends with death. This simple truth must be appreciated to fully enjoy living as a human being. Rembrandt also experienced many personal disasters in his life, yet his paintings shine with the light of empathy for the human condition. As the quality of his life slowly deteriorates, the spiritual light in his paintings only grows stronger and more tender.

His profound understanding of *Being* and what it meant to be human, along with his unbounded faith is still visible in paintings. Many artists have tapped into the emotional wisdom of the body. Artists such as Vincent van Gogh and Rembrandt, whose paintings educate the eye and speak to our inner feelings. The tragedy of van Gogh's life has been well documented and also how he transformed this sorrow into paintings that transcend the history of art. Similar to Rembrandt, van Gogh used colour and line to communicate his love of nature and the suffering of humanity. Like his illustrious predecessor, van Gogh aimed to make visible the full range of human values and emotions and in the process he transformed sickness and disappointment into a beautiful work of art.

Intentionally wanting to depict serious sorrow, he paints what was in his heart and his deepest and most tender emotions become visible for all to see. Like Kiefer's symbolic alchemical process, the act of painting becomes the filter for the purification of Vincent's pain and sorrow. Other artists such as Kollwitz also understood that the ethics of living as an authentic human being involved confronting the shadows in life.

Hans Kollwitz, her only surviving son, wrote in his introduction to his mother's diary, that Kollwitz uses the creative process to illuminate the terrible living conditions of the poor as a courageous challenge to the Fascists' desire for more war. Inspired by the suffering she encounters in her life, Kollwitz's art is a tribute to the endurance of the human spirit. Her goal was to reveal universal truth in aesthetic form that showed everyone feels pain, sadness and fear. Distilling form to its barest essentials, her art shows the divine spark of *Being* that lies hidden within each human being. But these images of women and children go far beyond cultural specifics and touch contemporary viewers as strongly as when they were first exhibited.

THE EXPRESSIVE ARTIST

It is through creative engagement with their innermost being that people discover the light of *Being*; the spark of divinity within that connects us to all existence. The ancient Greeks called it *genius* and we intuitively recognize this quality of enlightenment in a great work of art. Becoming consciously aware of the unique spark of light within requires a willingness to risk stepping over into another way of thinking. But going within often reveals the existence of unconscious and sometimes painful memories that can be expressed in aesthetic form. By making this hidden aspect of human nature visible, you must have faith and be willing to plunge into the abyss.

The abyss of consciousness, the unknowable where opposites are reconciled and innerness is revealed. This oceanic consciousness cannot be rationalized. It seems to be a separate part of the psyche that requires temporarily letting go of what is known and familiar. Stepping into the abyss requires an act of faith that *Being* will be disclosed as the artist is guided by the imagination through the creative process and trusting their intuitive emotional responses and the images that emerge from the inner world.

As aesthetic form manifests itself, bringing these archetypal images into consciousness seems to have a transformative effect. By showing one's inner truth, aesthetic form reconciles the mind-body split and illuminates the world as it is with all its joy and sorrow. Awareness of the beauty in nature as well as in our lives connects a person to a greater source of inner wisdom that often has many layers of metaphorical meaning. The emotional message opens up a special kind of original representation that has both personal and mythological connotations.

My own exploration of inner shadows comes to full expression in the painting *Lamentations* (1992). The image that materialized can be seen as an emotional outcry that reveals the despair and loneliness of the solitary artist.

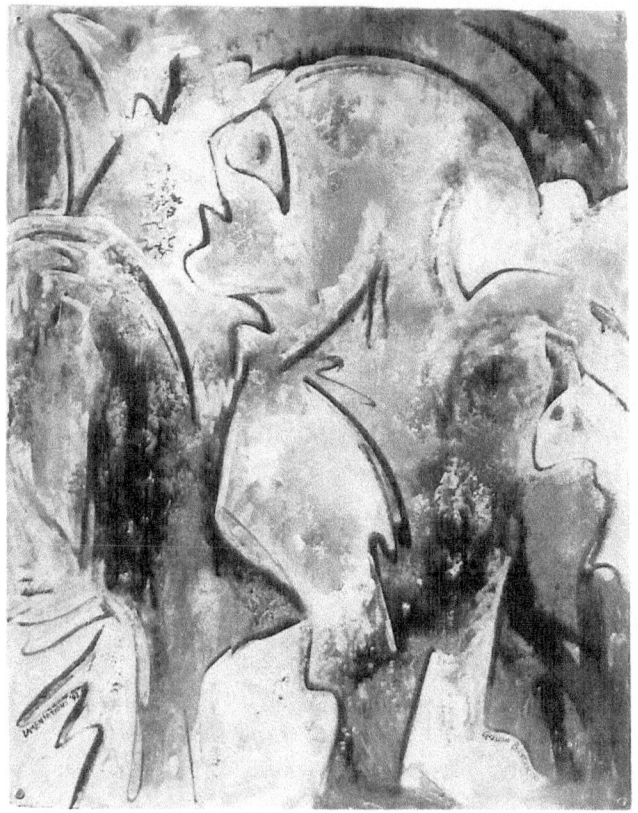

Lamentations (1991-1992)

The title refers to the Lamentations in the Hebrew bible, where the prophet Jeremiah mourns the destruction of the temple in Jerusalem. Traditionally, this book is recited on Tisha B'Av, the saddest day on the Jewish calendar. This image is symbolic of problems in my life at that time as well as events that were happening in the world. The sorrows of more war, more hunger, and more pain were transformed into a statement that can be understood on an intuitive level by all. This image speaks of the universality of the sorrow that surrounds us and threatens our survival. But it also speaks of unity. A harmony between the sensuous body and intellectual part of mind develops as the imagination discovers authentic aesthetic form.

When inner truth manifests itself, the canvas becomes an arena whereby meaning gives birth to itself. This discloses the interplay of difference yet at the same time also shows the unity of all existence. However, Western culture since Descartes has lived with a mind-body split that rejects the natural, intuitive wisdom of the body. Whereas other cultures still remember how to unify intuition and the intellect through its mythology, visions and sacred rituals. In certain places, dreams in particular, provide valuable insight into the existence of the divine. The dreamtime of the Australian aborigines immediately comes to mind. It is true that this connection to *Being* cannot be rationalized.

This divine light can only be grasped in an imaginative synthesis that reconciles sensibility and the intellectual part of mind. But the artist may discover this divine spark of *Being* in an aesthetic form that provides a unique type of knowledge that was previously unknown. Seeing beauty is an experience that requires silently listening to a message that can only be communicated through engagement with a beautiful work of art. Many great artworks are saturated with intrinsic meaning.

Knowledge that informs people how to live humanely in the world just as it is. Perhaps this is so because art has the ability to articulate the underlying simplicity of the existence of *Being* that at the same time also reveals what it means to be human. The body intuitively responds to beauty's purely aesthetic message with a surge of pleasure. Aesthetic pleasure directs both the artist during the creative process and viewers who participate with the unfolding message of *Being* as they engage with a work of art.

Success depends on the artist's power to communicate the essence of *Being* in simple objects To show the vitality of being alive through the exposure of innerness within a great work of art. Take van Gogh's passionate, ecstatically expressive paintings for example. These beautiful images speak of loneliness and sorrow, yet his work also communicates the love he saw in everything around him. His vivid use of colour and the vigour of his brushstrokes remain as a legacy of his overwhelming love for humanity and all living things. His unique expression of inner moods and feelings has been projected into the paintings for all to see.

Perhaps van Gogh's loneliness gave him the freedom to explore his inner feelings in a sincere personal quest for God. It shines out from his work. In any case, if truth is to be revealed, the artist must be faithful to what has been disclosed in the medium,. The revelation of *Being* requires an open relationship with the medium as personal innerness is brought into the open. Aesthetic form depends on a correct relationship between knower to the known, which Heidegger refers to it as the essence of truthful disclosure. He perceives this aesthetic knowledge essentially as the schematization of chaos, describing it as the 'hiddenness of unmastered abundance of becoming and the rhythmic flux of the world as a whole'.

Many expressive artists start their search for aesthetic form in the abundance of unmastered chaos. For me, letting colour flow freely while working helps form develop. If you let it, the paint itself will show you what it wants to be. It's a natural process that develops as the hands, mind and heart work in unison, as the painting *Rain Forest* shows.

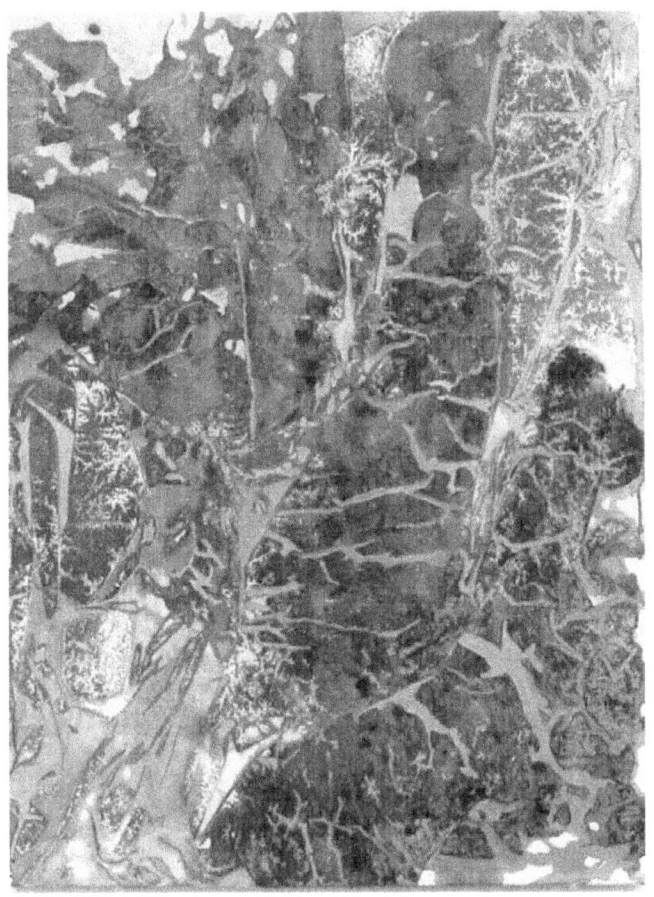

Rain Forest (1986)

As different forms emerge, I sense how these images were connected and contained a message or story. Once the image has been stabilized, aesthetic form speaks of things I may not have been conscious of before. These images often contain a deeper wisdom that I didn't know I possessed but that can be shared with others through art. It is true that the artist may have specialized knowledge. Many tend to live a rather different life from the societal norm. For one thing, many creative people seem to live closer to the earth, have an intimate relationship with their surroundings and are more open to the sacredness of nature. They are often people who live and love on the earth.

As mortal beings, they work hard to cultivate the land and build and maintain their dwellings. However, these people also know that the reality of human existence is more about remembering and responding to a call from *Being*. They know that establishing truth in their art involves bringing forth a unique form, one that has never been seen before nor ever will be again. It feels a lot like giving birth when the essence of innerness comes into form; much like being delivered of a child.

For Heidegger, artistic creativity as well as aesthetic appreciation of aesthetic form lets truth originate. By a founding leap aesthetic experience connects us to the essence of our innerness. It's a cognitive leap to the source that provides a fundamental insight that all is as it should be. The foundation of this profound truth consists of its coming-out-of oblivion, where this knowledge was waiting in the shadows of body memory. This leap into consciousness happens at the moment the forms that have emerged connect in a meaningful way.

At that moment, intuitive wisdom is reconciled under an intellectual concept, which brings harmony of mind, if only temporarily. This mental leap provides a feeling that everything is exactly as it is supposed to be, as if the pieces of an intricate puzzle suddenly fall into place. This transcending sensation brings an indescribable inner satisfaction that makes everything good, no matter how bad things seem to be.

The British philosopher Mary Warnock agrees that the recognition of aesthetic truth is both immediate and emotional but stresses that it is the role of the imagination to provide these valuable insights when we engage aesthetically with aesthetic form. For Warnock, a work of art articulates a collective language that appears to be rooted in shared human principles that are commonly understood on a spiritual level. These values can be given visual expression by going deeper into consciousness to reveal humanity's mythic-poetic nature.

People have been making are since prehistoric times and art originated as sympathetic magic. For millennia, artists have evoked archetypal, mythological form to bring forth works of art that carry special emotional appeal for their community. Inside the caves at Lascaux for example, many images of bison and horses were painted on walls in the belief that these animals would allow themselves to be caught by the hunter who had given them form. These paintings appear to be archetypal, mythological images that represent our innate humanness and shared existence on the earth.

The images may vary from culture to culture, but not their essential meaning. Although culturally determined, these symbolic images reveal that the underlying truth of *Being* and being human in the world is shared by everyone. As aesthetic form is made visible, these images give a profound satisfaction that restores both the artist as well as the culture. The transformative nature of art is a powerful tool for facilitating emotional participation therefore the arts are the legacy of the best that a culture has to offer the next generation.

Take for example, the painting *Transformation (2002)* that plays with the idea of the passage of time and the seasons of our lives.

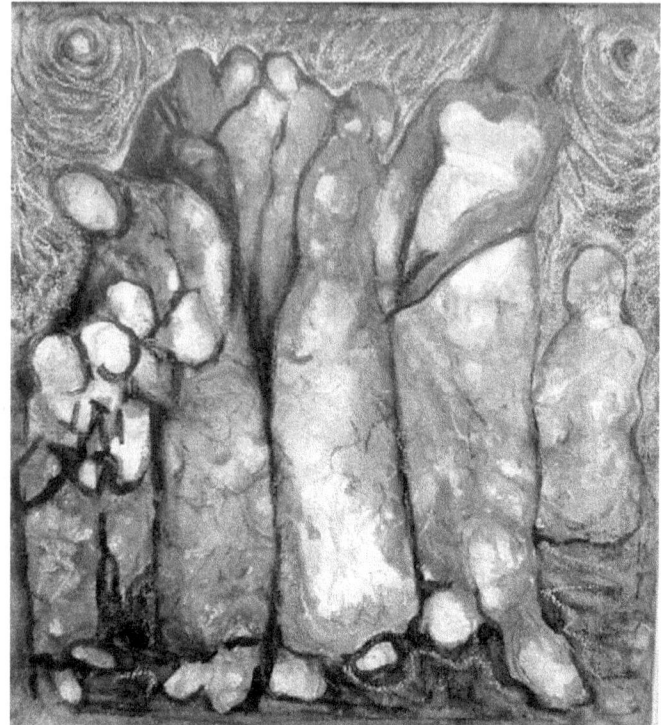

Transformation (2003)

This painting reminds me of medieval religious paintings that depict various important events on the same canvas. In this case it is somewhat autobiographical as it shows the various stages in my own life. The old seated woman on the right looks serenely over her shoulder to events of the past, and remembers. She remembers the young woman she once was, full of hope for the future, the mother who protectively embraces her children. The three graces look on in the background, symbolic of past, present and future. The sun shining high in the left-hand corner as the moon to the right seems to stand guard over them all.

This painting is loaded with personal as well as shared experience that speaks of the passing of time in the life of a woman, and familial relationships that transform over time. The theme of transformation is a recurring one in my artwork that I see as a confirmation of the path I have chosen. This image reconciles and celebrates the seasons of a woman's life and by giving it form, provides meaning to it. It's a reminder that the past cannot be undone, what is done is done. It is only in the present moment, that we can learn from the past in order to change our world.

The creative imagination understands on an emotional as well as on a cognitive level that a manifestation for a new future may be created from the past. A work of art may speak of living a good life while it preserves the artist's emotional response to living in the world for future generations. As new form is discovered, a reciprocal dialogue is made possible between one generation and the next and one culture to another. This dialogue serves to deepen our understanding of others and shows there is freedom in diversity.

Artistic creativity and imaginatively participating with a work of art is invaluable. Aesthetic experience encourages participants to explore the potential for knowledge that lies hidden within the psyche. As people connect to their inner world, they discover to their surprise, a spontaneity that opens up a place where the search for innerness is rewarded by a larger view of what it means to be alive. This process of self discovery is the beginning of the journey to *Being* and being human in the world.

Informed by a greater sense of who they really are, many artists look for the special gifts that wait to be discovered and given form. With the pleasure and delight of this sacred quest to know themselves, they understands that all life on earth is cyclical and that without sorrow there would be no beauty, truth or art. It is the expressive artist's job to interpret and bring innerness into aesthetic form that communicates the experience of being present in this time and place.

The aim of such artists is to create representations that others can understand as the light of *Being* revealed and shows what cannot be expressed in words. The essence of existence is difficult to articulate in any another way. It is no easy feat to bring forth this secretive knowledge that originates within body memory and bring it into form. What if what has being revealed is genuine emotion, it usually contains profound meaning, both for the artist and culture in which they live.

By making a representation of innerness, they create new meaning that can be grasped by a viewer's affective response. We feel truth of *Being* when we encounter it. It is felt within the body and our emotional response guides us to our own inner spirit. Artists who truly express innerness do not copy, imitate or look for personal glory. The purpose of artistic creativity is to create something of value that invokes a deep sense of recognition; an emotional response that is not just personal but also touches others in a profound way.

John Berger understood the artist's courage and their need to stand aloof from the struggles of their time. In addition, Berger believes that it is the duty of the creative artist to express, to the best of their abilities their unique personal and introspective truth. Naturally, learning the rules and skills of a given medium plays a large part in how successful they are in doing so. The painting *Fallen Angels (1987)* for example expresses the idea of the fallen state of humanity.

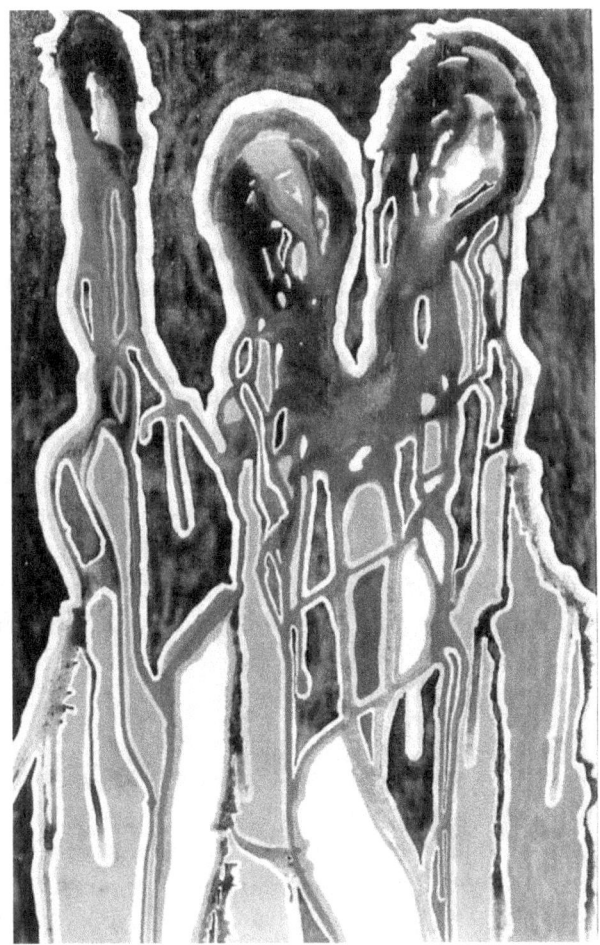

Fallen Angels I (1987)

In a sense, we are all fallen angels, having been cast out of paradise long ago. Expressing private inner thoughts and feelings brings aesthetic form into the public domain for all to see. That is the risk the artist takes in bringing one's own inner emotional life out into the open and it takes courage to expose one's emotions to the judgment of others. But a work of art will always be influenced by the time and the culture in which it was made. Art is never created in a vacuum.

Studies have shown that artists share certain personality traits that may help them maintain their focus. Many are vigorously ambitious and share a tendency to be stubborn, even in childhood. They usually have a strong need to excel when faced with obstacles. This is not surprising as it requires dedication and perseverance to continue to create art year after year, while they develop the necessary skills to successfully represent the inner knowledge that lies hidden within the heart.

Although life is often difficult, artists like Rembrandt and van Gogh persevered year after year with the confidence and assurance that painting the moodiness of nature and within human nature is a reasonable thing to do. Many like them continue to make art throughout their lives without social support. The inner journey is often fascinating and for most, making art seems to be its own reward. Another trait that many creative people have in common is a tendency to be balanced between masculine and feminine tendencies.

This characteristic may to some extent, resolve the Cartesian mind-body split. Having a more imaginative personality will most assuredly bring balance between emotional knowledge and the intellect. This equilibrium may also provide inner strength to withstand public criticism, which they may encounter in their quest for meaningful aesthetic form. Yet everyone has the capability to be an artist and connect with the core of their inner 'genius'. That spark, the source of our individual existence, no matter whether we are men or women. Artists are motivated by this spark of genius in the sense that the ancient Greek thought of genius. It informs all artistic creativity.

This divine spark motivates them to persist with stubborn determination and to succeed against all odds. A keen perceptiveness, an endurance to produce and influence others is also associated with artistic achievement. The tenacious and often difficult search for meaningful form may seem daunting to a young artist just starting out. They need role models to emulate who can encourage their individual journey to give expression their own unique perception of their humanity. Unfortunately all too often this much needed encouragement is sadly lacking.

Like Plato, many people see the artist as half mad, ecstatic, and possessed, even as a danger to societal norms, perhaps because they can communicate a greater knowledge than mere insight. Others point to the artist's unpredictability and social isolation but people don't realize that they need to be alone much of the time in order to reach within the psyche to find the forms that need to be expressed. The hustle and bustle of daily life can be distracting and take away from the required solitude needed to do their work. But there is a price to pay for this isolation, as society often looks on the artist with suspicion. All too often artistic creativity is associated with mental instability.

This may be the reason society often shuns the expressive artist, while later shamelessly celebrating their achievements after they are safely in the grave. John Berger remarks that the artist has two options today; to serve fashion or arrogantly search for truth alone. Art does not imitate fashion and artists often work in obscurity and isolation. Sometimes, what an artwork shows may not be popular or easy to understand but the artist knows when aesthetic form must be expressed for it to be true. In my own work, original visual forms are often symbolic of larger issues that are both cultural and personal. Take the painting *Coming to Meet* (1995). It represents a confrontation between masculine and feminine energies, two distinctly different ways of knowing.

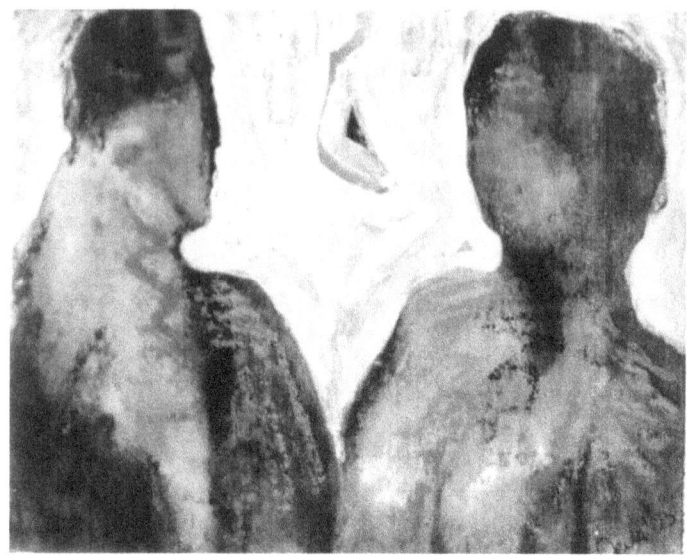

Coming to Meet (1995)

Their meeting, though fraught with suspicion, may serve to rebalance, both personally as well as for others. In this painting, its form as well as the title can be viewed as a metaphor for a necessary dialogue between these two polar opposites so they can begin to comprehend each other. For me, this image represents a reparation of the Cartesian mind-body but its title also refers to number 44 in the Book of Changes. The I Ching, one of the oldest of the Chinese classics, is all about balance, in nature as well as in society. Coming to Meet represents the Creative; Heaven above and the Gentle, Wind below. This hexagram also related to the return of yin or feminine energy. She comes from below to meet the male. This painting serves as a reminder that innerness needs to be balanced by the intellect.

It is true that artistic authenticity and self expression is not often appreciated by others until the artist is long gone. Perhaps that is why a great artist like Rembrandt appeared humble and self effacing. But the British art historian, Kenneth Clark qualifies this statement by saying however humble Rembrandt may have appeared, he was well aware of his own genius. This was also true of van Gogh and others who worked from authentic authenticity. These artists intuitively know that their work has value and that helped motivate them to keep working year after year.

Not only does art mirror one's own existence, it often holds up a reflective mirror to society. Its emotional impact is meant to deepen our reflection on reality and broaden our insights. The philosopher Charles Taylor in *The Malaise of Modernity* laments that art today speaks a mysterious language using a 'forest of symbols' whose meaning is no longer understood by the general public. Therefore artists must create their own symbolic language in an artwork that whispers of elusive thoughts and emotions. He describes the inner search for symbolic form as a quest for meaning that is inherent in nature and is not based on accepted conventions.

Taylor believes that a work of art articulates something beyond the self that goes much deeper than the individual. He described the creative act as an attempt to reconcile our fragile humanity with all existence; past, present, and future. The search for symbolic meaning within aesthetic form speaks directly to others in a language that seems linked to the sacredness of nature, people formerly thought of as 'god'. Taylor laments that we no longer see ourselves as part of a great chain of *Being* like in the past. But people still need to feel connected to a larger order that holds value beyond themselves. Most people today seem to have lost their connection to *Being* and sacredness of life.

However, artistic creativity and aesthetic appreciation can compensate for losing this much needed feeling of belonging to something bigger than ourselves. The creative process is an emotional dialogue between innerness and the medium that discloses, in an authentic representation, this feeling of being connected to the natural cycles of life. At the same time, this aesthetic experience also reveals the commonality of the being human.

We know with inner certainty that resonates deep within the emotional body when inner truth has been brought into form. It is this affective component that guides our response to a work of art. By giving the imagination freedom to roam between sensibility and the intellect, the artist discovers meaningful images and brings them into form. Then a work art reveals us to ourselves in a timeless image that provides courage to go on and persevere in an often hostile world, in the face of all obstacles, and live life to the fullest.

SELF-PORTRAITS: A PERSONAL VIEW

But an artist truly shares innerness with the viewer in a self-portrait. A depiction of oneself is the artefact they leave the world as evidence of their inner search for meaningful form within one's own flesh. This requires the ability to synthesize psychological and pictorial elements simultaneously. It also requires empathy and audacity to represent what is perceived honestly, as the image of one's own features emerge out of the interplay of shadow and light.

Throughout the ages, artists have discovered great truths by exploring their own features. The insightful self-portraits of Rembrandt, for example depict an all too human face emerging from the painted surface. These self portraits eloquently express his quest for that divine spark of humanity within himself. Berger notes that for Rembrandt, painting his own face was a search for an exit out of darkness. To find out who he really was, as an individual but also in relation to his shared humanity. Knowledge only found by penetrating the dark shadows within body memory.

Rembrandt was able to observe and depict himself honestly, with humility and a profound empathy for the human condition. Rich with this mysterious undercurrent, these self portraits reveal his painfully candid appraisal of himself as a deeply spiritual, meditative and dignified man. Using the contrast between light and dark, he created a mysterious atmosphere that half conceals and half discloses both the tangible and intangible with a sublime trace of philosophical humour. The painter's observations are so intense and their emotional impact so great that these paintings still delight yet intimidate the impaired sensibilities of postmodern society. The potential for self expression in a work of art inspires much philosophical reflection, like the painting *Fallen Angels III (1987)*.

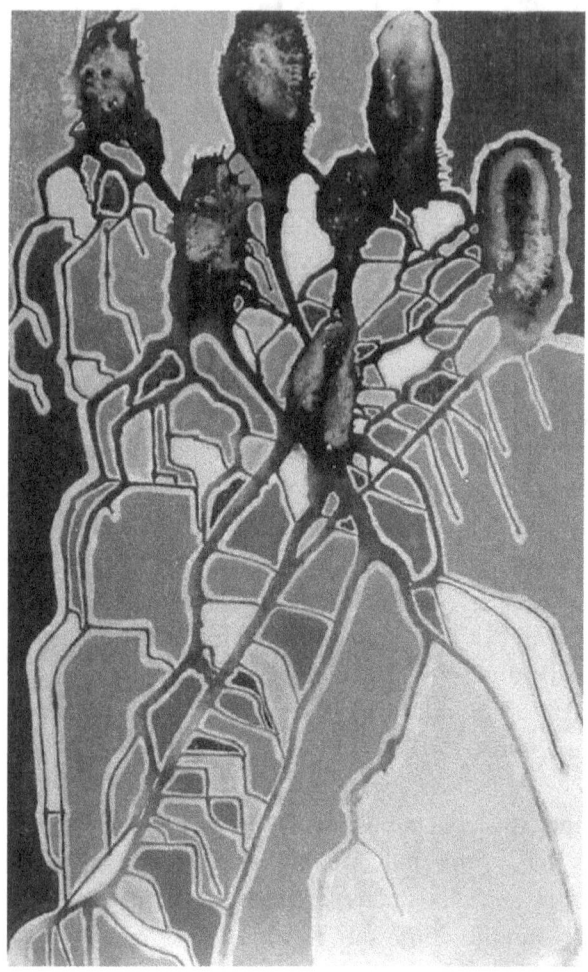

Fallen Angels III (1987)

This image, like the one in the previous chapter, contemplates the fallen nature of humanity. It also related to who I am in relation to my Western cultural heritage. Its title was inspired by the natural liquidity of the paint as streams of colour travelled across the canvas, leaving their tracks behind. It suggests an aerial perspective, as if seen from above. From an airplane, or bird's eye view high above the landscape. Although abstract, the meaning behind its form is defined by using specific colours as a visual metaphor; a bright blue sky juxtaposed by dark, jagged figures, splayed across the green landscape. It brings to mind the myth of Icarus who flew too close to the sun, aspiring to great heights, although warned not to. But the heat of the sun melted his wings and he tumbled into the sea.

However, colour, form and its title also imply that this image is also an allegory of the mythical war in heaven that ended when the rebellious angels were cast out by God. Although this painting is not a self portrait per se, it does express an inner philosophical thought about who I feel myself to be. Rather than using gold enamel to pull out form, as in other paintings, gold was used as under-painting and left visible to define the emerging figures. Using gold as a base is also reminiscent of *cloisonné*, an ancient technique that involves painting with enamel over metal and then firing it in a kiln. This creates a vibrant effect similar to stained glass.

Enjoying the inherent goodness of aesthetic form is a crucial component of being human. Appreciating beauty in art or in nature is vital for the well-being of both artist and the entire community. Vincent van Gogh often found inspiration in painting portraits. Paintings that are a testament to a man who worked very hard to succeed but who had also come to terms with failure. The beauty of these paintings synthesizes his all too human need for recognition with his lonely and sometimes arrogant search for artistic authenticity. His penetrating eye saw the inner spark of genius in others as well as himself. He paints the essence behind the skin with radiating energy that seems to shine from between his furrowed brow.

A decade later, Kiefer also used his body to create self-portraits that question and challenge Germany's past. As a young art student, he photographs himself standing erect in various places around Europe, with his hand held high in a Nazi salute. Placing himself strategically in the landscape, he explores his Teutonic heritage in order to understand what drove his ancestors to commit horrendous atrocities during two world wars. The emotional impact of linking his body to the Nazi past was his vehicle for personal exploration.

This imaginative synthesis enabled him to come to terms with the darkness of human nature that his culture tried hard to suppress. By bringing these unpleasant memories into aesthetic form, they can be contemplated and learned from to avoid these tragedies from happening in the future. Bringing aesthetic form into consciousness helps process the shadows that hide within. The exposure of innerness is the universal essence of a great work of art. Authentic aesthetic form is like birthing something new.

Inner feelings become visible that are rooted deep in the emotional body. Then the artwork is a new revelation of what it means to be alive in the world that amplifies the metaphysical structure of the flesh. A work of art then becomes a shared experience of essential truth of being human that involves us in a dialogue between perception and felt emotions. Take the painting *Exposed (1991)*, for example. As form emerged, I knew that this image was definitely autobiographical. As with many other paintings, I immediately recognized the figures as they appeared in the paint. Images of people I have loved over time but for one reason or another lost contact with. But this painting also reveals that within the psyche, these memories are as potent as ever.

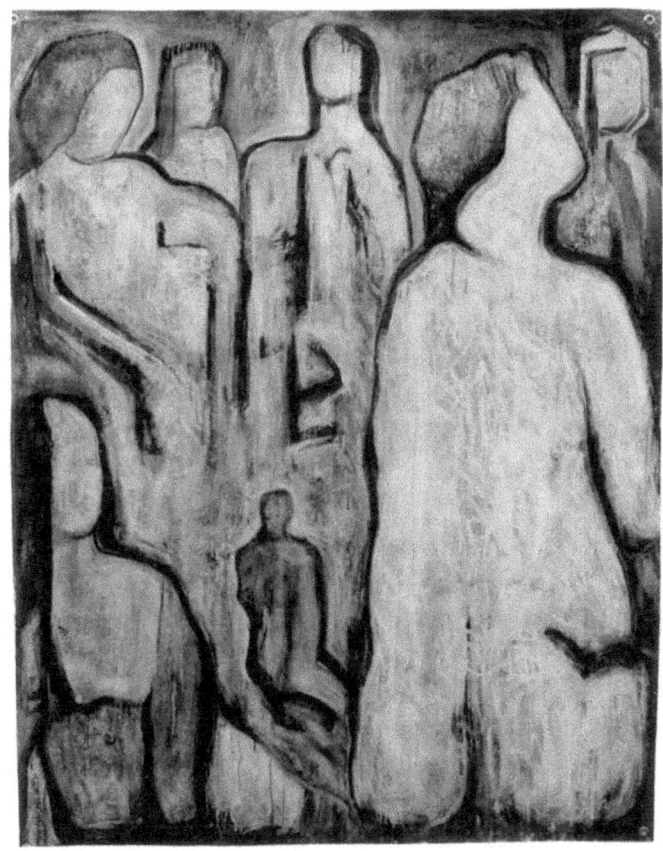

Exposed (1991)

And I did feel exposed when the painting was finished. Not liking it much at the time, perhaps because it said too much. This painting is also an exploration of the aging process as the body changes over time. Rembrandt also painted self portraits that show the passage of time. How his facial features changed over his lifetime. With a detached eye, he shows how this physical and spiritual transformation and links these changes to nature and cycles of temporal existence as he aged. But Rembrandt's intelligent eyes remained alive and deeply penetrating to the essence that lay beneath the skin. From his self-portraits, one gets a sense of the artist's vitality and love for life. Portraits that show the artist was able to see himself with brutal honesty, even as a young man until he was very old. The authenticity of his character was embedded in the paint for all to see.

Vincent van Gogh's self portraits are also a part of his artistic legacy. Like Rembrandt, he used the painted image as a means to express his innerness. These paintings are intensely emotional and autobiographical and have a strong impact on viewers who connect to the exposure of *Being* and inner truth. These portraits invite viewers to participate in a dialogue with the artist through the artwork. To stand in the place of another and see with their eyes as inner sensibilities are exposed and recognized on the surface of their skin.

The spectator's body remembers its own experience when confronted with the subtle language of aesthetic form. Berger calls this reciprocal dialogue with a work of art a corporeal experience that is shared by all participants. There is a type of remembering that is lodged in the sensibility of body memory but it requires time and solitude to be heard. To be truly present in the moment and in the sensuousness of the body and attending to form as ideas come to consciousness. To be in that place where one is truly present and aware.

A timelessness that brims with sensual wisdom, laid bare in the beauty of colour and paint on canvas or in a haunting melody. Breathing is crucial in this sublime experience of being fully alive in the body. The flow of air that goes in and out sustains, relaxes and soothes so the imagination can play with ideas that come to mind. This enables the artist to shift their perception of time and space in search for aesthetic form. Therefore many artists tend to live playfully, abandoning themselves to curiosity and wonder like children do naturally as they explore the medium of their choice.

The creative process offers the opportunity to rediscover the joy of being a alive that comes from within and frames our relationship to the world. Then the body and mind are in harmony, and images and memories surface into consciousness with a sense of rapture that echoes deep within the psyche. A wondrous sense of inspiration and rapture is experienced as one reflects on the possible meaning of form as it develops. Heidegger as well as Nietzsche describes this rapture or *rausch* as an aesthetic bodily state, which is intensely personal, yet at the same time involves the entire human race.

The blissful experience of rapture physically permeates the soul with a quintessential sense of belonging and being loved. Joy that speaks to our emotional being and reveals that on one level, all is unfolding exactly as it should. Rapture, like inspiration is intuitive and requires a shift in awareness. And a blind trust in the creative process, which enables the often non-rational leap it demands. An artist has to trust the process and follow the imagination wherever it may lead.

Rapture feels as if the windows of perception have been opened, allowing us to extend our vision beyond the self. An ecstatic relationship with a greater sense of ourselves is grasped, along with a sense of being more fully human than was the case before. A profound joy emanates from imaginative unity between hand, eye and mind. The painting *Kali (1987)* developed from this inspirational unity.

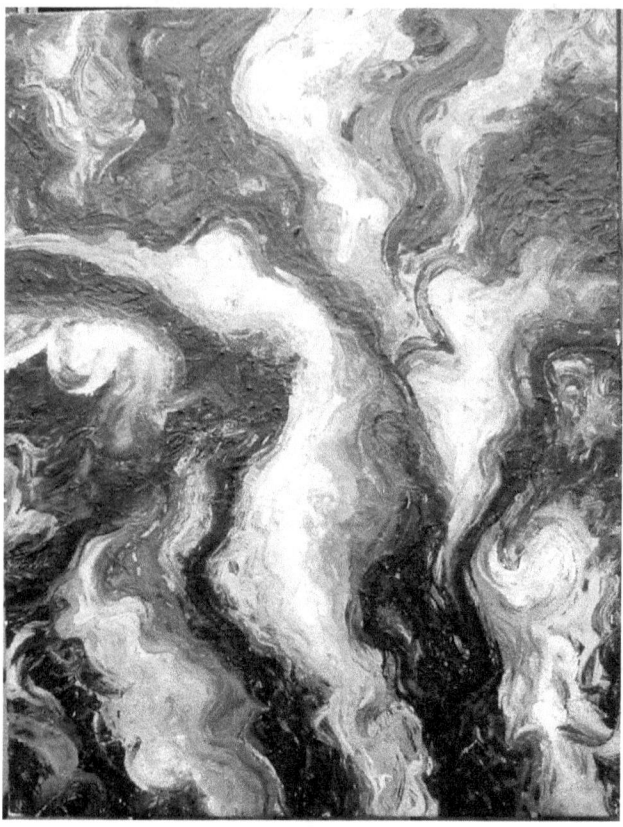

Kali (1987)

Fluid colours were poured from cans onto a canvas that lay flat on the floor. By playing in the wet paint, gesture, feelings and thoughts soon came together and as if by magic, figures began to appear. As the paint moved across the canvas, it was intriguing to see aesthetically pleasing patterns in the marks left in the paint by the texture of rubber gloves. With practice, I soon learned to manipulate these pleasant surprises that happen during the creative process. It feels like rhapsody when the meaning of what

had been revealed is understood, both on an emotional as well
as intellectual level.

I soon recognized this image represented Kali, the Hindu
goddess associated with empowerment. She is black time, death
but also eternity. She is the goddess of Time and Change and for
some she is the ultimate reality or Brahman revered as the
redeemer of the universe. In this painting, she is dancing the end
of the world as we know it. But there is also a deeper meaning
that refers to the Kali Yuga, the last of four stages of the world as
part of a cosmic cycle. The Kali Yuga is now at an end and the
world is at threshold of the Satya Yuga, a new golden age. An era
where truth is seen as the purest ideal and humanity will live in
rhapsody, appreciating goodness and beauty once more.

Rapture is a feeling of plenitude that is above all forms of being
attuned; the ecstasy of knowing for certain that truth of *Being*
and being human resides within ourselves, as well as in nature.
Feeling as if nothing is foreign to the mind is an aesthetic
pleasure; to experience really seeing, not only oneself, but others
more clearly. Many artists have had a glimpse of this new world
era. In a single moment, these creative people are acutely aware
that they and the other are one. In this space where I and the
other meet, realizing that our separation is but an illusion.

In the meeting of our differences that Heidegger calls the abyss
of being, truth, beauty and aesthetic form is found. The French
postmodern philosopher Maurice Merleau-Ponty, in *The Visible
and the Invisible* calls this encounter with difference the
intertwining; a chiasm where wisdom may be found within
corporeal sensibility. Merleau-Ponty describes this encounter as
the thickness of flesh that lies between the seer and the thing.

Flesh separates us from each other, yet being in the flesh is the
means by which we interact. Our flesh is at the limits of the body,

and it is in the flesh where we meet and experience life. This knowledge is an aesthetic experience, whether creating a work of art or appreciating its aesthetic form. Seeing the world as it is with a compassionate eye, aesthetic form makes sense of our being in it. Most expressive artists create from the body but none so evidently as the painter whose gesture is left as an invitation to share in the creative process.

Gesture unique to the artist is established in a great painting and remains alive long after they're gone. Most artists respect these marks left by the body as an aesthetic quality that brings up ideas from the subconscious. This natural and original mark belongs to a specific person and is instantly recognized as being authentic. Then the image is not the object of repression, but the subject of a particular constitution. Gesture is an important part of aesthetic form and become part of the creative expression of the artwork itself. Gestures develop spontaneously as body and mind play with the subtleties and implications of corresponding ideas and suggested meaning.

For me, a visual metaphor will often come to mind that goes far beyond gesture and surface of paint on canvas. These ideas may change as images come into form, and then disappear again as other ideas emerge. The image may appear to be one thing but then turn out to be something entirely different after the paint dries. The aesthetic delight that often accompanies artistic creativity has the power to open the doors of perception of how things truly are. Aesthetic form holds up a mirror, both to ourselves and to society as a whole.

Take for example the painting *Tears of the Sun* that utters a blunt critique of colonialism. The title, inspired by the Inca word for gold, implies the atrocity of plundering native cultures during the conquest of America. Form as well as gesture can be seen as a visual metaphor for the devastation of the original inhabitants of the Americas.

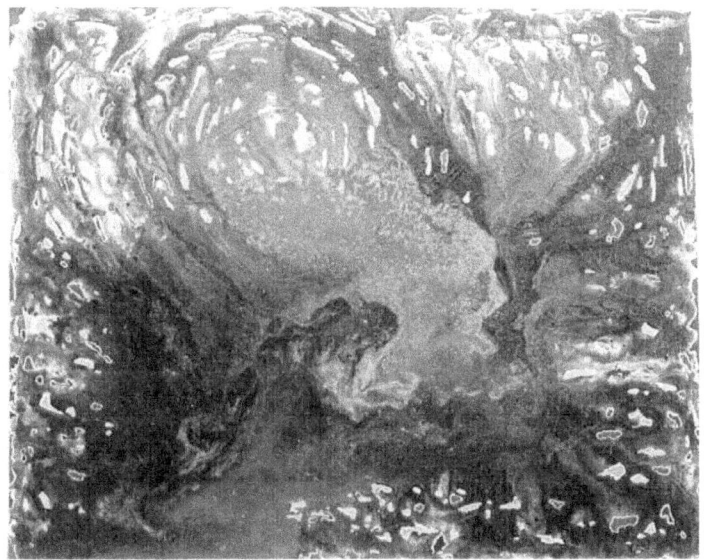

Tears of the Sun (1987)

The painting depicts a large, fractured sun on a gold enamel background, shedding a river of blood. Although highly abstract, there is a suggestion of a landscape destroyed where the paint coagulates into a putrid brownish green. These colours and shapes refer to the abominable cruelty of the conquistadors whose greed for gold all but decimated the native population. This devastation extended to every aspect of life; not only did they rape and kill the local people, but the landscape as well. For me, this painting shouts of the horrors of conquest and colonialism. The violent subjugation of other cultures that still goes on today and for much the same reasons.

Gesture also exposes the artist's sense of rhythm and mobility, inviting the viewer to partially experience the physical movements of the body embedded in the work itself. These gestures communicate on an emotional level across time and place and are intuitively understood. But it may take several attempts to feel satisfied with aesthetic form that has revealed itself. Intuitively, artists know when they have caught something of value. Then the intellect may take over the editing process and decide which potential forms will be kept, and what will have to go to make a painting work. It is the artist's function to bring these images into form as best as they can.

Making authentic innerness visible has a transformative and healing effect, perhaps because these images come from a collective consciousness. Aesthetic form is rich with meaning of a greater consciousness that underlies everyday reality. As form manifests itself in the medium, it seems we are better able to express and interpret personal experience. Yet these images also seem to connect to a mythic-poetic level of being. A greater wisdom that resides within that speaks on a universal level of lived experience.

Aesthetic form is a spontaneous expression of the body that reveals nature is the original artist. Every gesture or bodily posture expresses the artist's primal relationship to being present in the world. There is a wellspring of hidden knowledge that is the fundamental foundation of creation and source of the essential meaning of life. Heidegger describes it as a form-like presence, which is not just personal but represents the *Gestalt* of humanity, a principle basic to all human beings. These images seem to be pre-formed in the human psyche and appear spontaneously during the creative process. Although the painting *Dance of Life (1990)* looks spontaneous, this image took quite some time to make.

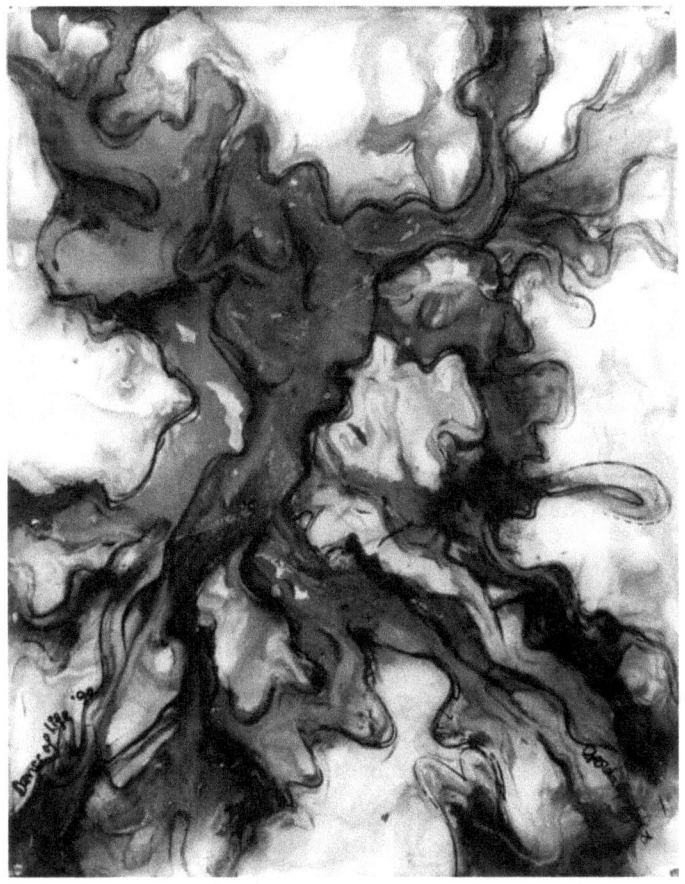

Dance of Life (1990)

However, it's not always easy to grasp the essential meaning of aesthetic form as is appears in the medium. Sometimes it takes days or even weeks before I feel inspired. I may put the canvas somewhere out of the way while I do other things and then suddenly forms will jump out. That signals the creative act, which at times requires a long incubation period. Time for the imagination to play with potential before form is recognized. The artist must be willing to temporarily bypassing the intellect so they can bring these images out of themselves and into the artwork. This process may take them to the edge of awareness where conscious awareness meets unconscious sensibilities.

This cognitive borderland between sleep and being full awake is where aesthetic form is often found. Artists play these underground games of the mind in order to engage with universal *Gestalt* images that bubble up from the depth of their psyche. Time and again, these images show the existence of a collective consciousness, which is the source of all meaningful form. This cognitive state everyone returns to each night as they sleep. Every being must sleep eventually. No one can remain in a conscious state for long before the body must return to the unconscious state to regenerate.

Archetypal *Gestalt* form is a meaningful revelation of both personal and collective information that adapts itself to the medium. *Gestalt* images are a phenomenon Heidegger describes as the 'coming-to-pass of non-concealment' that opens up a new way of seeing the world as it has never been seen before. Bringing these meaningful images into aesthetic form is a private act of going inward that at the same time connects with and projects the *Gestalt* of the culture in which the artist lives. As the artist learns too open to *Gestalt* form, images may appear either during the incubation period or the creative process itself as they try to see the relationship between forms; individual, culture and this unknown and unknowable consciousness where *Gestalt* images seem to originate.

There seems to be a link between inner perception and collective cultural memory at a peripheral level of remembering .that cannot be separated. At this level of awareness, aesthetic form is reduced to its very essence. Simplified and compressed into intuitive meaning, which is the source of an authentic work of art. These timeless images have a primordial quality, yet contain wisdom that is as valid today as this knowledge was for our prehistoric ancestors. To discover these archetypal and mythical images, one must shift their perception to the periphery of consciousness. I find while painting, it sometimes helps to view the work from the side or even hold it upside down.

This may be what the postmodern painter Georg Bazelitz was getting at when he painted his portraits upside down. Seeing a painting upside down shifts the viewer's perception from what they would like to see, to what is actually there. Their perception has changed so the peripheral eye can connect to the oldest, most primitive part of the brain that deals with instinct and emotions. This ancient instinctual part of mind may be the source of the artist's unique way of seeing the world. Some link intuitive instinct with originality and understand that this affective relationship is solidly rooted in the earth.

Often, there is a sudden feeling of happiness, a sense of a "Eureka" moment when we see with this inner eye. This illumination is usually followed by discovering a distinct pattern, as *Gestalt* images come into form. Manifesting these previously unconscious ideas and making the invisible visible, aesthetic form brings a treasure of hidden wisdom out of the dark and into the light for all to see. The universality of aesthetic form informs not only the artist, but many scientists as well. Physicists also visualize beautiful patterns around magnets and understand that these sensuous curves in space relate not only to magnetic force, but also to electricity. Aesthetic form exists everywhere.

Sometimes an image is just playful, as with the painting *Watery Beings (1987)*. Playing with form and preserving a particular colour or shape just because it appeals.

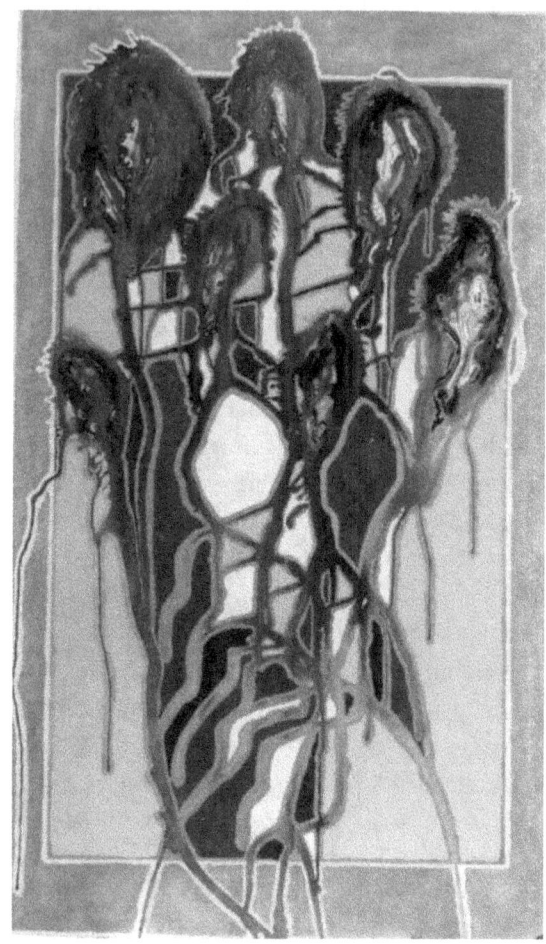

Watery Beings (1987)

Artistic creativity is not subject to the will, and can seem illusive unless one is willing to forfeit ego control and really listen and enter into a dialogue with the medium. This requires a shifting our awareness and trusting that the creative process will produce something worthwhile. These truths can be found in the perceptual vision of the artist. The artwork expresses their particular interpretation of space and time.

Gestalt form requires that we enter into a different state of being when they work; a place within themselves where intuition guides the dialogue and collaborative relationship that has been established with the medium that allows form and figures to enter into the visible realm. As these images come in and out of focus, their ability to trust the body's emotional responses helps to illuminate the patterns that deepen the aesthetic meaning inherent in the work. One must be willing to follow where the imagination leads, deep into personal and collective memory. As the artist learns to listen and respond to the wisdom of the emotional body, they develop the ability to improvise and skill that allow the manifestation of the ineffable.

In these *Gestalt* images, the essential truth of *Being* and being human is often found. Archetypal *Gestalt* images are simplified schematic forms that contain true perceptual elements that are held together by cognitive linkages. Some philosophers call these cognitive memory strands 'sound pictures' that contain both individual and collective symbolic form. The imagination helps to bring this complex hierarchy of schematic shapes under a general concept so the meaning of a work of art may be grasped.

The imagination is the guide both artist and viewer must follow to truly see with the mind's inner eye. The poetic imagination is the intellectual lens through which people see an aesthetic idea taking shape while playing with colour and form. To follow the imagination into a realm of unconscious form shapes a uniquely personal perspective of reality. As the 'I-Eye' of the world, a work of art makes visible an original perception of the world. This unique expressive potentiality each person has underlies all philosophical ideas of authenticity.

Visually playing with aesthetic form provides a feeling of pleasure and joy that at the same time opens up many levels of interpretation. Not only does a work of art contain different possible meanings but our interpretations may also change over time. This does not take away from the initial meaning, but seems to make the aesthetic experience richer than before. For the artist, there is often a period of incubation that precedes the creative act when they ruminate on a creative idea. The period of incubation is much like the world of dream, where the restraint of logical reasoning is temporarily suspended.

Arthur Koestler refers to the incubation period as 'thinking aside' which allows the mind to wander fluidly, without prejudice and adaptable to change. Temporarily suspending judgment and trusting the imagination to facilitate the creative leap is often experienced in a feeling of euphoria. Aesthetic form shows itself in miraculous flashes of insight that seem like short-circuits of reasoning. These are Eureka moments; creative leaps that are experienced on a very personal yet also on a collective level. These insights are often expressed in simplified form

Essential form seems to draw viewers into a reciprocal process with the artwork, a far richer experience because it requires using their imagination. But it may not require an imaginative viewer to interpret form if they recognize it in a different context. For example, the painting *Floating Venus* is readily understood as a depiction of the Venus of Willendorf, a tiny prehistoric statue. Thought to be between 25,000 and 40,000 years old, it's one of the oldest sculptures in the world. I painted it large as a personal tribute to the goddess but this image also expresses a broader perspective of the cultural history of European art.

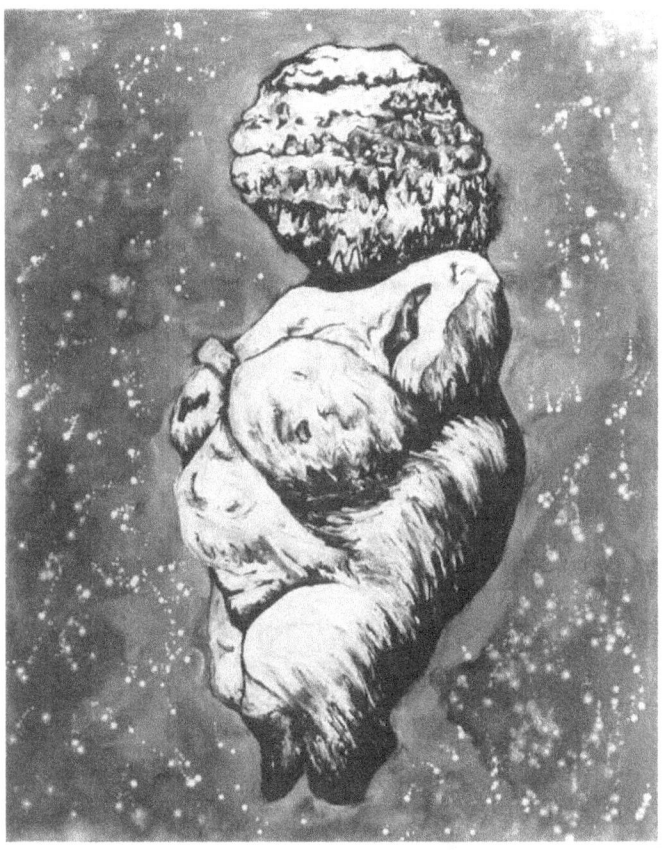

Floating Venus (1988)

For many women today, the Venus of Willendorf has become an icon, representing one of the oldest cult objects made in honour of the ancient mother goddess. Although this tiny sculpture fits in the palm of the hand, its size does not diminish the monumental power of its aesthetic form. By painting a much larger representation, my hope was to avoid the possibility of plagiarism, and merely imitating another work of art. This larger format was also intended to pay tribute to the influence this image has had on my own work. And on a more general level, the tremendous self awareness of feminine history this little Venus has given to contemporary women.

Another reason for its much larger scale reflects my conviction that people, and women in particular, need to be reminded of the personal and social values of the idea of an ancient mother goddess. Perhaps relearning respect for the feminine in general may facilitate balance in the world. I also wanted to represent this Venus figure as floating among the stars because it seems that it is where she belongs. Painted larger than life among the stars, this image of the Venus of Willendorf makes reference to the planet Venus, as a visual metaphor of peace and love, expressed in aesthetic form.

As an artist attempts to disclose what lies concealed in the sensibility of the body, they also make visible emotional knowledge that lies hidden in the collective consciousness of the culture. Artistic creativity is not just about self-representation, but that of the world as well. By reflecting on the mystery of self-disclosure, people also reveal important information about their society. Why are there no 'great' women artists? Were there no women artists? Why; what happened? These questions surfaced during the time this painting was made as it did for many other women.

After a period of incubation, the work is often rapidly executed, often without pausing to reason or think about details. The body knows what must be expressed, and artists trust the imagination as aesthetic form becomes visible. The actual execution of the work is often experienced as a rapid flow of imaginative thinking when it is not practical to stop. As soon as one stops to rationally contemplate what they are doing, the images immediately begin to fade away. Therefore trust inner feelings and instinctive intuition, and only later revise form, if necessary. Trust is an important part of the artistic process as is a temporary relinquishing of conscious control that liberates the mind. These cognitive restraints may be necessary to maintain disciplined routines of rational thought but they rapidly become an impediment to the creative leap.

The imagination must be free to play in order to connect the images that express inner ideas but this process also depends on knowing the rules and skills of the medium. Artistic creativity is a unifying associative process that puts the patterns together that reveal *Gestalt* form that contain valuable insight. Suddenly seeing the right fit or link between different concepts provides new meaning and relationship between pattern and form. Artistic connectivity is an intuitive cognitive process that cannot be learned. It is always original and creative. Everyone has this ability to see with the mind's eye but few have the courage to follow where it leads.

Although each culture may see things differently, appreciating aesthetic form is a shared human phenomenon. Everyone is a potential visionary artist if they stop for a moment to listen to their inner voice and activate their imagination. Once the imagination is free to play and the artist begins to trust the creative process, there is a supreme energy from within that van Gogh described as a fire that he could not put out. Authentic artistic creativity reveals that there is a powerful cognitive and affective drive to follow the inner call of *Being* with childlike faith and naïve sincerity.

Art reaches far beyond what is established and leads those who are will to risk transformation to a better social vision, as Maxine Greene once said. The painting *Naked before the Goddess(1988)* illustrates this point.

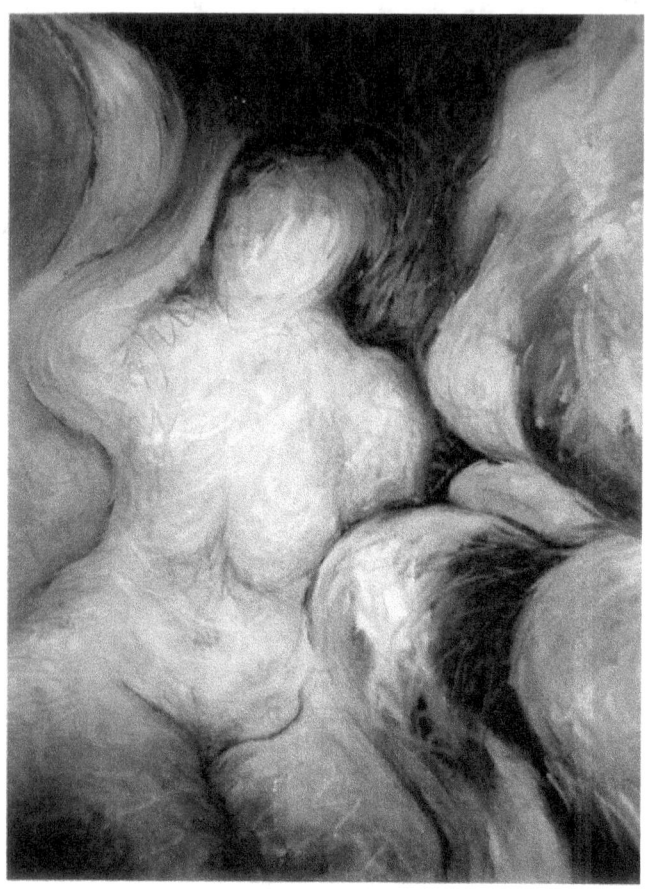

Naked before the Goddess (1988)

This image speaks of an alternative view of human spirituality; one centered on a feminine conception of the divine. At the time this painting was made, it had become increasingly clear that the predominant masculine conception of 'god' had done tremendous damage to the status of women and the natural world, with devastating results. This painting gives form to the idea that 'god' could just as well be feminine, which was a daring new concept at the time; flying in the face of everything I had been taught. But I was learning that the notion of the feminine in human spirituality as well as in art, history and philosophy, had been actively suppressed for millennia in both the Protestant and Catholic Church.

However, during the 1980's many books were published that challenged this predominant masculine concept of the divine. Merlin Stone's *When God was a Woman* and *Ancient Mirrors of Womanhood,* along with M. Esther Harding's *The Way of All Women* and *Woman's Mysteries* had tremendous influence on my work. Contemporary literature and film showed images of the goddess in her many forms. Her image reflected both cultural unity, as well as celebrating the diversity among human beings. Although her image often changes from place to place, some variation of the feminine divine can be found across the globe.

The abundance of available texts and images since the 1980's, has made the notion of 'goddess' veneration public knowledge, inspiring many artists to explore this 'new' aesthetic concept of the feminine within a spiritual context. Especially along the West Coast of North America, many artists had discovered an appropriate aesthetic form by which to express an important idea whose meaning still contained much personal and cultural currency.

This painting may be interpreted as somewhat autobiographical. The woman in front of the half hidden goddess personified the beginning of a lifelong, personal transformative journey towards greater self consciousness and aesthetic understanding. This image also articulates a critique of the dominance of the masculine over the feminine in Western culture. Neglecting the artistic and philosophical contributions of women over the centuries has become an issue some artists and philosophers have tried to address. Not only has the feminine been marginalized but the artistic and philosophical contributions of other cultures have for the most part also been excluded from the historical record.

By reaching deep inside oneself, people find what is true for them, but their subjective truth may also be objective truth for others. After all, no one works in a vacuum and artists are no exception. They usually build on past accomplishments and may have been inspired by their predecessors, as art is always, to some extent, culturally determined. Heidegger points out that a work of art changes our relationship to the world because aesthetic form transcends everyday existence. A great work of art lifts people ecstatically out of their mundane lives in order to connect them to an essential inner truth.

Take van Gogh's painting of a family of peasant farmers eating potatoes they had toiled to grow. Their facial expressions speak volumes about human dignity and suffering. Silently, their faces stare out at the viewer, with a pathos that still has power to move even a hardened postmodern audience. Most everyone can relate to the emaciated features and the fierce pride in these people's eyes. The artist has shown without saying a word what the world of a peasant must have been like in those days. A great work of art shows the inner light of the human spirit and shares it with others in a language most people intuitively understand.

Aesthetic experience makes people aware of the original disclosure of the source of *Being* and what being in the world really means. Take the painting *First Degree (1991)* for example. One senses from its colour and form that this image depicts a tribunal. A group of matrons surround a woman huddled naked on the floor. The figures, heavily outlined in black, have featureless faces that suggest anger and isolation.

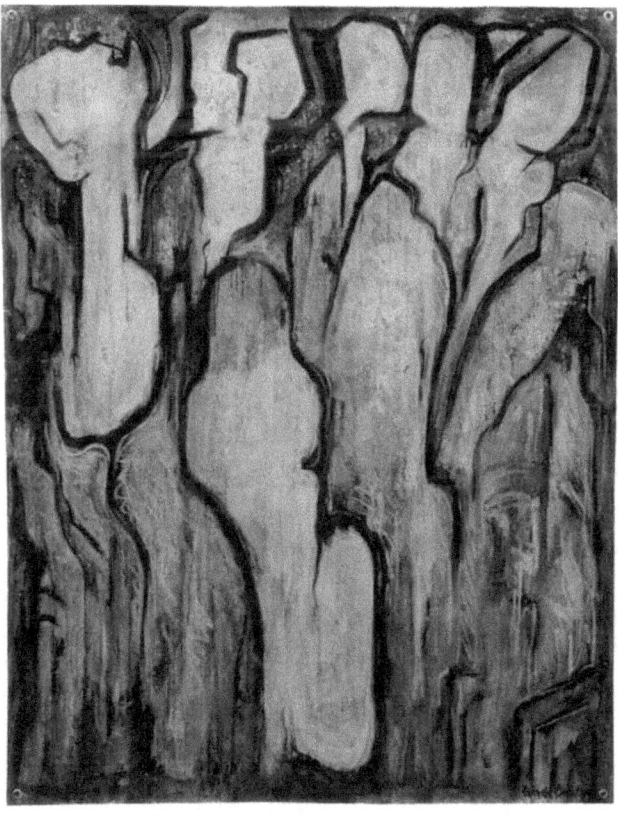

First Degree (1991)

As a viewer many years later, I feel her abandonment as if it is my own. Which it is because this image shows what was hidden within at the time it was painted. Aesthetic form reveals personal and collective emotions long suppressed that needed to be reflected upon if there was to be a better future. The image speaks in a silent emotional language of a collective consciousness that demands a personal and immediate response. This is the fundamental truth that Heidegger refers to as *Dasein*, which is established between the disclosure and concealment of aesthetic form.

Dasein originates in art as a rift between innerness and illumination. Darkness brought into visibility that Berger describes as that space filled with the potentiality of every form; a reflection of inner emotions that articulates humanity's collective destiny. This light of *Being* flickers between these archetypal images that reside in the mysterious darkness of body memory. Aesthetic form makes these inner reflections visible by bringing them into the light.

Rembrandt's paintings speak that same aesthetic language. His masterly use of *chiaroscuro* lifts his subjects onto a different plane in images that speak a subtler language that elevate a commonplace sentiment to the highest level of poetry. That is why a great work of art can withstand changing fashions of time and place. Aesthetic form opens up a dialogue that transcends history. We are emotionally affected when we engage with a work of art that exposes the light of *Being* and being human, which lies at the heart of authenticity.

ART'S SOCIAL FUNCTION

Although aesthetic form expresses the artist's personal reality, it also illuminates the state of the culture. As an artist projects and expresses their inner reality into a work of art, an essential quality of collective truth is also actualized. Therefore a work of art provides a glimpse of a timeless and universal foundation that supports and lies beyond everyday reality. This truth of a greater consciousness is inherent in every great work of art. The British writer and philosopher, Iris Murdoch believes a great work of art has the power to propel us beyond the banality of everyday experience.

This revelation of a higher truth resonates within the emotional body and is instantly recognized by our affective response to the work itself. A work of art represents a unique perspective on the world that is shared with others. Artistic creativity, as it were, wipes clean the aspect-ridden window pane of life yet the artist never ceases to be a limited ego. Rather, they must tap into an expanded consciousness to bring forth an original interpretation of cultural reality. It is through a synthesis of the imagination that the mind is able to reach this higher level of cognition.

When the imagination is free to play with ideas inherent in aesthetic form, two totally different ways of thinking cooperate and become more than their sum parts. But it takes activating the imagination to be able to empathize with others. Putting oneself into another's shoes requires taking a thoughtful leap forward. Activating the imagination facilitates the ability to empathize on a universal global scale. The act of creating a work of art feels like ascending, as if in flight, as the imagination reaches deep within body memory.

Paradoxically, reaching within seems like a religious experience that goes beyond the horizons of consciousness. Raising consciousness to a higher level that the painting *Ascension (1989)* illustrates.

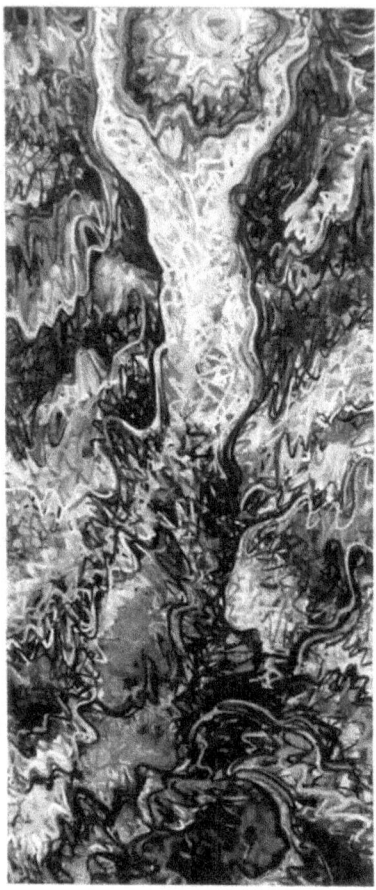

Ascension (1989)

Shaping aesthetic form is not just a private search for significant meaning but it is also cultural in nature. Social themes often come up in the arts; to give voice to critique, or comment on social aspects of culture. People may not be born as cultural beings, but culture is an absolute necessity, if humanity is to survive. By interpreting society, a successful artwork conveys meaning to bodily existence, and expands our experience of *Being* and being in the world.

In addition, there is much to learn from the arts made by other people. A work of art explains and illuminates similarities as well as differences that make each culture as unique as the people within it. Sharing our cultural achievements with others creates a cohesive community. As participants begin to appreciate the aesthetic values of other perspectives, they learn to celebrate their own. Social and political attitudes are often embedded in a work of art. Aesthetic socialization exposes the community to a shared experience of difference in a enjoyable way.

As a personal expression of innermost thoughts and feelings, aesthetic form embodies a social message that defines the ideology of the society in which the artist lives. Take Rembrandt's paintings for example. He lived and worked in Amsterdam, a prosperous and colourful international seaport. During the seventeenth century, Amsterdam was one of the richest cities in Europe but the wealth of the merchant and upper classes did not filter down to the urban peasants. Although he never travelled far, there is no doubt that the painter was aware of the abject poverty of the labourers and their families.

This social upheaval was the result of peasant families leaving the countryside to find work in the cities. The hardship suffered by the Dutch working class was comparable to the poverty in England during the Industrial Revolution a century later. Although Rembrandt never became alienated from society as such, the painter withdrew into seclusion later in life. More and more he found inspiration for his religious paintings in faces of his Jewish neighbours and the downtrodden urban poor. He was inspired by the plight of the disenfranchised, the cripples and tramps. Many of his paintings are visual statements that clearly express what he thought about social injustice. Many great artists throughout history have been acutely aware of social problems and often confront these issues in their art.

Like Rembrandt before him, van Gogh felt that the purpose of art was to convey a social message. He believed that peasants and the working poor were the proper subject of art and states this conviction repeatedly in his letters. His sympathies were with the urban peasants whom he glorified in his work. Expressing hope that his art might comfort them, he felt a moral obligation to paint these ordinary people with a deep feeling of respect and empathy. The destitute painter saw himself as one with them, in their difficult struggle to survive.

Artistic form speaks a 'subtler' language, making thought visible and public in order to express what cannot be spoken of in words. For example, the painting *Ishtar with Moon in her Lap (1989)* articulates an aesthetic idea not easily communicated in words alone. This celebratory image of the ancient Sumerian goddess was personally reassuring because many of my other paintings at the time were dark and chaotic, and strangely incoherent. Challenging the status quo had created powerful conflicting energies in my work, as well as in my life, shaking the very foundations of what I had believed to be true. But there was no turning back, and it required tenacity and courage to continue this artistic journey in order to bring these aesthetic ideas into the public domain. Bringing a idea into visible form meant that its image could then be reflectively contemplated and understood.

The image of the moon is a reoccurring motif in my work, perhaps because of its feminine character, whose monthly phases mimic a woman's menstrual cycle.

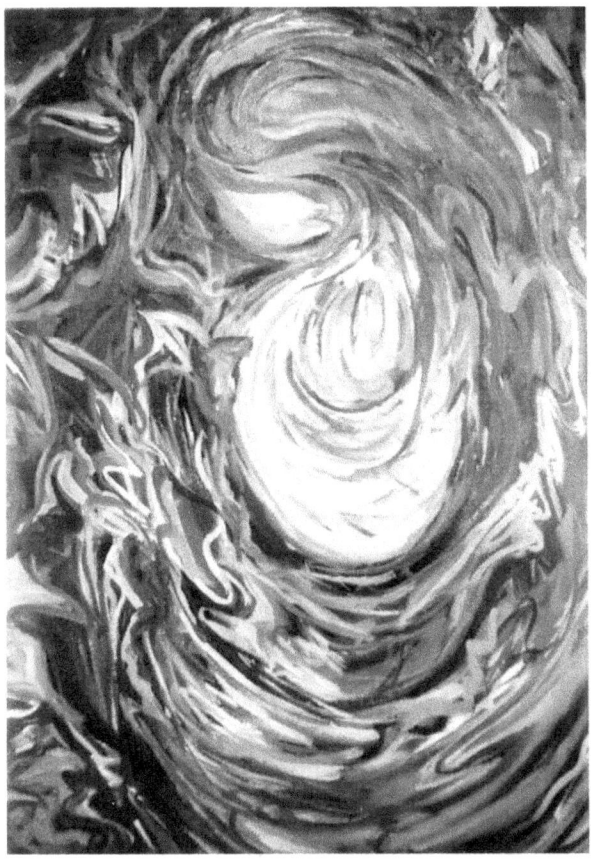

Ishtar with Moon in her Lap (1989)

In many cultures women still refer to this time of the month as 'moon time', as they rest and gossip with other women friends. In contrast to contemporary Western culture, these few days are a time of quiet contemplation to reflect on the special regenerative power of nature. The moon has always held a particular fascination, provoking the imagination to escape its limits as we look up into the night sky. Its three-fold character and the waxing and waning of the moon may also be viewed as a metaphor for the feminine life cycle; as maiden, mother and crone. In addition, it also suggests the natural cycles of decay and regeneration in an endless cycle of birth, death and rebirth.

Many expressive artists do not hesitate to use aesthetic form as a social commentary on the politics of the day, often at great cost to themselves. Kathe Kollwitz found inspiration in the plight of the urban poor in Germany, and the horrendous effects of the war on women and children. Her work speaks to us on a universal level as she depicts the devastating consequences of war on the families in Berlin. These images are a social critique of the morality of a culture that glorified war at the expense of its people. Her art never gives form to the enemy, only to the stark faces and gestures of women holding their dead children in their arms.

Kollwitz creates powerful images that speak the truth about oppression and the need for a better society. These images articulate on an emotional level, which needs no words to convey her social message of pacifism. Her work illuminates a reality whose meaning goes far beyond the experience of the mundane, to bring the plight of ordinary people into focus. She openly critiqued German society for allowing such misery, using her art to state an undeniable truth that resonates deep within the emotional body as well as in the mind. Most viewers respond instantly, with intuitive understanding when they recognize the despair in the other.

Like Kollwitz, Anselm Kiefer also uses his art work as a social commentary and critique of societal issues. Through the creative process, he explores the dark shadow of the Nazi past that contemporary German society prefers to forget. Born in 1945, his generation questioned the legacy they inherited in post-war Europe. Artists and intellectuals of this generation were confronted by a questionable past and a future that seemed so threatening that it tends to create despair.

Kiefer looks at Germanic mythology and Europe's historical past for personal insight. He courageously confronts the collective guilt and dark shadows of two world wars that some people in Germany tried hard to suppress. His paintings are a revelation of a fundamental truth that the culture had been wounded when it destroyed a segment of its people. Exposing the dark shadows of absolute power, which is a deep wound of Germanic history, Kiefer's paintings illuminate the light of reason so the culture may begin to heal and renew itself.

Although cultural history will eventually judge the authenticity of a work of art, its truth begins with the individual artist who must strive to find their inner and authentic voice. It is through the individual eye and heart that this universal essence is manifested. Yet artists build on a historical background of past cultural achievements in their search for inner truth. Authenticity always rests on the foundations of what has come before. A successful work of art carries on the old ways of an established tradition to bring a new aesthetic expression into manifestation that has lasting value and significance.

Throughout human history, works of art have left a moving and emotional testament of being alive in a particular time and place, for generations to come. Since before the caves of Lascaux were painted, art has provided meaningful form that speaks of *Being* and being human and shares its significance from one generation to the next. But aesthetic understanding requires the emotional participation of viewers, and a society that is willing to preserve and pass on the artwork itself. The painting *Valley of the Masks* shows what I mean. This painting draws its inspiration from the distinctive art of the West Coast First Nations' people.

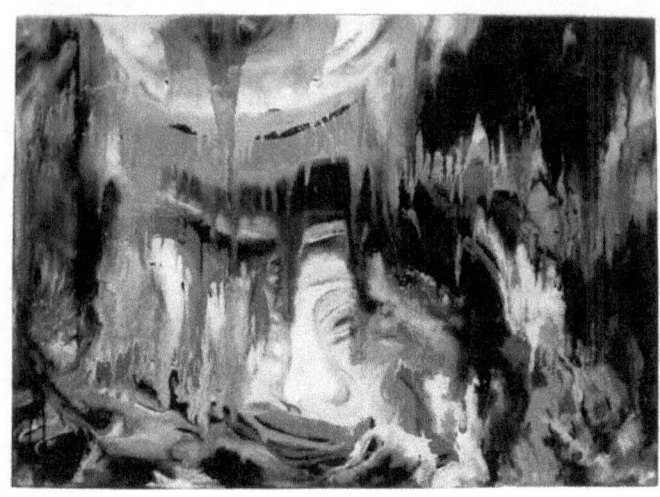

Valley of the Masks (1989)

This image pays tribute to the traditional masks of the native people of British Columbia, without expropriating or imitating their unique style. This painting was begun by pouring diluted oil paint on the flat surface of the canvas. The colours were encouraged to mix together in what appears to be a random manner. When the application of paint was finished, the canvas was lifted then up to let the paint drip down. Its 'tear-like' forms speak of the negative impact of colonization on the indigenous people as well as the environment of the Pacific West Coast.

These beautiful hand-carved masks, unique to Canada's West Coast, embody tremendous cultural meaning for the indigenous people. Stylized natural forms depict family crests, and each clan's animal totem is a uniquely crafted artistic form. For these people masks are considered to be family heirlooms to be passed down from the elders to the younger generation. In this culture, owning a mask gives someone special privileges along with a special name, and specific social obligations. Masks are a valuable part of the ceremonial regalia, worn during the winter season communal dances as well as at family celebrations. In addition, masks are believed to embody special spiritual power; therefore they are highly valued and kept in a special place of honor within the home.

Not only in America, but all over the world including many places in Europe, masks are believed to contain special personal and cultural power. Usually worn over the face, masks have been used since antiquity for both ceremonial as well as practical purposes. Many people today still wear masks during carnival and masquerade parties, as well as during seasonal and family celebrations. Although some First Nations communities use masks for healing purposes, they most often are meant to embody a specific spirit and are considered priceless artifacts to be cherished.

When art touches people like that, aesthetic form speaks in a language that resonates in the deepest part of body memory. Then aesthetic form imparts the lessons that people need to know to live a humane life that is in harmony with others. Although many primitive societies still remember, this knowledge has been suppressed in the west for centuries. Contemporary culture still endures the Cartesian separation of mind over the body, rejecting the emotional sensibility of the body in favour of intellectual rationalism. But some artists and philosophers realize that intellectual rationality must be balanced by intuition and inner wisdom of the body.

It is through the creative process that artists constantly reconnect to innerness and the affective part of *Being*. They bring back artefacts of this experience and express it in a work of art that bears witness to this inner journey. The ancient Greeks understood this mysterious aesthetic language as the revelation of *Being* that resides within. Since ancient times, this dark power of bodily wisdom was honoured in the culture's rituals, mythology and art.

There is a correlation between the mind and the world that represents an underlying collective consciousness that dwells beyond everything else. As images become visible during the art-making process, aesthetic form often seems to refer to this timeless collective consciousness. As the imagination weaves inner emotional knowledge into an aesthetically pleasing pattern, these images may make reference to the prehistoric, primordial origins of the universe. This celestial memory of humanity's cosmic origins lies hidden in the recesses of inner body wisdom, waiting to be brought into consciousness.

Always people of their own time, it helps if artists have a curious nature, especially when it comes to the crucial issues of their culture. They need to be securely rooted in the present and have the necessary emotional and psychological balance to penetrate and comprehend the images that emerge from the depth of consciousness. It takes audacity to articulate the emotional memories of the past that emerge. But if a work of art is to have value for others, the artist needs the ability to visualize a better future for humanity.

There is no doubt that a work of art is influenced by culture, however aesthetic form goes far beyond cultural specifics to bring a timeless reality into form. This was the aim behind the painting *After Lascaux (1990)*. Lascaux, in the south of France, is world famous for its Palaeolithic cave paintings of prehistoric animals, which are estimated to be about 17,300 years old.

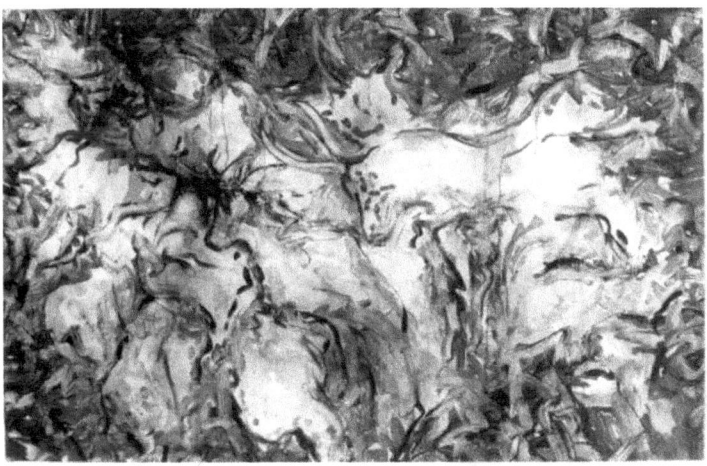

After Lascaux (1990)

Discovered in 1940, the cave walls are covered with animals, human figures and abstract symbols. One cave contains nearly 2,000 figures such as pregnant horses, stags and bison. These timeless images seem to refer to the hunt and procreation and may have been used for seasonal or hunting ceremonies. Although it may be true that art is a historical construct, most artists throughout the ages have created aesthetic form from a timeless perspective. But a work of art is historical in the sense that it is a personal reflection on life in a specific time and place. In an essential sense, the artwork grounds history because it always represents a particular point of view.

Visionary artists have always worked within a historical context that often reserves posterity until long after their death. Ironically, art history demonstrates that those artists who were most despised while they were alive, often receive the greatest appreciation later. Be that as it may, most artists are keenly aware of the politics of their day. Art often has a political undercurrent that critiques social inequality; often shocking society. If a work of art is authentic, it can't help but expose injustice. In *Ways of Seeing*, John Berger points out that art does not cover anything up but reveals what it must. Therefore aesthetic form may articulate a political message, which often makes the artist appear to be rebellious and nonconformist.

There was an element of the rebel in Rembrandt that shows even in his earliest portraits and he remained a rebel throughout his entire life. He grew up and attended university in Leiden, one of the wealthiest cities in Europe and centre of the textile industry, Intellectuals from all over Europe mingled with the urban poor. The underpaid and illiterate workers lived a marginal existence. From an early age, Rembrandt was very aware of the gap between rich and poor and loved to paint the lower classes in society. Capturing their essence with great insight into the soul, he paints the poor and the old exactly as he saw them, with dignity and penetrating observation.

Art can make a social statement but aesthetic appreciation also has the power to build communities through audience participation. For many indigenous people, artwork in the form of masks and button blankets are a crucial aesthetic component of the communal gatherings. The painting *The Great Divide* pays tribute to the traditional button blankets that the First Nations people of British Columbia use in their rituals and ceremonies. Similar to the masks, each blanket represents a family totem animal, which is hand appliquéd in uniquely flowing patterns and distinctive colours.

This painting echoes the standard colours of red on a dark blue background, found on many blankets originating along the West Coast and Fraser Valley. Further north, the colours are more often bright yellow on a background of cerulean blue. However, the flowing pattern and design of the clan's totem animals is a common characteristic of both types of blankets, regardless of where they were made.

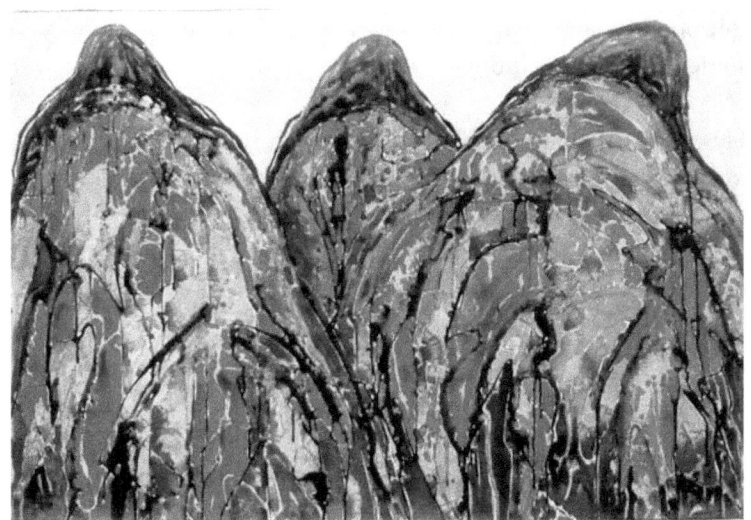

The Great Divide (1989)

As with *Valley of the Masks*, my intention here was not to imitate or expropriate artistic form but to make reference to the significance of West Coast indigenous art, and articulate my respect for the goodness of Canada's native cultures. In addition, this painting also honours the feminine nature of the mountainous landscape of British Columbia. The title of this painting relates to an actual place deep in the Rockies where a mighty river separates and flows either west to the sea, or east towards the prairies in Alberta and beyond.

Furthermore, the unity of three sisters as landscape, articulates the three-fold nature of feminine experience which was referred to earlier. The idea of three sisters recurs over and over in my work, perhaps because it reflects the connective relationship I have with my own two sisters. I see blankets in general as a commonly understood artistic form because blankets are used in every culture for utilitarian reasons as well as for ceremonial use. Blankets are used to comfort and protect the body from the cold. But blankets also bear witness to a person's dreams, as well as to some of their most intimate secrets.

My aim in making this painting was to unite a particular artistic form with a universally understood aesthetic idea, anticipating that a viewer would intuitively understand the complexity of its meaning. Although people may not be consciously aware of the cultural meaning of the animal patterns used on the West Coast button blankets, on some level art speaks to everyone who takes time for contemplative reflection of its aesthetic form. As one works over the years, certain recurring themes seem to appear time and again. Forms that develop express a uniquely feminine perspective of equality between people, regardless of race, age, gender or state of their bank account.

The plight of the urban poor and the even greater poverty on the land due to its depopulation, continued well into van Gogh's time, and still happens today. Many were painfully aware of the poverty and disease that the peasant migration brought to the cities and countryside alike. Several of van Gogh's landscapes literally confront us with a scarred countryside whose pre-emptive wounds were caused by the expanding city. His paintings also depict the dignity of the poor.. He paints the urban workers and peasants working the fields with great love and respect.

From predecessors such as Gustave Courbet, he learned that the ordinary working classes were a worthy subject for art. But van Gogh went a step further. He believed that the working poor should also be the recipients of his art and not the rich merchant class whom he shunned. Vincent wrote that he would be pleased if ordinary people would hang his paintings in their room or workshop. Van Gogh had other revolutionary ideas with regards to the social inequality of women in his time. Like Degas and others, he acknowledged the inhumanness of a culture that forced its women to support themselves by selling their bodies on the street.

He found inspiration in the sorrowful lives of these marginalized women, painting Sien, his lover over and over again to express the suffering of this unfortunate woman. He also believed that freedom and equal rights was needed between men and women. This was a revolutionary viewpoint and ahead of his time. Vincent also understood that many social problems were caused by people's separation from the land where families had lived and worked together in order to prosper. City life irrevocably changed the relationship between genders as men increasingly began to dominate over the women and children.

Like Rembrandt, van Gogh rebelled against society throughout his short life. Both artists spent their life giving form to the sad reality of peasant life and the urban poor, who propped up the wealth of the nation, yet reap none of the rewards. This sentiment can be seen in the painting *Refugees (2002)* that silently expresses the profound misery of the homeless in the blank faces and gestures of the women holding their children. Yet these women stand together and support each other. In simplified form, this image communicates my resistance to more misery caused by war and aggression.

Its starkness is a universal image of suffering, readily understood by everyone who thinks about its truth.

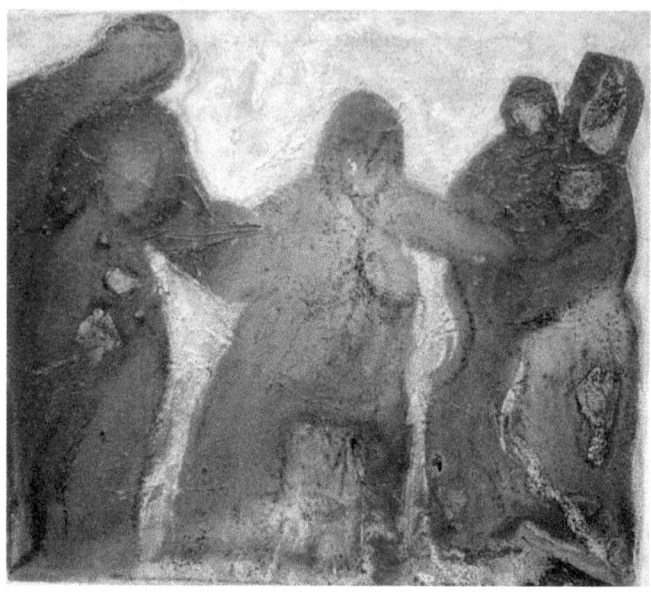

Refugees (2002)

Kathe Kollwitz was also strongly affected by the social problems of the poor living in Berlin. With an enlightened eye, she records the hardship etched on the faces of women and children who came to her husband's infirmary. Her artwork clearly articulates her empathy for the less fortunate in powerful images of hungry faces that become the focus of her art making. Kollwitz used aesthetic form to make a persuasive political statement against the prevailing politics of her day. In poignantly moving images, she bravely denounced the violence that was erupting in Germany. Although it was dangerous to do so, Kollwitz publicly expressed her opposition to the carnage and the recruitment of more young men to fight for Germany.

The bold expression of Kollwitz's convictions in her work stands as a powerful statement of the horrors of war and its debilitating consequences for the people. Even after the Nazis fired her from her teaching position, she continued to create humanitarian leaflets and posters for distribution. Kollwitz' art resonates with heart felt compassion. These moving images speak of the terrible conditions that the German people endured during two world wars. With her work, she makes an appeal on behalf of the disenfranchised women and children she saw in her husband's infirmary. Using her art as a form of protest, she clearly articulates the criminal social conditions that prevailed in Germany at the time.

The generation of artists that followed, also create art with a political message. Anselm Kiefer's work for instance, critiqued German society for refusing to confront its Nazi past. His art intentionally shocks the senses in order to force viewers to face up to half-buried memories of the past that refuse to go away. For some people, Kiefer's art is a thorn in their side. Much of post-war society would much rather forget Germany's past history, preferring to focus on more mundane issues of the day. His work not only challenged social convention, but Kiefer himself has also been viewed as a rebel in the progress of modern art.

In an era of increasing abstraction, his paintings reintroduce pictorial representation and even make reference to pre-modern Western art and philosophy; particularly, his reference to the role of the artist as shaman and transformer. Rejecting the prevailing fashions of the avant-garde, he creates aesthetic form that is intensely symbolic of European history. In some of these images, he explore pre-scientific and more fluid modes of visual thinking and in so doing, he brings ancient symbolism into postmodern aesthetic form.

Kiefer uses aesthetic form that the imagination discovered in the shadows of body memory as a metaphor for the transformative power of art. He compares the ancient alchemical arts to the creative act of painting, acknowledging that aesthetic form is always shaped by a personal perception of the visible world. his paintings are thought provoking personal reflections on German history in conjunction with ancient mythology. His subjects express the deeply rooted shadow of Germanic heroic culture that has brought unspeakable suffering to its people. These multi-dimensional paintings have an emotional impact that broadens our insight into the past. They are the heroic testament of an artist who attempts to come to terms with the collective guilt, which has haunts his generation.

These images seem to regress into a historical past that speaks directly to the emotional inner body. Viewers intuitively recognize the sorrow that lies buried in the German collective consciousness as he searches for insight from within. But his paintings also critique contemporary politics because society encourages the proliferation of nuclear energy. His painting, *Heavy Cloud* (1985) makes reference to social and health problems that are inherent in the inevitable pollution of nuclear waste. At a time when the issue of nuclear energy was contested in Germany, this image suggests that yellow radiation has leaked onto the landscape. Kiefer poses important concerns about the individual relates to the past and how this affects the present.

His work confronts us with the consequences of our short sighted political actions in humanity's press for progress. His art also make reference to the chemists, the ancient scientists who understood that the world in which they lived has limitations. This realization of the limits of nature is as valid today as it was in the past. Contemporary society must learn to accept the limits of the world as it is. The earth, air and water are finite and vulnerable. These natural elements require balance and respect, or humanity will be faced with the inevitable consequences. These elements that make up the natural world have not changed with time, and this simple truth is as relevant to life here today as it was back then.

ARE THERE NO GREAT WOMEN ARTISTS?

There is a peculiar lack of female artists included in the predominantly masculine history of Western art, yet legends claim that the art of painting was invented by a woman. In both eastern and western culture, convention has it that the origin of painting was attributed to a Corinthian maiden by the name of Dibutades. The ancient philosopher Pliny, records the legend of the young woman who traced her lover's profile on a wall in her room and then filled it in with colour. She was the daughter of Butades, an accomplished potter. Her painting inspired her father to work the image up into a sculpture.

This legend of the first painter, who was also a woman, became a popular theme in the history of Western art but the fact remains that before the age of modernism, few women were able to speak publicly about how it felt to be an artist. Wendy Steiner in her book *Venus in exile the rejection of beauty in Twentieth-Century art* wryly observes that if the official version of art history is to be believed, there simply were no female artists, period. This negation of artistic creativity in women gives a peculiar one-sidedness to Western art.

Increasingly, the female body was perceives as a source of titillation intended for the male viewer alone. Contemporary artists of both genders have challenged this notion in their search for more appropriate representations of the female body. Shaping aesthetic form require an imaginative unity between sensible intuition, which is associated with the feminine and the masculine attribute of intellectual understanding. Both ways of knowing is essential in discovering meaningful aesthetic form.

Take for example, the painting *Motherhood (1990)*. This image came out of the sensuousness of the paint, in tandem with intuitive ideas that entered my mind as I worked.

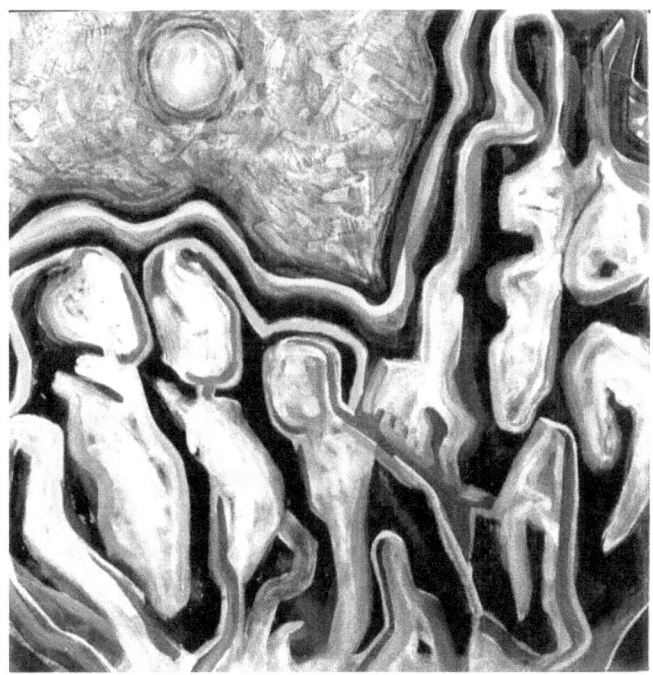

Motherhood (1990)

As this image took shape, these aesthetic ideas began to organize themselves under a general concept of a mother and her children. This painting recalls some of Picasso's later paintings, where he stylized the female figure, depicting her as if seen from within and without simultaneously. Similarly the mother figure to the right suggests an X-ray perspective, while the disembodied forms of the children articulate the frustration of fragmentation and separation. However, there is also a note of hope in this image.

The sun shines brightly over the heads of the children in an energetic cerulean blue sky, as the woman serenely watches over them. Heavy bands of colour envelop the mother and her children, connecting these figures to each other as if in a protective womb. This womb-like structure was meant to suggest an iconic depiction; perhaps as a talisman for protecting absent loved ones. This painting may also be interpreted on a more universal level, as an infinitely recurring theme of motherhood in general. A sympathetic viewer, who takes time to reflect on the many possible interpretations the artist may have consciously as well as unconsciously intended, should be able to grasp the complex meaning behind this abstracted and fractured female form.

Artists as diverse as the ones mentioned in the previous chapters used the female figure as a personal metaphor for expressing a higher collective conception of inner truth: They worked hard to expresses their subject's inner spirit, no matter which gender they happen to be. The search for symbolic meaning in depicting the human body speaks honestly about the artist's lived experience. In the process of depicting the surface of the body, inner truth is often revealed that reminds both the artist and viewer they are not alone. Everyone is a vital part of all existence.

During a time when the female body was seen as merely an object of desire, van Gogh painted the women in his life with a compassionate eye. His reverence for the sanctity of women was revolutionary in Western art. Not interested in depicting obvious beauty, van Gogh would rather express the lived experience that left traces on a woman's body. In his paintings and drawings, he expresses his attraction to his lover Sien, whom others detested. When he was confronted by his family who wanted to know what he saw in her, he replied that for him Sien was beautiful because real life had marched over her body.

For Vincent, her beauty lay in the pain and visitations that had marked and left scars on both her skin and her heart. With profound empathy and honesty, van Gogh sketched and painted the women in his life in a direct confrontation to the bourgeoisie notion of propriety. His paintings celebrate the real world of the working poor that burgers would rather ignore. But it is the paintings and drawings of Sien in particular that evoke a strong emotional response from anyone who encounters them. An 1882 lithograph called *Sorrow* makes a powerful statement about the wretchedness of life for lower class women in modern industrialized society.

Alcohol abuse and prostitution was a huge problem in the inner cities of Europe. If women weren't prostitutes, they worked at menial jobs to earn enough to feed themselves and their children. Van Gogh saw only their beauty, especially in Sien, a prostitute addicted to alcohol who was often sick from starvation. When she was well enough to work, she scrubbed houses for the bourgeoisie and took in their washing. When she was too sick to work, she sold her body on the street like her mother had done before her.

He paints Sien honestly; as she was, without idealizing her, showing a woman who had seen it all. His love and empathy shines through the images he made of his lover, as the painting *Relationship (1990)* does for me. This image shows the discursiveness of inner feelings about the last days of a marriage that had ended long before. It depicts the masks we all wear in public and in our daily life in order to keep the peace. This painting also expressed my suppressed rage at a man who wanted to control my life and the patriarchal system that condoned it. But outside marriage and the protection of a male, many women resort to selling their body on the streets, as Sien did. Prostitution is a dangerous business, even today.

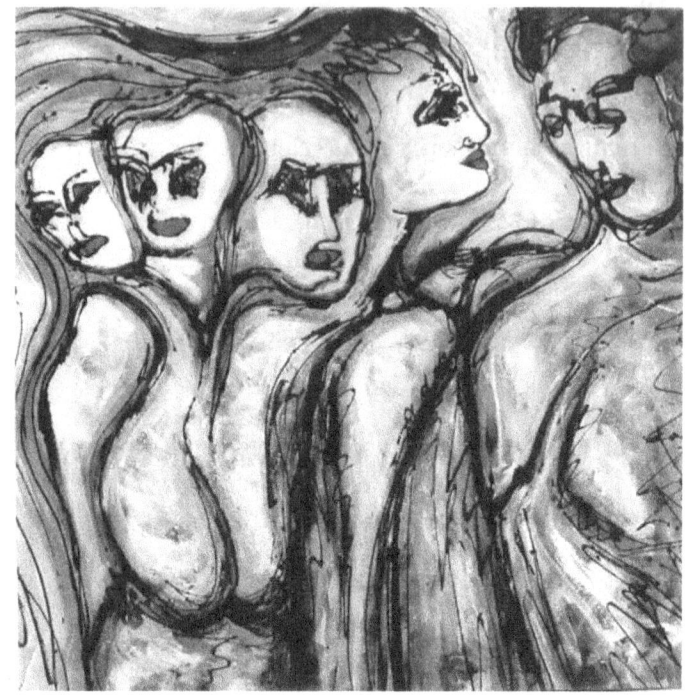

Relationship (1990)

Kathe Kollwitz was familiar with the plight of prostitutes, sick with venereal disease and hunger that came to her husband's medical practice in Berlin. Like van Gogh and Rembrandt, she expressed her compassion for these marginalized women and found inspiration for her art in the dignity and despair written on their faces. Kollwitz' haunting images of these women holding their children are a heart-rending testament to the trauma that is often stored deep within body memory. Viewers can only respond with empathy to the stark faces of women who have seen it all. These powerful images force viewers to really listen to the silent message that critiques a society so corrupt that it allows such misery, and that this must be changed. But her subjects also speak of beauty and the rhythm of the body and

their inherent strength to protect their children at all costs.
These women may be sick and hungry, but they stand fearlessly
together to face the aggressor.

These moving aesthetic statements articulate a primordial love
that women have for each other and their children in their
common struggle to survive during a time of war and social
upheaval. Kollwitz has given to western art a timeless expression
of what it means to be a woman and mother, with all the
compassion that is involves. A vocal advocate for the rights of
women, she demanded support from the educational system for
a woman's right to receive an equal education in the arts long
before it became fashionable. She taught at the Berlin Academy
for the Arts until her dismissal by the Nazi regime. Throughout
her life, Kollwitz synthesized her social, political and feminist
views and had the courage and endurance to use art to fight back
and survive.

Although Kiefer does not address gender inequality directly, he
does refer to an ancient conception of time as being feminine and
circular. This perception of the passing of time is still found in
primitive matrilineal societies around the world. Nietzsche was
also aware of the cyclical notion of time, where both past and
future met in the present moment. But in some of his paintings,
Kiefer does refer to an all powerful earth goddess who exists as
the foundation of the world. His painting *Margarethe* is a self
conscious effort to suggest the quintessential woman in a
landscape of earth, straw and lead.

The artist as transformer imitates the alchemical quest for
transforming base metal into gold. He transmutes various
minerals, substances that originate from deep within the earth.
Like the alchemists, Kiefer starts with the shadow and works
from darkness towards the light, perhaps as a metaphor for the
birthing process of aesthetic form. The challenge for

contemporary artists is to create an authentic representation of the female body that is free of misogyny so prevalent in the modernist tradition.

The artist must re-imagine women as equal partners in aesthetic pleasure. But this would require a new mythical conception that teaches reverence and respect for each person, regardless of gender. This radically new attitude towards the female goes hand in hand with respect for the earth that gives us life. But how can society expand its conception of feminine beauty without falling back on the traditional notions of male dominance, female victimization and a false consciousness of separation? Perhaps a new mythology can articulate the dance between feminine and masculine energies, in nature as well as within ourselves.

A renewed vision of the feminine divine may be able to emulate the rhythms of nature, rather than support continuous conflict. The painting *The Encounter (1990)* articulates this hope for the possibility of peaceful coexistence. Despite the aggressive application of paint, the meeting between the bull and stag seems copasetic. These horned animals symbolize the masculine and feminine energies in the world as well as within human nature. Activating the mythic imagination seems to rebalance these opposing energies so they may enhance each other rather than hinder.

A respectful dialogue between the two may be initiated that make use of the strengths of both points of view. Some oral cultures still remember the stories of the ancestors when women were honoured and respected.

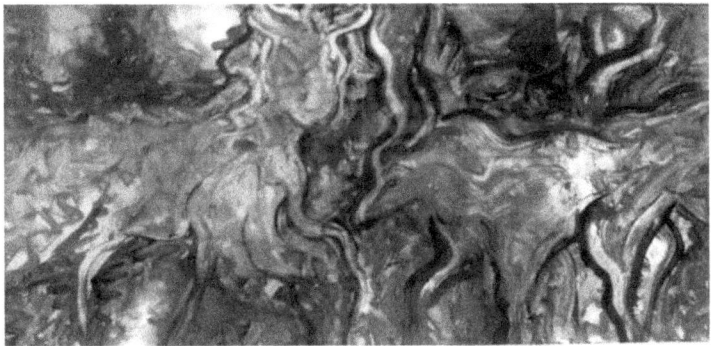

The Encounter (1990)

Respect for the feminine goes hand in hand with peaceful coexistence on the land. Many indigenous people maintain a humble respect for Mother Earth who sustains them. In these cultures, the elders are the keepers of mythological wisdom. Mothers and grandmothers recite the age-old wisdom the next generation needed to know in order to survive. Through mythic stories, the elders explained the obligations each person had to themselves and to the community.

Participation in the mythology through art and ritual gave meaning to one's life within the context of the group but it requires an aesthetic response from participants. This emotional involvement with aesthetic form, whether in stories or a song, communicates important knowledge from one generation to the next about how people survive. These myths and stories justify the cultural norms and designate the place each individual has in its survival.

These stories preserved cultural memories of important events that have happened on the land, so others may find their own meaning. Throughout time and place, a people's mythology taught the next generation the ethics and morality of a particular group. With a strong ethical and moral foundation for the equality of human existence, women will again be valued and revered, bringing a new harmony into the world. In such an ideal society, artistic creativity and the imagination will again find its rightful place with images of the feminine body that are saturated with meaning and humanity's place in nature.

Heidegger understood the reciprocal nature of the unfolding of human existence on the earth. Knowing, as the old saying goes, what goes around comes around. He observed that technology had reduced the earth and the atmosphere to mere raw material, a commodity to be used and exploited. Since the Industrial Revolution, even human beings were perceived as raw material and are therefore expendable. As nature and the environment increasingly are devalued, and the incessant desire for more technology relentlessly drives global consumerism, the future growth of a modernist society cannot be predicted.

Long before the age of nano technology, Heidegger points to the danger of ignoring the transformative nature of a culture that extends to changing even the essence of humanity itself. In a time before post humanism, he understood the need for a great chain of *Being*. In the past, the mythology of a people taught the next generation that they have moral and ethical responsibilities. Often this was illustrated in a work of art. Art satisfies the human need for archetypical images articulate valuable knowledge needed to live in a good life.

Engagement with a work of art reinvests the natural world with mystery. This atmosphere of uncertainty puts enchantment back into our lives. However, it is true that the search for the hidden truth of *Being* has its perils. One must have faith in the outcome to continue the journey inward to the Self. But aesthetic form only becomes accessible by exploring innerness where a hidden well of vital knowledge lies waiting to be tapped. By making these archetypal images visible, aesthetic form shows that existence is indeed infinitely circular. Understanding the cyclical nature of our being is the most important message an artist can give to others.

Every living thing comes and goes, it grows, dies, and is born again. By mirroring the natural world of regeneration; growth as well as decay and death, a work of art illuminates the truth of being in the world. Everything changes and the theme of transformation recurs time and again in my work. Each time, the artwork articulates this revelation anew; aesthetic truth and shares this vital knowledge of eternal transformation of everything that exists here on earth.

The expressive artist continually searches for new ways to articulate this inner wisdom by paying attention to form that spontaneously appears in the medium. Bringing these images through and into the light requires an unconditional love for knowledge. It also requires a deep irrational faith that the imagination will find aesthetic form can adequately represent these shadowy ideas. The inner search for hidden wisdom involves stepping over the threshold of consciousness and to risk emotional exposure, when these fleeting ideas or images come to mind.

Yet if one is true to the medium, they respect these sometimes painful images and strive to make them visible for all to see. By giving form to personal truth, a work of art reveals that a vast oceanic world underlies everyday reality. This greater sense of Self or *Being* informs both on a individual as well as level. When *Being* reveals itself in a work of art, aesthetic form clearly articulates what it means to be human in a particular place and time. It reveals us to ourselves, and whispers a subtle message of how things are that everyone understands.

WHY SORROW?

John Berger wryly observed that the present pain of living in this postmodern society is unprecedented. He has a point. It does sometimes seem as if social and personal values have all but eroded. Our elders lament that cultural norms of ethics and morality have almost been lost from one generation to the next. But perhaps we should view the world as the ancient Greeks once did. They saw the violence and victimization in society as part of the regenerative cycle of creation and thus part of the revelation of *Being* and being human.

The Greeks reconciled themselves by celebrating this regenerative power of nature through their mythology and art. The Greeks made great works of art that gave form to the various archetypal forces that underpin the psyche of humanity. Bringing these archetypes into manifestation and into the light of day made it possible to come to terms with these conflicting forces between the individual and the culture. Artists and philosophers realized that reconciling the polar opposites of 'good' and 'evil' brought psychic harmony for the individual as well as for society as a whole.

The ancients personified these archetypal forces in the stories of the exploits of a variety of gods and goddesses. These sacred myths not only taught people how to live well, but they also explained the often contradictory elements of *Being* and being human. Unfortunately, after the fall of the Roman Empire, Christianity rejected the notion of many archetypal deities in favour of one omnipotent god. As the idea of one almighty masculine god took hold in the western psyche, it became increasingly difficult to maintain equilibrium between these opposing psychic forces and humanity has lived with the results for centuries.

The painting *The Burning Times(1990)* illustrates the anxiety of long forgotten world events.

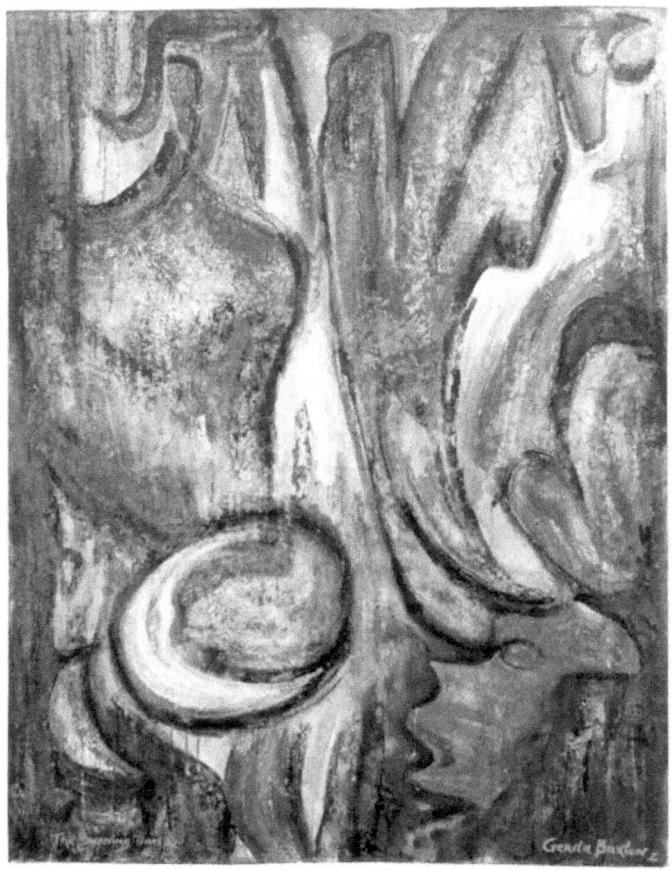

The Burning Times (1990)

This image is a personal interpretation and response to Western culture's misogynous history. It alludes to a time when women in Europe were murdered in droves and whose memory seems to reside deep within our consciousness. The title refers to a historical period when scores of women were accused as witches, and consequently burnt at the stake. This image recalls the fear of pain and death that permeated throughout much of Europe when the Inquisition and the Church tried to suppress women in general and the old pagan nature religion in particular.

Bringing these aesthetic ideas into form felt like an act of *at-one-ment*. The implications of truth that had been made visible could then be rationally reflected upon. Although there is a pleasant tension between the lusciousness of colour and texture of the painted surface, the jagged anxiety of the figures suggest a certain ambivalence concerning the implied meaning of this image. However, the title reinforced this idea by making direct reference to historical events that have had tremendous influence on the treatment of women for centuries to come.

Although early Christianity tried to rebalance the disparity between masculine and feminine energies, with the advent of Roman Catholicism a disturbing onesidedness took precedence in western thought. With the rejection of the feminine part of *Being* and being human, the unnatural suppression of the two-sidedness in nature increasingly became an ethical and psychological problem in society. Some philosophers have argued that the negation of the archetypal forces of nature has resulted in a tragic collective guilt that hides in the shadows of western cultural consciousness.

Mythology and religion can no longer explain these powerful archetypal energies but artists know that it is their role to bring these hidden psychological forces into aesthetic form. Some contemporary artists directly address the shadow that hides in the psyche of their culture. Kiefer, for instance attempts to come to terms with this psychological blemish that exists on the soul of humanity, especially the psyche of Germany. But it seems artists have been inspired by sorrow for centuries.

Rembrandt, who lived in one of the most affluent cities in Europe, also saw much inequity and suffering in the lives of his neighbours. In his personal life as well, the painter suffered far more than the ordinary man but he bore his misfortune with the utmost nobility. Vincent van Gogh and Kathe Kollwitz also experienced much sadness in their lives, and like Rembrandt also found inspiration in the suffering of the working poor. Perhaps these artists had a sense of solidarity with the sorrow of others and expressed these feelings in aesthetic form. Their work speaks of this shared pain with great compassion.

Both the artwork of van Gogh and Kollwitz show the sorrow that war and poverty brings, especially to the women and children. Both were aware of the abysmal lives of the weavers and used their work to critique the European textile industry, which was renowned for its notoriously poor working conditions and low pay. While the capitalist owners became wealthy, the working poor went hungry. Their art articulates loud and clear the terrible consequences of poverty in images that are there for all to see. Aesthetic form silently speaks in a universal language of inner feelings and emotions that all human beings understand.

Artists and philosophers understand that suppressing inner thoughts and feelings is futile and dangerous. The painting *The Other (1990)* illustrates how an appropriate artistic form can describe this aesthetic idea. The figures in this painting spontaneously emerged from the colour and paint, one shape coming out of another. As the paint was moved about, aesthetic meaning began to take shape, driven by the active imagination and the art-making process itself. It seems as if the mind reorders lived experience, and by making thought and feelings visible, a work of art can articulate important personal and cultural truth.

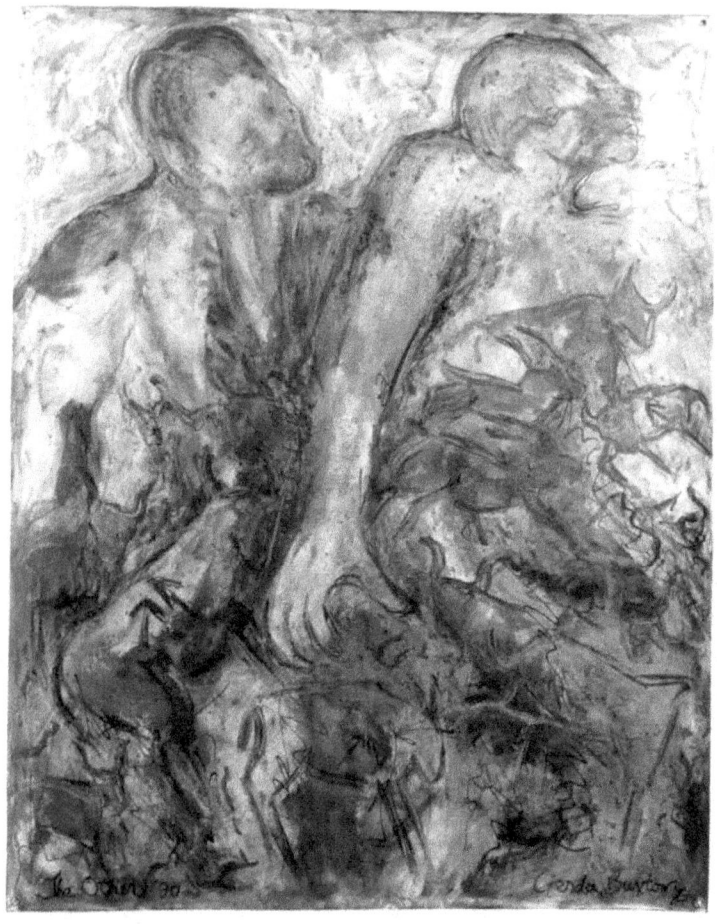

The Other (1990)

The meaning of this image may be interpreted on many different levels, but for me, the biblical story of Jacob wrestling with an angel comes to mind. Perhaps on one level, these two figures represent the universal tension between individual needs and the general demands of the culture. Animal forms dominate one half of the canvas as a visual metaphor for the animal passions, as the woman turns her back on the puzzled curiosity of the man.

This image in particular seems to reach back deep into personal memories of a long forgotten past, bringing these suppressed yet intuitively recognized feelings into a fresh new context and aesthetic form.

On a broader level, this painting expresses the oppositional relationship between the masculine and feminine, both apprehension and attraction. However, the energizing tension between these two figures, which is painful, has to be reconciled by an act of the imagination. Although pain and sorrow do seem to separate us from others, sharing these feelings can also join people together in a harmony of opposites. Expressing pain and sorrow in a beautiful work of art is at the foundation of aesthetic pleasure. This pleasurable tension is resolved by the imagination's ability to unite these opposing psychic archetypes.

Heidegger saw pain and suffering as separating humanity from the world yet at the same time joining the body to all that exists. The philosopher describes sorrow as the seam that 'binds the world and things together in the middle of their intimacy, thereby drawing human beings towards one another'. Imaginatively engaging with sorrow, expressed in a beautiful work of art, can be the connective basis for a sense of belonging, together in the intimacy of finding common ground. Sorrow is something everyone understands. Even if not experienced directly, we feel a strong sense of recognition when confronted by the suffering of others.

Facing pain and suffering in aesthetic form often elicits a compassionate and emotional response. As opposing archetypal energies meet at the place of common ground, the essence of humanity's shared existence is revealed. A shared communal aesthetic experience of innerness is the original mystery visionaries describe as the dark silence that surrounds the light of *Being* and what it means to be human. Artistic expression of suffering draws these opposites together in a work of art and thus provides people with a greater sense of what it means to be alive.

Many of van Gogh's paintings demonstrate this imaginative synthesis of the dark mystery of inner pain with the demands of the external world. The painter conquers this opposition by perseverance and his great love of humanity. In one of his letters, Vincent wrote that he wants to devote his life to expressing serious sorrow that he sees as the poetry hidden in things. Expressing the bitter sweet mystery of sorrow exposes the shadows to the light. Only then can the innate wisdom of the body be grasped, as the timeless significance of sublime beauty becomes crystal clear.

Sometimes a work of art is meant to shock, as when the imagination discovers an image that expresses deeply suppressed feelings and intuitions. Take the painting *Kali's Feast* for example. Kali, the Hindu goddess of empowerment, is also the goddess of war and destruction. In this painting, she straddles what appears to be a bomb while feasting on the bodies and blood of the dead. Inspired by an actual political event, this painting intends to express a critique of globalized aggression, greed and war. Aesthetic form makes personal thoughts and feelings tangible in the patterns of agitated brush strokes and acrid colour.

Sharp jagged shapes and aggressive scratches of paint on the canvas intentionally articulate my disgust at the mindless destruction and hatred of yet another confrontation between opposite ideologies.

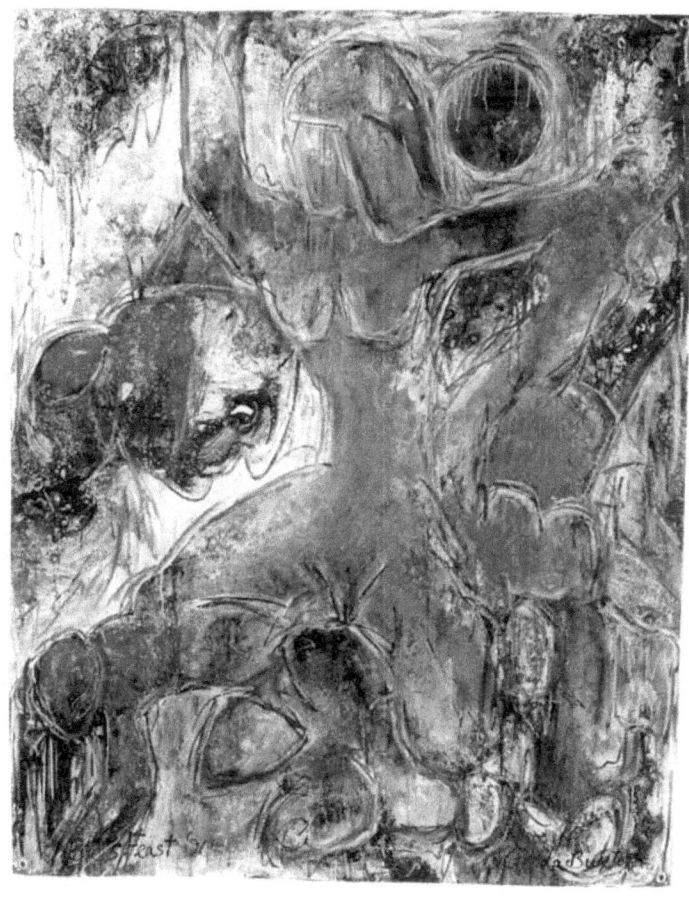

Kali's Feast (1991)

Hovering over Kali's left shoulder hangs a blue moon, an ancient feminine symbol representing profound sadness and despair. On a more personal level this painting articulates suppressed thoughts and a deep feeling of despair during a time when my mother lay dying, and my marriage was rapidly disintegrating. It was a time of chaos when it seemed that the world, and certainly *my* world was about to enter a frightening abyss. However, once these feelings of fear and anger were brought into visual form, it provided meaningful understanding of the universal human dilemma.

By making thought and feeling visible, the complexity of meaning can then be rationally interpreted on a personal, as well as collective level. Aesthetic understanding often provides a broader perception of experience, viewed in a global context. Aesthetic delight arises when the imagination has brought harmony to the mind. This often has tremendous personal and collective power that goes beyond good and evil. Goodness and evil after all, have existed side by side throughout history. The unity between these two opposing perspectives inspired many great artists and philosophers. They knew that together these archetypes represented the full range of emotions within the human psyche.

Many artists and philosophers today believe that the eternal interaction between yin and yang energy brings harmony to their work. This ancient concept of natural balance, which is ever changing is still remembered in the orient. Eastern philosophy is based on the yin–yang principle where masculine yang energy represents the light from heaven, and feminine yin energy represents darkness and comes from within the earth. This imaginative juxtaposition between opposite forces is a metaphor for a meeting between two totally different worldviews that is reminiscent of Nietzsche's notion of thinking beyond goodness and evil.

Kiefer's *I-Thou* series, which he painted in 1971 is also based on the concept of this eternal dance between opposite archetypal forces. In an interview in *Art News* in1987, Kiefer admits that he was very aware that the yin-yang archetypal energy is the power behind his work. In an essentially postmodern way, he plays between these different psychological domains to create aesthetic form. In the encounter with aesthetic form, the artist asks viewers to visualize a coming together of two different planes of reality that intersect but do not coincide. The imaginative synthesis of intuitive wisdom of the body with the more rational approach of the intellect often happens when our mental focus is on something else.

Freeing the intellect from absolute control liberates the mind, which can then make the cognitive and emotional connections. The best ideas about art making often come while doing something totally unrelated, like doing dishes or weeding the garden. It seems that by thinking about something entirely different, the imagination connects the yin energy that hides in the darkness with the yang part of the mind. Both Nietzsche and Heidegger realized that expressing the pain and suffering of the world in aesthetic form is where these two opposite worldviews intertwine and embrace each other.

These archetypal images are intuitively grasped with a profound knowing that aesthetic form has made these powerful forces visible so the pain of living in the world can be better understood. A new revelation of *Being* and being human may be discovered when these opposite ways of knowing come together and are to some extent reconciled. It is a bitter-sweet sensation when the masculine and feminine confront and meet each other on an equal footing and realize their difference. The rift of difference, which is the source of all suffering, makes the limpid brightness shine again. As what is within and without penetrates each other, aesthetic form holds it in place. These sometimes painful images contain tremendous philosophical value for the artist as well as the viewer. The painting *The Betrayal (1992)* articulates this confrontation between opposing archetypal energies.

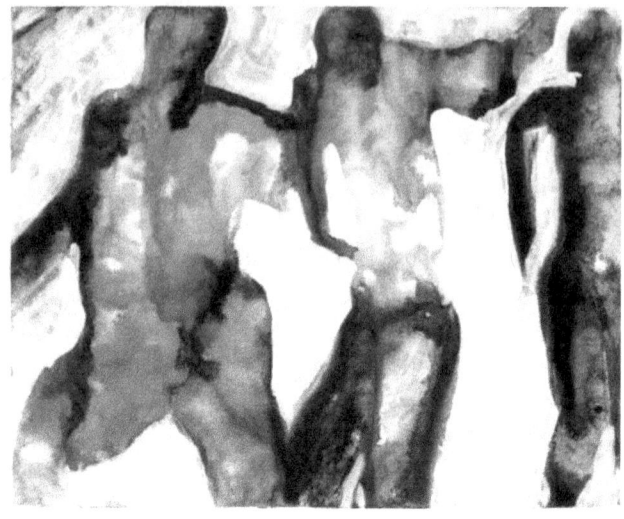

The Betrayal (1992)

The value of a work of art lies in the fact that aesthetic form reveals a part of the human condition that was not previously known and preserves this knowledge for others. Rembrandt's paintings are hundreds of years old, yet they still retain a rich and profound mystery and a haunting undercurrent, a quality that never ceases to touch people's hearts anew. His penetrating and enlightened eye painted the subject's innerness that lies hidden beneath the surface of the skin. With respect and empathy for the human condition, this great painter created works of art that have stood the test of time.

Searching his inner depths, he juxtaposed light and shadow to create an atmosphere where a glimpse of the dignity of the human soul may be caught. Aesthetic form makes visible what was previously hidden from view. The brilliance shining out from the inner shadows clearly shows that the seemingly opposite worlds of happiness and sorrow are inseparable. Greater understanding comes to light when two different realms of being human are reconciled. But sometimes a work of art presents a reproachful image that brings tears to the eyes.

Some contemporary landscapes depict the tremendous damage that has been inflicted on our collective home, be it through war or through industrial globalization. Greed has almost destroyed the atmosphere and the brutal rape of nature is unprecedented in the known history of the world. Many artists and philosophers express a profound concern for the future of the planet. Yet some of them also celebrate the fecundity and regeneration of nature, if given half a chance. They realize that our initial experience of life is through the senses and understand the world through feelings and experience encountered in the body.

Everyone sees with their eyes and hears with their ears. But, as Merleau-Ponty points out, the world is only visible up to the limits of our vision. Our personal point of view is always informed by being alive in a certain place and time. Our knowledge of the world is limited to the confines of the material body, which ultimately defines and exposes a person's creaturely existence to visibility. It is the boundary of flesh that limits human consciousness but the corporeal body creates an openness that reflects the invisible truth of human existence and brings this knowledge into manifestation.

The body makes it possible to be present, here and now in this time and place. The sensuous eye is the horizon of our being. The body is the place where past and future meets in the here and now. In the flesh of physicality, each person is the I-Eye of the world and everyone experiences the world from a different perspective. It is interesting that the word 'body' has a dual meaning. It can be either singular or collective; a body as an individual personality or a universal body that we have inherited from our species. It is also worth noting that the sensuous body connects people to their ancestors. Reminding them that as time passes by, death approaches and they are but a single wave on the ocean of humanity.

The body not only connect people to their ancestors but it also projects them forward to future generations, in an endless cycle of birth, death and regeneration. It is true that all life ends in death but that only makes life more meaningful as the beginning of life is always recast again with each new birth. Awareness of the sorrow of the decaying body also sets limits to all personal experience of existence as a person journeys through the seasons of their life. The essence of artistic creativity is the reconciliation of inner sorrow of the vulnerable body with an experience of the essential truth that all life is cyclical and reciprocal.

It is within the power of a great work of art to transport people beyond their limited self into a new realm that transforms this sadness of temporality. Aesthetic pleasure is inspired by engaging with art, but ultimately comes from within and informs all our relationships with others in the world. Throughout time and place, artistic creativity has celebrated lived experience and joyful participation in the magic of aesthetic form, no matter what medium it is, transforms sorrow into joy.

The painting The *Long Goodbye (1992)* expresses my relief of finally being free.

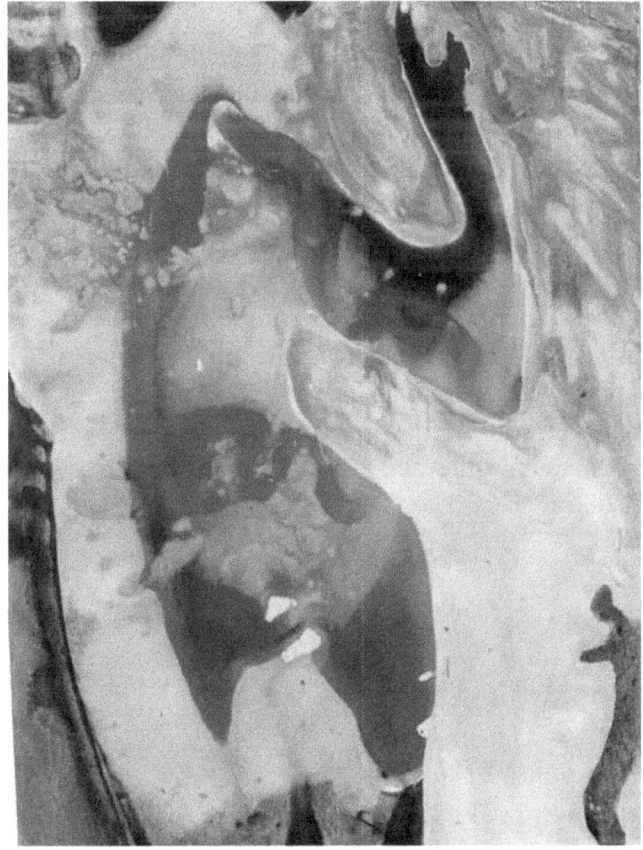

The Long Goodbye (1992)

Still divided as to how I would survive on my own, this painting shows there is light at the end of the tunnel. The anger is gone and the vibrant colour seems to celebrate my release. This image still makes me happy even after all these years. Aesthetic experience lifts us up and out of our obliviousness so we can see beyond our limited horizons. As we engage with aesthetic form, we rediscover the joy and mystery of being alive. All knowledge springs from aesthetic experience. The arts connect inner wisdom to the outer cognitive world.

People recognize the revelation of the ineffable and they can feel this artistic sincerity resonate within the body as an ecstatic sense of rapture and inspiration. It is this meta-awareness that grounds the individual with their inner being and within their culture. Perhaps this is why so many artists have been inspired by human suffering. In their art-making, they are able to transform the sorrows of the world into simplified form that speaks of pure harmony that is as consoling as music. Be it a tragic play or a great symphony, inner responsiveness to the illumination of *Being* is immediate and intuitive. A revelation of fundamental truth in art projects participants out of their everyday, mundane life and for a moment, they can see the infinity of existence.

THE FUTURE OF ART

In the not too distant past, the arts were the very foundation of society. Aesthetic form was a celebration of the social values of the group and cultural cohesiveness depended on the underlying premise that everyone shared these values, which were collectively accepted to be true. Mythology, religion and sacred rituals informed the individual of the rules that were required to live in harmony with other beings in the world. Since discarded the notion of a grand narrative, there has been a systemic erosion of a commonly understood mythic structure that held the world together. As postmodern society rejected the artistic and philosophical ideal of *Being* and being human, people lost contact with the natural rhythms of the earth.

The mythological foundations that had connected living generations with their ancestors, and taught humans how to live with each other, were forgotten. Without a mythological connection to the sacred earth, the world has become a hollow and flattened place. Rather than a connection to the environment in which they live, Western society opted for selfish individualism. In his book the *Malaise of Modernity,* the philosopher Charles Taylor laments this loss of a grand narrative. He sees this loss as an aspect of egotistical individualism that puts the focus exclusively on the self. This exclusive focus on the self has created a fragmented and pluralistic culture where there is only choice, but no individual power.

As our attention is solely on self-fulfilment, commitment to the broader society diminishes and people increasingly feel alienated. Taylor points out that a richer understanding of the relationship between the individual and the culture is urgently required. There is a critical necessity to re-examine our commitment to each other and to the planet that gives us life. Perhaps, as the painting The Goddess Remembered (1991) suggests, rediscovering the ancient mother goddess would go a long way towards rejuvenating postmodern society.

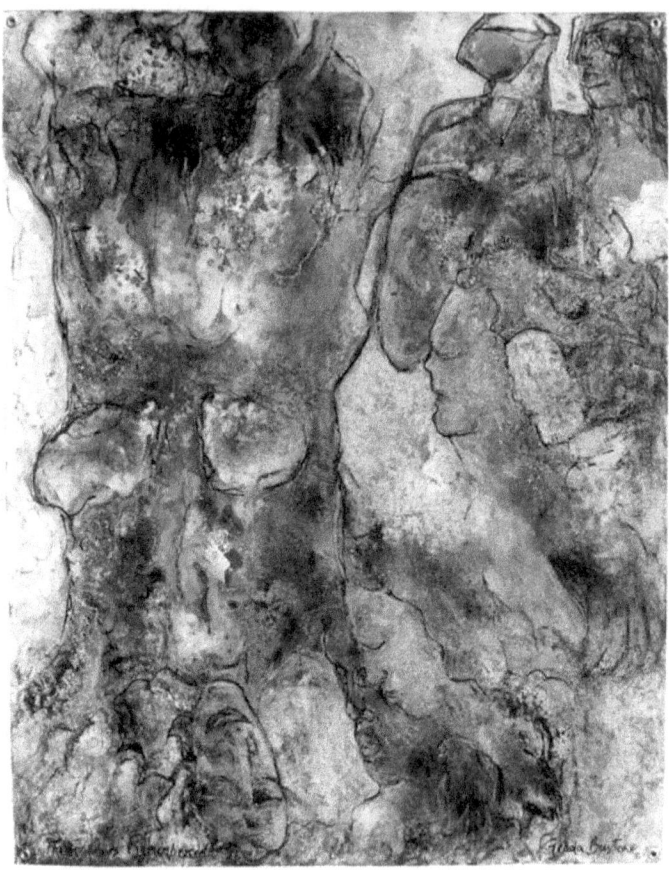

The Goddess Remembered (1991)

This painting articulates a growing serenity and acceptance of personal and cultural limitations. Although painted around the same time as *Kali's Feast*, this image depicts the ancient goddess in repose, as if asleep. The Venus of Willendorf, in stylized form, makes an appearance in the background. Perhaps in support of the women whose faces display quiet contemplation and respectful reverence for the prostrate feminine figure. Western art has a long history of the reclining female nude. For centuries, the reclining nude was a source of titillation for discerning male viewers. But the woman was usually not upside down.

I chose to represent her hanging, upside down, reminiscent of a contemporary Bazelitz painting. The goddess' elongated pose seems restful and at ease as she smiles contently with her eyes closed as if in a dream. This image makes me think of St. Peter who insisted he be crucified upside down, feeling unworthy to die like his master. However, here the goddess may also be hanging upside down because of the continuous chaos of personal and cultural events in the world at large. But the expression of anger and conflict inherent in *Kali's Feast* has been replaced by a sense of quiet serenity.

A reassuring sense of acceptance has crept into this painting, telling me once again that progress has been made. The sandstone colour is reminiscent of the beauty of the Arizona and New Mexico landscape where I had the good fortune to spend a few weeks. My paintings were on exhibit in a gallery in Phoenix and after the opening, I rented a car and set off to explore the 'four corners' area of the American South West. The opening had been an extraordinary celebration of the power of art to speak across personal and cultural difference. The next few weeks became an odyssey of personal transformation filled with many aesthetic encounters of both ancient and contemporary works of art.

Traveling through vast deserts and Indian reservations, I learned about the cultural history and art-making practices of the Navaho and Hopi people. I also enjoyed the beauty and spiritual symbolism of the wax covered religious sculptures of saints found in the Spanish mission churches that have stood for hundreds of years in this part of the world. While standing on top of a mountain south of Phoenix overlooking the city, it occurred to me that life would never be quite the same again. This painting embodies this feeling of empowerment in the colours of the architecture and landscape of the American South West.

Although a casual viewer might not know the personal details and reasons behind aesthetic form, on some level these meanings may be grasped, if only in part. But only the artist knows the depth of personal meaning that a work of art holds, which is difficult to put into words. Although it is true that personal identity requires recognition, dialogue with others in the community gives life meaning. Some postmodern artists create aesthetic artefacts that symbolize a renewal of cultural values, and express these ideas in depictions of the female body. Some feminist artists are inspired by ancient images of a great mother goddess who personified the wisdom of nature. Through the emotions of the body, these artists recognize that what people do to one another, they do to humanity as a whole.

As history shows, a culture that centres mainly on self gratification and negates and distances people from each other is on its way down. But the benevolent matrix of the earth waits patiently for her people to recognize their personal connection to all living things. But a person can only begin to change society if they are willing to begin the change within themselves. The painting *Mediterranean Goddess* was inspired by ancient wall carving that had recently been discovered by archeologists in Greece. It depicts a sacred feminine image of a local goddess.

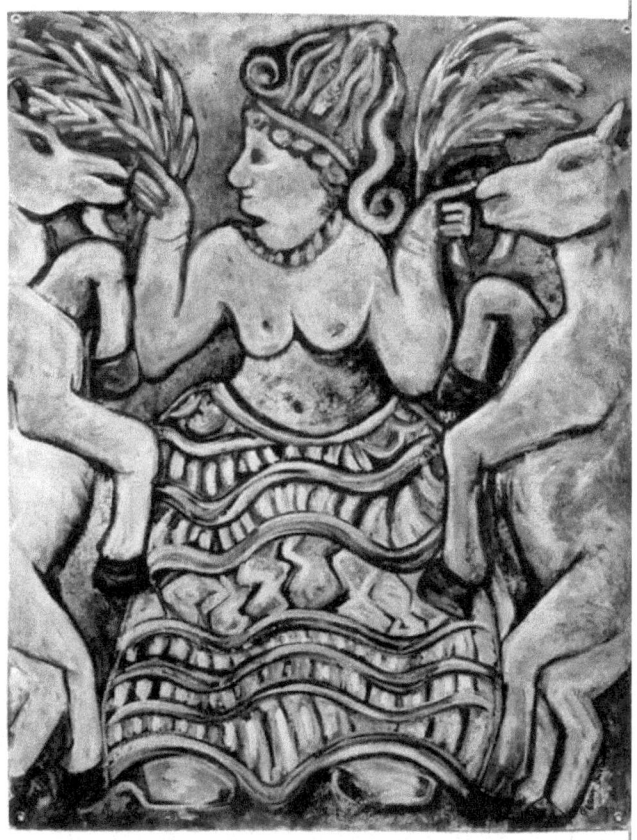

Mediterranean Goddess (1991)

Bare-breasted and proudly female, this image looks back to the ancient past for contemporary inspiration. The goddess holds palm leaves in her hands as if in benediction, while blessing two bearded goats as she averts her eyes from the viewer. I remember how much fun it was to paint her skirt, and I like the sense of playful celebration this painting seems to embody. This painting may be interpreted and understood on many different cognitive and affective levels, if viewers reflect on what its artistic form may mean.

The imagination is inspired to find rational understanding in the beautiful pattern of a snowflake, as well as in a painting whose meaning the intellect alone can never find. Artists and philosophers know that it is only a matter of time before people come to their senses. In the mean time, a work of art transcends the sorrow of our mortal existence, leaving only a sublime beauty that goes beyond paint and canvas. This has great significance for contemporary society because creating and enjoying aesthetic form shares this vital knowledge of necessary balance between two opposite ways of thinking and shares it with future generations.

Members of a democratic society recognize the equal status of different cultures and know that no matter what colour, race or gender, each person deserves to be treated with dignity and respect. In an increasingly interconnected world, it is crucial that people respect difference as being part of the diversity of all living beings on the planet. It is by engaging the imagination that people learn to appreciate their shared human values, while celebrating the diversity of other cultures. It is the function of art to manifest the universality of *Being* as well as well as the diversity of being human in the world.

Sharing aesthetic experience with others facilitates a mutual dialogue between different people who can appreciate beauty and inner truth that is inherent in the arts, no matter where it was made. Sharing a work of art reconnects participants to the intrinsic wisdom of the emotional body. Engagement with a work of art activates the imagination to respond intuitively to archetypal form that the artist discovered within the medium. Good theatre for example, whether a tragedy or comedy, gives voice to inner thoughts and feelings that may be too traumatic to face in the real world.

The aesthetic pleasure encountered by engaging the inner world through aesthetic experience happens as we discover a profound truth of *Being* and what it means to be human that facilitates emotional and intellectual growth. Whether making or enjoying a work of art, aesthetic experience facilitates a notion of culture that far surpasses our present knowledge of *Being*. Rooted in the sensuous and emotional responses to beauty unites innerness with the intellect and brings a sense of balance to the mind. Whether it is the collective culture or a singular human mind, consciousness must be anchored in the compassionate body to be authentic.

Participating in the arts connects directly to the body by engaging people's affective innerness. They intuitively respond to, and recognize authentic truth when it is informed by innerness. But contemporary culture has rejected the sensibility of the body in favour of intellectual rationalism and this negation has brought society to the brink of disaster. The world became a waste land when our connection to nature was severed long ago. Yet all our experience comes from living on the earth in a human body. Aesthetic experience can reconnect people to their inner being, healing the pain of existential alienation.

Some artists propose a more holistic way of experiencing existence that embraces both the intellect and innerness. They imagine a world where inner wisdom is not ignored in favour of intellectual rationalism. The painting *Paradise Lost (1992)* interprets a personal situation in terms of the Old Testament story of Adam and Eve's expulsion from the Garden of Eden. This well known biblical myth found in *Genesis* has inspired many great works of art over the centuries.

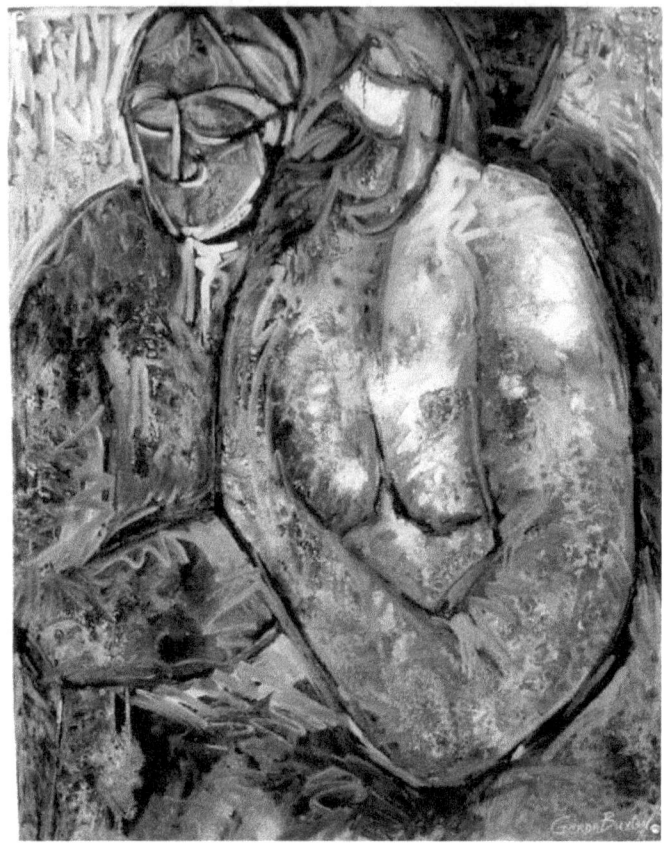

Paradise Lost (1992)

This ancient story also has its darker side. The fall of Eve became a reason for Western culture's misogyny and hatred of women. The colour and brushwork suggest unhappiness and loss, as the two figures turn away from the dark form in the background who might be an arch-angel standing guard at the garden gates. Again, there are complex layers of interpretation concerning its form, because the painting articulates aesthetic ideas whose meaning may be comprehended on many different levels.

On a more personal level, this painting expresses the slow disintegration of a relationship that had died long ago. In addition, the predominant use of dark blue reinforces the general sense of defeat this image seems to articulate. The pleasure of aesthetic appreciation is produced by a feeling of harmonious unity between one's mental abilities when the mind spontaneously grasps the meaning of what has been revealed. A work of art can and often does illuminate the ideals of a culture and demonstrates faith that the future will be a better place. The arts are the foundation of all culture.

Artists and philosophers who truly seek to know truth of *Being*, reach deep into the shadows of the psyche to make the mythic, eternal and sacred images visible. For me, painting creates a visual image of an aesthetic idea about experience that the mind has reworked into an original work of art. Artistic creativity is an attempt to express this idea in the context of a general concept; in aesthetic form that surpasses the limits of personal knowledge. Collectively, the arts represent the communal values of its people.

Therefore, society as a whole must ensure that this history and prior artistic disclosure is preserved. It is in sharing the essential knowledge, which is often contained in a work of art, that society can show the next generation how to visualize and give form to the future. A work of art can manifest invisible thoughts and feelings that cannot be communicated in any other way. Aesthetic form consolidates and gives structure to our inner emotional world and connects deeply private thoughts and feelings to daily life.

However, the arts have a social as well as emotional function within the community. Understanding and appreciating the underlying mythology, which is often the supreme source of artistic creation in many places, can facilitate empathy for the human condition. Imaginative participation with art creates cohesion within the group. Aesthetic experience requires activating the imagination to reconnect to inner feelings rather than respond in a computerized, mechanical way that is incapable of human empathy.

An emotional response to a work of art can bring enchantment back into the world but people have to be conscious of their own as well as the artist's innerness. One has to be in tune with the body and listen to inner emotional promptings and this requires imaginative participation. Engaging with a work of art requires that participants feel, not only empathy for others but also joy and excitement. It is a pleasure to experience the diversity of artistic creativity that celebrates living in the world.

Aesthetic experience requires an agreement and consensus by the entire group to determine if a work of art shares an authentic cultural value. Therefore a work of art must be inclusive and multifaceted to adequately represent a multicultural community. A work of art requires not only individual artists to create it, but art also needs the support of a community to receive and preserves the work. Preserving a work of art consists of standing within the openness of *Being* that has been presented. Its form shows what progress (or lack thereof) a culture has made. By engaging with art, others are able to imagine a new and better future, not only for themselves but also for the planet.

Taylor argues that people need to rediscover the ideal of authenticity and I agree. Each person can be true to themselves and still feel connected to a more communal horizon of significance. I like it when my work makes reference to other cultures, as in the painting *The Buddha Meditation (1992)*.

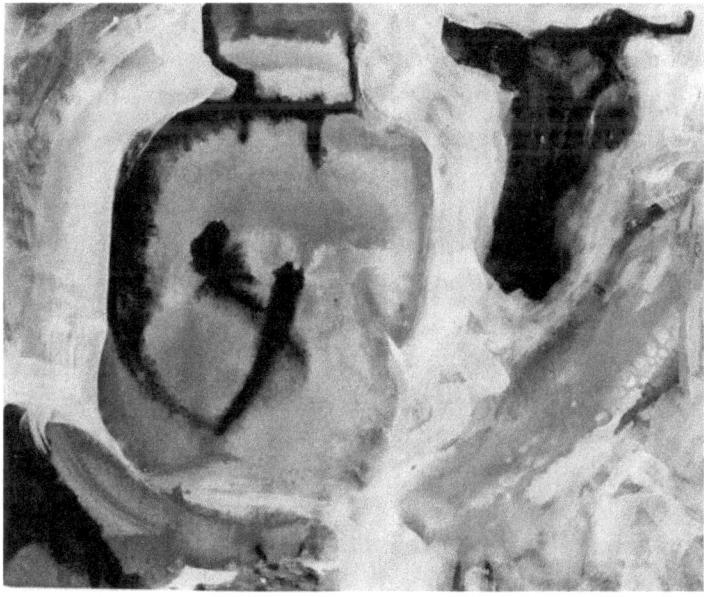

The Buddha Meditation (1992)

Communal decisions regarding the value of art are often based on whether a new vision of both society and the essence of human nature have been revealed. If it has, then the work will be appreciated for giving people a start along a new path of cultural development. People who are encouraged to search for self fulfilment and express innerness creatively are more likely to grant that privilege to others. In this way, the individual who seeks enlightenment and self expression within their chosen medium may also impart valuable cultural knowledge that reflects the community.

The arts act as a mirror on the world by revealing inner emotional and sensuous experience that cannot be communicated in words alone. Engagement with art demonstrates that inside body memory, there is a place people can go to get away from the problems of the world. A work of art shows that there is a metaphysically safe refuge from the vicissitudes of life inside each person, but to get there requires activating the imagination. Only then can a person respond with feeling to the emotional and intuitive experience of artistic expression.

A human being is far more than just their individual ego. Everyone has a unique insight to give their community. This special gift is the purpose of our life's journey to fulfil. It is a gift for the artist as well as the culture in which they live. Following the ancient Greek dictum 'know thyself', it then becomes clear that tragedy and comedy are just two sides of the same coin. The arts across cultures reveal that other people have valuable aesthetic knowledge but it is often negated. Some societies are more in tune with the fact that there is valuable information in the shadows of body memory, which is able transcend the mundane, everyday world.

In the east, various meditation techniques have been used for centuries. All over the world people have gone inward in search of the spirit of *Being* and gain greater understanding of what it means to be human. But sometimes a work of art is an emotional outcry that reveals the despair and loneliness of existence for a solitary artist. The sorrows of the world; more war, more hunger, and more pain, are transformed into an aesthetic statement that is understood on an intuitive level by everyone. Aesthetic form often speaks of the universality of suffering that surrounds us and threatens our very survival.

A work of art has been described as a shelter that has come into existence because the images speak to the artist's basic human instincts and their need for reassurance. By depicting a small part of the world, a painting makes the real world less frightening. Artistic creativity consoles and shelters the artist and they feel closer to the rest of creation while shaping aesthetic form. Art that express this need for shelter from the vastness of existence provides comfort to both the creator and the spectator.

Manifesting *Being*, art has the power to restore a person's lost connection to the world because aesthetic form explains what it means to live an authentic life in this sometimes frightening world. A great work of art challenges our preconceived notions about humanity and shows us who we really are. Art initiates a dialogue that restores the severed connection to inner thoughts and feelings by opening the heart and mind to the wisdom embedded within. It is a delightful experience when the imagination connects with and understands this inner wisdom made visible in a particular medium, be it a dance, a concerto or a painting.

It is the key purpose of art to make this knowledge visible. By focusing our attention exclusively on aesthetic form, the mind creates a pattern from the sensuous and emotional stimuli that impinge on the body. Then the imagination can open the windows of perception on potential possibilities that transcend the limits of what was previously possible. The synthetic imagination reveals that feelings and reason are not separate but intertwined and mutually dependent on each other. Visual form that it discovers in the shadows of the body memory is often symbolic of larger personal and collective issues.

Sometimes aesthetic form represents an imaginative meeting between opposing energies that serves to rebalance the artist as well as the culture. Then the creative process becomes a metaphor for a necessary dialogue so these two polar opposites can begin to comprehend each other. This imaginative dialogue within a work of art unifies intellectual rationality with sensibility.

The philosopher Mary Warnock notes that truth in art must be grasped by an act of will so that the original vision becomes our own. She points out that it is this shared imaginative creativity that leads to the discovery of a timeless and quite general knowing. Whereas Taylor is critical of the focus on the self, Warnock believes that the imaginative quest for self-expression is a valid ideal. However Taylor thinks that western culture has put too much pressure on the notion of individuality and unique artistic expression. He claims that this pursuit of individuation has lead to the fragmentation of contemporary culture.

Taylor claims that the malaise of modernity has degraded the integrity of the ideal of the individual. People may have freedom of choice today but few are willing to accept the responsibility that comes with this freedom. However, he believes that the cultural ideal of authenticity needs to be retrieved in a less selfish sense and that the development of individual freedom was western society's greatest achievement. But personal liberty and self determination implies that the right of self expression does no harm and others are free to do the same.

A work of art exists as an invitation to share this inner quest of discovering this timeless and general knowledge, which is full of possibilities. The painting *A Face in the Crowd (1991)* articulates that being fully conscious and alive involves communicating with others as well as with our own inner sensibilities.

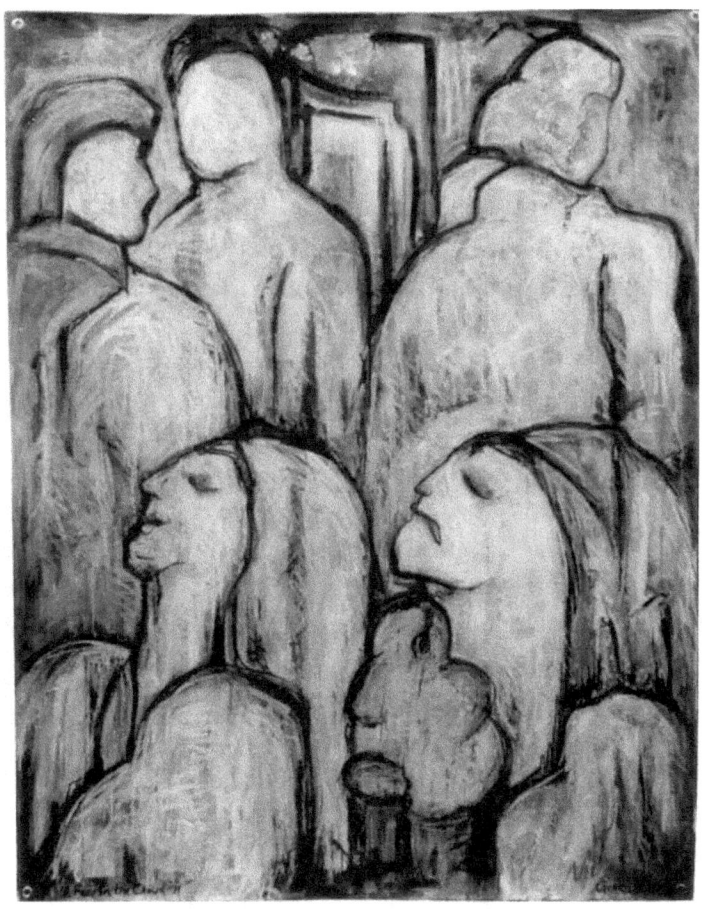

A Face in the Crowd (1991)

This image catches a moment when I and the other meet. On a crowded street, a flash of recognition of an apparent stranger could potentially change one's life. The imaginative interaction between intuitive wisdom and intellectual understanding is the source of aesthetic delight. The imagination conceptualizes order and purposefulness from the myriad of impressions that the body gathers. As the imagination penetrates the multiple layered connotations that are presented in aesthetic form, the body as well as the mind respond with awe and wonder, and the human spirit is renewed.

A work of art opens up a unique perspective of the diversity of self expression. These unique differences acknowledge that no one ever stands completely within a single world or upon a single earth. Although everyone experiences aesthetic form in a different way, artists hope that the underlying truth in the work will be universally understood. Aesthetic understanding transcends cultural differences because art is the language of our shared humanity.

Richard Anderson, in his comparative study of philosophies of art, looks at the different artistic practices of cultures across the world. Such diverse societies as the Australian aborigines, the Inuit in the Arctic, the Navajo in the American South West, the Aztec in Mesoamerica, and the Sepik of New Guinea. He also includes the Yoruba in West Africa and the San in South-West Africa as well as early Indian and Japanese aesthetics and compares these cultures to contemporary western art. Despite the complexity and variations of art's essential meaning, religion and spirituality was of the utmost importance.

In every culture, aesthetic experience transcends every day existence, taking viewers to a sacred inner world. Through the sensuous embodiment of beauty, aesthetic form communicates special intuitive insights and shared principles of goodness. When a work of art expresses authentic human emotions, such as in this painting Temptation (1992), everyone gets the message. We have all been tempted at one time or another to surrender to our feelings, knowing better. The overall structure of this image plays with the idea of opposition and duality.

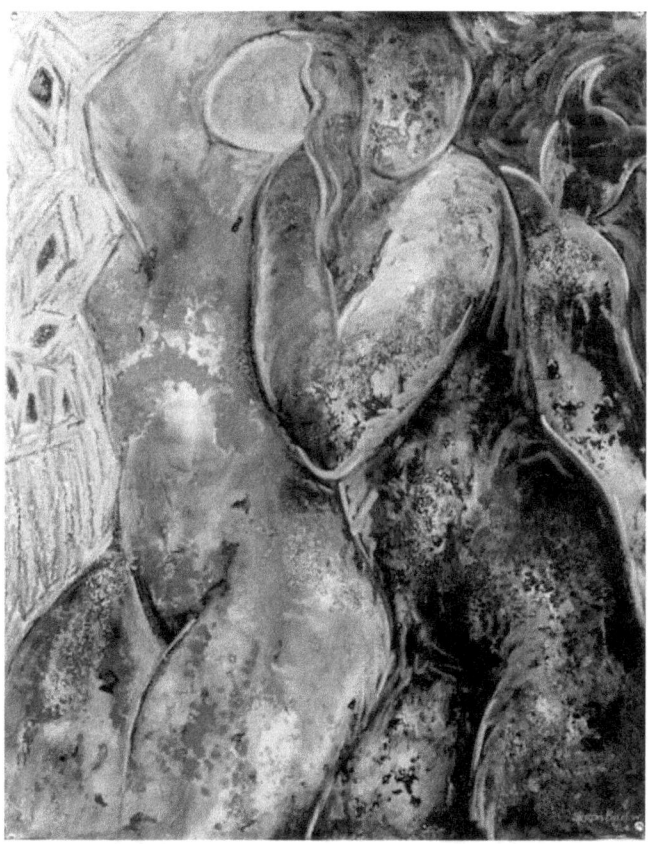

Temptation (1992)

By splitting the canvas almost in half, this image suggests a meeting between light and dark, as well as goodness and evil. The left represents the warm feminine side of sensibility and intuition, while the right side suggests the cool intellectualism of the masculine. The brightness of the female figure suggests joy and love, in contrast to the nocturnal masculine figure, which represents the darker side of human temptation. In the background, a devilish figure watches the two figures, as the male pushes the dancing woman forward towards the light. After all these years, there still remains unknown yet tantalizing psychological suggestions, whose message I don't fully understand.

It may be this mysterious prompting by the imagination that makes these images perennially interesting. Sometimes it may take years before the full meaning becomes clear, and can then be rationally articulated to some extent. This painting illustrates a return of the light after a particularly sorrowful time in my life. For me, form in a painting is a barometer of psychological states, whose meaning only becomes clearer as the work progresses. The devil personified in the background has haunted us all. It reminds me of Adam and Eve being cast out from the garden. Naked and afraid they face a bleak future alone.

One does not have to be Christian or know the story to understand what this image refers to. Colour here is symbolic of this deeply troubling emotion that can tear at one's life and rent it apart. This painting still pleases me because the image was also an affirmation that the healing process had begun. The painting's colour and texture was the result of a new technique that I was experimenting with, where the cement floor in the studio became an integral part of the painting process. As usual, fluid paint was poured on a flat canvas and manipulated on the ground using only my hands.

I had been working that way for a few years, and liked the development of form, which the colour and paint itself suggests when it was dry. But this time the wet canvas was pulled up and reversed face down on the cement floor and left to dry. This creates a pleasing effect where colour and texture interact to create form. The sensuous colour and forms tell a story, as in the painting *The Approach (1992)*.

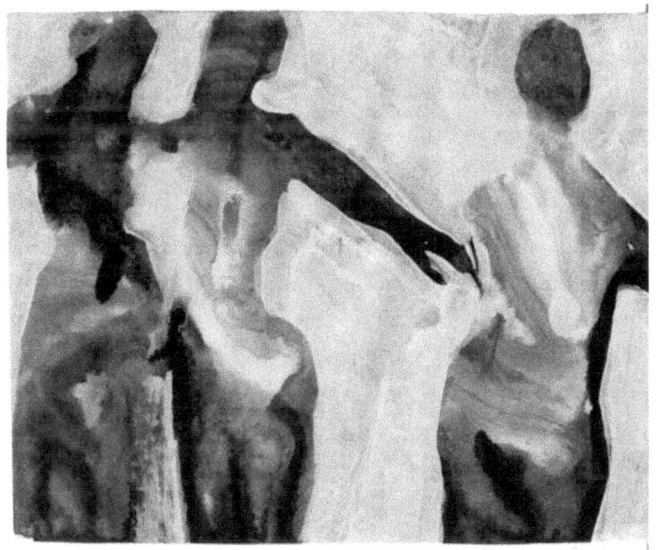

The Approach (1992)

The image presents a mystery, a story that we can only imagine but can never for sure. But feelings that everyone recognizes shown through gesture and figures that reach out to each other. Aesthetic form required emotional participation and being open to the message with an emphatic response to what the art work represents. This subtler language whispers softly to the heart and expands the mind to a richer understanding of human existence. This aesthetic language is intuitively grasped, as significant meaning resonates deep within the emotional body.

A work of art speaks to our inner *Being*. By listening to the language of aesthetic form, we begin to understand the essence of our common humanity. Richard Anderson found that Navajo sand paintings and Aztec art were gifts to the gods. Japanese Shinto art making incorporates music and dance as the perfect mirror to lure the Sun goddess out of the Rock Cave of Heaven. Anderson compared Indian art as a means to transcend reality much like Renaissance religious paintings that do the same.

Although the intrinsic message of a work of art may be understood differently, aesthetic form exposes diversity as well as to the similarities of others.

Aesthetic experience has always been a necessary part of the human equation. It feels good when we interact with aesthetic form. Engagement with the arts across cultures encourages empathy and respect for diversity of human experience. Sharing aesthetic experience initiates a mutual and beneficial dialogue as people delight in grasping the depth of personal and cultural ideas that are embedded in a work of art. This intuitive wisdom is the embodiment of a person's whole life. Therefore artists must trust their inner responses because they contain value of unknown immensity.

Aesthetic form exhibits how the artist made choices and accepts responsibility for the unforeseen consequences of those choices. Participating with art can show others how to access their own creativity and discover what needs to be expressed. Balancing the intellect with inner sensibility provides a strong foundation for the future that people can build on. There is often a feeling of synchronicity when inner wisdom is listened to and the cognitive pieces fall into their rightful place.

Everyone has the potential to access this sensuous and emotional knowledge. It is inherent in body memory and it is a source of greater insight into the possibility of regeneration. Artistic creativity is an important part of human cognition. By bringing fleeting thoughts and emotions into aesthetic form, each person is able to contribute their own unique and valued voice in the ongoing dialogue of human development. The imagination unites the invisible world of inner thoughts and emotions with the intellectual part of the mind and together these different ways of knowing inform our everyday reality.

An imaginative synthesis between the two ways of experience reveals that a greater reality exists beyond the senses and finite body. In a digital world, the primacy of instrumental reason makes people think that they should seek technological solutions even when something quite different is called for. It seems that contemporary society has lost touch with its roots in the natural world. Bombarded with images, people are unable to respond with basic human empathy to issues in the world. However, a work art provides joy and delight and a sense of wonder when we recognize pieces of ourselves in the patterns of others.

Art celebrates the self in a language that cannot be articulated in any other way. Aesthetic experience restores the emotional connection to the wisdom of the body because art communicates the very essence of being human. Aesthetic experience connects the individual to humanity as a whole and shows the cultural common ground that gives people a sense of continuity. Aesthetic form shows how to make the connections between various forms of knowledge. Artistic creativity is the very foundation of civilization and indispensable for living well.

KANT'S THEORY OF MIND

Sometimes, words and text are not enough to fully express a particular idea and it may be necessary to invent a new language game; a rich and composite statement whose meaning is embedded in aesthetic form. A work of art can express a special kind of knowledge, which is deeply emotional, capable of touching the heart as well as the mind. Therefore aesthetic engagement with art cultivates cognitive sensibilities and the ability to reason better. But full comprehension of what is perceived requires activating the imagination to unify sensibility with an intellectual concept.

Authentic artistic expression of inner ideas makes sensible intuitions visible in a complex and meaningful form that is grasped on an emotional level. A work of art articulates how the artist sees the world and expresses this unique perspective in a subtle aesthetic language. Understanding this subtler language requires that viewers use their imagination when engaging with the artwork itself. This opens the mind to reach beyond personal and cultural limitations and make good and innovative aesthetic judgments.

Aesthetic appreciation of goodness and beauty inherent in a work of art lifts the spirit and expands our awareness of quality and excellence. Aesthetic experience allows the mind to reach beyond the horizons of an otherwise flat and nihilistic world. It is a cognitive state where body and spirit, the intellect and intuition and primordial meet. The complexity of the human mind embodies not only intentionality and the will but also our wishes, purposes and desires.

Aesthetic form can encompass memory, recollection, remembrance and what we think and feel about our perceptions and experience, as in the painting *Ritual (1991)*

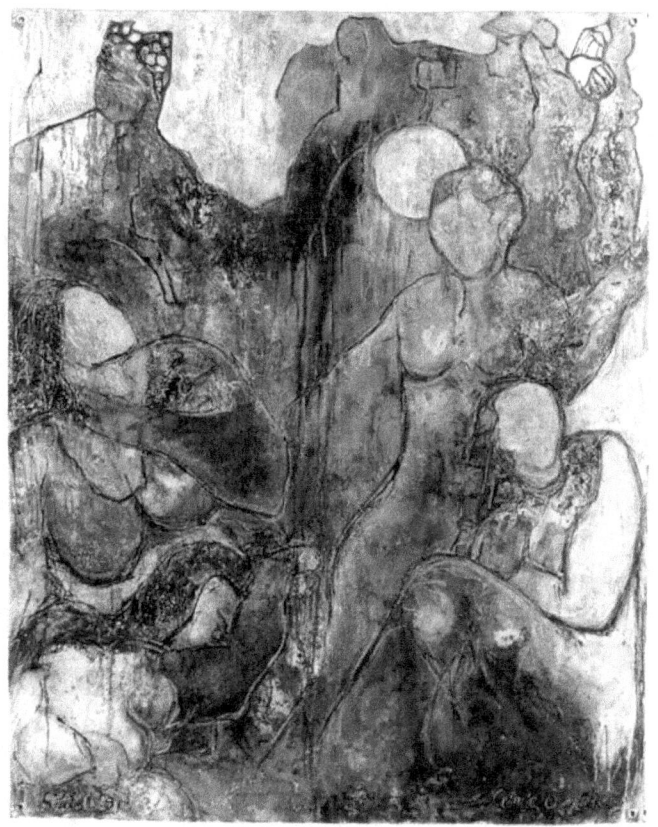

Ritual (1991)

This painting depicts a group of women gathered together in a communal celebration. Some have drums and appear to be singing, while others lie on the ground or sit simply enjoying the sight of the dancers. The faces have no particular features because they represent all women across time and place. For millennia, women have gathered to celebrate the seasons and cycles of life. Traditionally, these gatherings were intended to renew and regenerate fertility, of the people as well as of the land.

The newly discovered technique of letting the painting dry upside down on the floor was also used here. I like the 'natural' look the painting took on, its texture somewhat like the surface of rock. This way of painting creates the most remarkable colours. Being face down on the floor captures the paint so it can't run off the canvas. Some of the paint will stick to the floor, and bits of cement remain stuck on the canvas. This unusual texture reminds me of the ancient cave paintings at Lascaux, and the Anasazi rock paintings in the American South West. It also reminds me that people all over the world have left their mark on rocks or the landscape since anyone can remember.

It seems that intense attention to colour, texture and form leads to further reflection on the complexity of understanding, which often calms the mind. Emmanuel Kant was the first Western philosopher who grasped the complexity of human rationality. He understood that aesthetic judgment required the synthetic power of the imagination to bring harmonious unity between sensible intuitions and the intellect. His philosophy articulates a new cosmology that developed during modernity and he revolutionized western philosophy by taking into account the discursiveness of the human mind.

His revolutionary ideas initiated a debate not only among philosophers but also among artists. With the advent of a new age, many artists started to express a greater self awareness and artistic creativity rapidly became a new way of visual thinking. Although some analytic philosophers disagree with Kant's unifying theory of mind, his astute insight that different kinds of cognition were involved in aesthetic understanding remains relevant today. Cognition refers to the mental processes of acquiring knowledge through experience, by way of thought as well as through the senses.

Central to Kant's theory is that the synthetic power of the imagination brought mental unity between sensible intuition and the intellect. Unification between these two distinctly different and oppositional kinds of knowledge results in the harmony of reason. This imaginative unity brings a suitable concept or image into consciousness, making intuitive sensibility visible. For Kant, this mental harmony demonstrates the universality of general human concepts and aesthetic ideas. He understood that harmonious unity of mind facilitates the ability to reason better, so people can make good ethical and aesthetic judgments.

Kant's synthetic theory of mind explains the necessity of imaginative unity between two distinct and opposite cognitive powers. Kant's comments on aesthetic judgment are considered to be a major milestone in western philosophy. Warnock describes the history of western philosophy as 'pre-Kantian' and 'post-Kantian'. She believes that Kant's modernist theory was a turning point in the history of philosophy that reflects the new physics of his day, which challenged the predominant world view that the earth was the centre of the universe. Just as Copernicus reversed the long standing claim that the sun travels around the earth, Kant reversed the claim that the world gives its order to the mind.

Overturning long held assumptions that knowledge came from the world outside, Kant claims that perception and the different faculties of mind give order to reality. If the world has no structure except for what the mind gives it, as Kant's suggests, his greater insight was that two distinctly different types of cognition is involved in the acquisition of knowledge, which require an imaginative synthesis.The painting *Lughnasadh (1991)* shows what Kant meant.

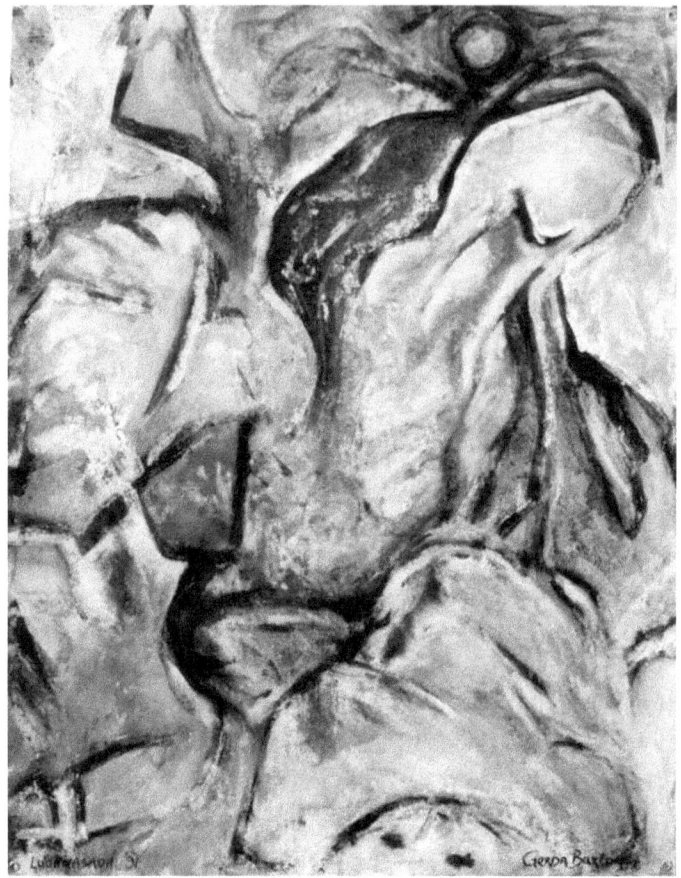

Lughnasadh (1991)

For me, the folklore of old Europe shows that a generous affection for the human condition may be hard-wired in human consciousness. The ancient Greeks articulate this affection in context of living a happy and balanced life within a community that is embedded within a particular landscape. Their mythology speaks of personal as well as collective duties and responsibilities to each other and to the land. These obligations were shared throughout the season in communal festivals. The title of this painting refers to one of the four main feast days of the ancient European calendar.

Lughnasadh is a midsummer festival when people gave thanks for the ripening of the first fruits in early August. Traditionally, it was a time of community gatherings, market festivals and family reunions. Weddings were often part of the Lughnasadh festivities. The abundance of flowers and vegetables in the summer gardens could feed many friends and relatives. However, this painting also suggests another part of the myth; that of the barley king's demise. While this feast takes place in mid summer, there is already a vague sense of impending death and the coming winter, in gathering the early harvest.

In this image, this indeterminate suggestion of death and decay may be felt in the prostrate figure that represents the barley king, who dies each year to feed the people, but comes to life again each spring. This interpretation seems to fit better with the qualitative stillness of this image, and the subdued colours also seem to imply a sense of pathos and loss. Regular artistic creativity develops the ability to perceive and comprehend the inherent meaning of form, inspiring the mind to reach beyond what it knows. Strengthening aesthetic perception and understanding provides unity and wholeness in the mind.

Kant's philosophy was based on the idea that when the imagination unifies sensibility and perception, a mental concept could be found. Therefore activating the imagination is crucial for a holistic understanding of perception and experience. The imagination functions as a mental bridge between the senses and intellect, unifying intuitive thoughts and feelings with an intellectual concept. This imaginative bridge allows the mind to reason clearer and grasp a fundamental idea of reality more effectively.

When visualizing this synthesis of the imagination, there has to be a distinction made between the part to which structure is given and that part giving it structure. It is the imaginative part of mind that gives structure and order to all our perceptions. An imaginative mental unification provides meaningful form from the chaos of sensible intuition that bombards the senses. However, these sensible intuitions are not just arbitrary stimuli. People see discrete things but the imagination is able to organize these random perceptions of various objects so the mind can conceptually categorize these indiscriminate stimuli and gain understanding of their form.

The imagination's connective nature unites two distinctly different types of knowledge so they can work harmoniously and rationally together. Artistic creativity and shaping aesthetic form also requires activating the imagination to bring unity between sensible intuition and intellectual understanding. Archetypal aesthetic form develops from the sensuousness of the medium, in tandem with intuitive ideas that enter the mind as the artist works. These primordial images seem to hover below the normal threshold of consciousness but can be accessed by the imagination.

It's as if the image unfolds by itself yet the artist is actively involved. The entire body moves as the eye joins hands with the heart and mind. It's an exhilarating experience that drives the artist to search time and again for aesthetic form that can then be interpreted. It seems that these infinitely recurring images spontaneously appear in the mind's eye, as in the painting *Maiden and Crone (1990).*

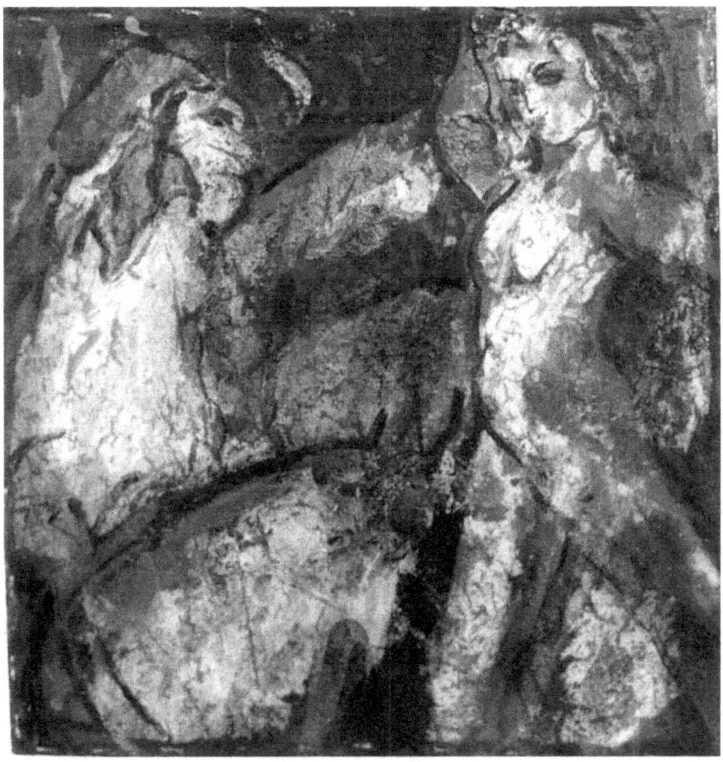

Maiden and Crone (1990)

As form took shape, aesthetic ideas seemed to organize themselves under a general concept as the image unfolded. Sympathetic viewers who take the time to reflect on the many possible interpretations the artist may have consciously or unconsciously intended, will sense the complexity of aesthetic meaning behind its form. If the imagination is given freedom to play between sensible intuition and an indeterminate concept, it creates harmonious order, which is necessary for making a rational aesthetic judgment.

Activating the imagination is the cognitive ability to think in the subjunctive mode *as if*. This conceptual shift makes it possible to conceive of unusual and effective solutions within a particular context. The connective imagination is productive and formative; bringing sensibility and intuition together under a general idea that is found in the mind. By pulling different feelings and emotions together under a concept, the imagination usually discovers something new, or produces something unique and valuable.

The free play of the imagination takes both intuitive thoughts and feelings and intellectual ideas into consideration and actively connects these opposing mental powers in a more or less harmonious unity. When neither sensibility nor the intellect dominates within the mind, people are more able to reason and grasp the meaning of their perception of things. Imaginative free play satisfies the mind's need for unity by presenting coherent aesthetic form. For Kant, there are three mental capacities that are distinct yet necessary for understanding all possible experience.

He believed that the power of the imagination to facilitate human reason was autonomous and a necessary part of cognition. Although some philosophers argue Kant's notion of different faculties of mind is untenable, for others his ideas regarding the complexity of the human mind continues to fascinate and inspire. Kant's theory of the synthetic imagination remains a useful metaphor for the unity of human experience because it explains the multi-faceted nature of the mind. Rationality requires the cooperation between two distinctly different and conflicting types of knowledge.

For Kant, there are also two different parts to the imagination that he describes these as being either *empirical* or *a priori*. The empirical imagination is the capacity that fills the mind with visual images whose details depends on personal experience, whereas the *a priori* imagination is 'given' and common to all rational creatures. For Kant, time and space are the only pure *a priori* intuitions 'given' to human experience. But the *a priori* imagination can bring an aesthetic idea into form that others intuitively respond to on a more fundamental level of understanding. Archetypal *a priori* form seems to be entrenched in personal and cultural folklore and mythology. These mythical images appear spontaneously in the mind's eye during artistic creativity and shaping of aesthetic form

The *a priori* imagination discovers aesthetic form, which is often securely rooted in a long forgotten 'mythological' past. Imaginative free play with the fluid nature of the medium offers many creative opportunities for expressing aesthetic form. For example while painting, colour and texture may suggest things like blood, as rusty red paint drips over gold enamel. Aesthetic form triggers both personal as well as collectively shared memories of events and experience. Many interesting associations pop into consciousness as one colour is applied over another.

The painting *Artemis (1992)* illustrates what I mean. As paint is moved around the canvas, forms that appear and disappear continuously suggest fresh, new ideas and possibilities of self expression. This painting was inspired by the ancient Greek myth of Artemis, the goddess who protects the wilderness, as well as the hunt. Artemis is often depicted carrying a bow and arrow but in this painting she is unarmed.

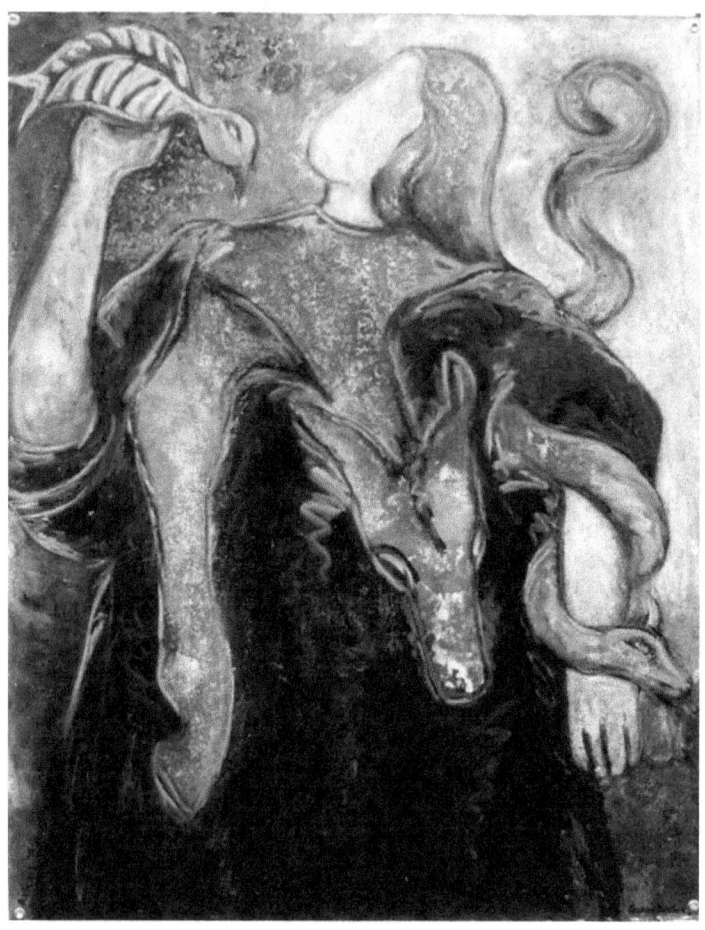

Artemis (1992)]

A snake coils around her arm, and in her right hand she holds a white bird, perhaps a dove. The only suggestion of the hunt is a deer-skin draped over her shoulders, but the overall feeling in this painting is one of peace and tranquillity. Perhaps this sense of peacefulness reflects another aspect of Artemis, who was also venerated as the goddess of healing, who protected women during childbirth. Paradoxically, she also represents purity and chastity because her father Zeus bestowed on her eternal virginity. Although Artemis is usually represented with a crescent moon above her forehead, this image makes only an abstract reference to the light of the moon in the background behind her head. Since long before the ancient Greeks, works of art have had the power to move us, to feel awe and wonder at the beauty of artistic form.

During the creative process, one thing tends to lead to another as the imagination makes the necessary connections. A cognitive and affective synthesis between past memories and intellectual concepts usually leads to an appropriate image that expresses this newly found idea. It seems that the imagination can be trusted to find a suitable visual image. One that can convey previously unknown depths of knowledge found within the mind. Imaginative unification between sensibility and the intellect uncovers an aesthetic image and brings it to consciousness so its message is better understood.

If the imagination guides the artist's thoughts and feelings as well as the hands and eye, there is usually something of value expressed in the finished work. Making innerness visible and therefore understandable develops our ability to make good value judgments about objective experience. Connecting sensible intuitions under an intellectual concept joins subject and object, thereby harmonizing the particular with the universal. Intellectual understanding alone limits the ability to learn new things. Only the spontaneous free play of the productive imagination can extend human awareness, allowing consciousness to reach beyond the self.

There is a delightful aesthetic tension in maintaining a harmonious balance between intuitive sensibility and intellectual reason, only the imagination can reconcile. When the mind succeeds in bringing these oppositional cognitive capacities together, it brings with it a profound sense of awe and wonder. Most people take pleasure in their ability to reason and think about the infinite possibilities of human experience. Perhaps this is because the capacity to reason well liberates consciousness from the limitations of personal and cultural horizons. Harmonious unity between mental abilities provides a sense of affinity. An aesthetic pleasure that brings with it the realization that all knowledge is personal, yet also grounded in shared human concepts.

The notion that the pursuit of knowledge is a quest for self-knowledge is part of Kant's non-philosophical legacy. It was Kant who introduced the idea of the 'I' whose point of view creates the world of experience. To my way of thinking, understanding the intricate nature of the human mind and the unity of experience is all the justification his synthetic theory of the imagination requires. Unification of opposite mental abilities by the active imagination allows conflicting ways of seeing to work together, bringing out the best in both. Releasing the imagination gives the mind freedom to search for a concept or appropriate visual image to express the meaning of personal and collective events.

Inner sensibility and the intellect, brought together by the cohesive imagination, forms the essential ground for the unique way each one perceives and interprets reality. When these opposite and uniquely different energies stand in contrast to each other, the encounter produces a pleasurable friction. This synthesis confines the imagination to a broader general concept, making our perception of things knowable and communicable.As in the painting *Androgynous (1992)*, these two distinctly different ways of knowing energize each other.

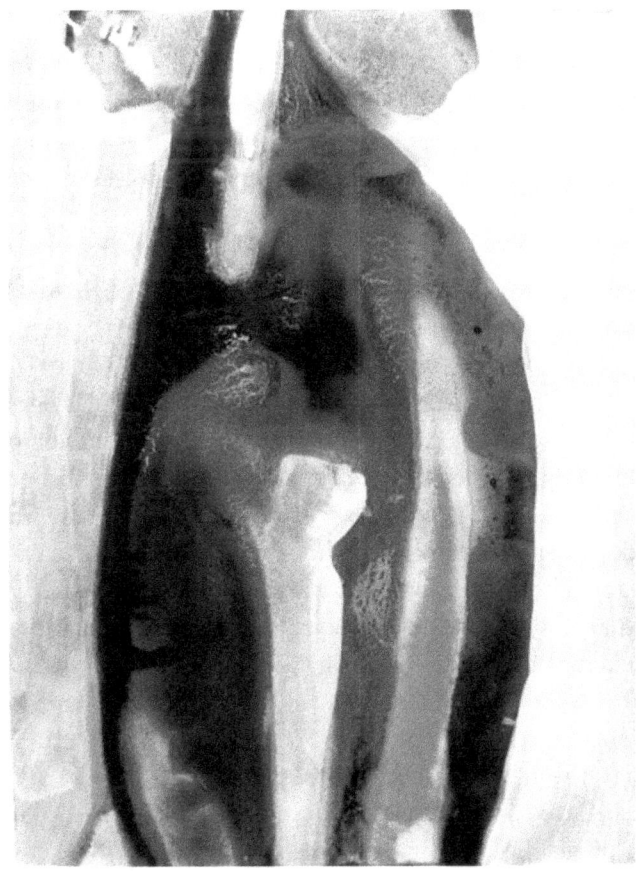

Androgynous (1992)

Although all human experience in the objective world is subjectively perceived, the meaning of things and events are understood according to general cognitive concepts and applicable laws. These concepts are common to everyone but may be grasped differently because people's understanding is determined by personal and cultural variation. When the imagination discovers an appropriate form to articulate a personal perspective on general human values, the idea that it presents can then be shared with others. The imaginative part of mind searches for a suitable image to bring a universal concept into meaningful form. As form appears, in the fluidity of colour and paint for example, it articulates an aesthetic idea that may concern the nature of personal growth. This happens during the transformative process of art making itself but its message can be reflected upon later.

The organic nature of aesthetic form is indicative of the natural process of transformation inherent in all lived experience. In painting for example, the contrast between light and dark suggests the idea that positive as well as negative feelings need to be expressed so these psychic energies are better understood. The human mind requires imaginative harmony in order to reason well. So the intellect can grasp the meaning of the forms that make inner thoughts and feelings visible and to some extent understandable. Therefore, intuitive hidden wisdom and intellectual understanding are equally important and must be reconciled for the mind to function at capacity.

It is important to remember that Kant's theory of the synthetic imagination went up against philosophers from Plato to Hume, who all believed intellectual reason should dominate the inner wisdom of feelings within the sensuous body. However, Kant realized that rational development of cognitive abilities does not require the subordination of inner feelings to the intellect. Rather the reverse; full cognitive understanding requires the harmonious interaction between these opposite ways of knowledge.

There is always a certain amount of tension involved when the imagination unites intuitive sensibility with a concept as the mind intellectually grasps the meaning behind an aesthetic form. This cognitive friction has been described as a push-pull effect between two old friends. They don't much like each other, but can't live without each other either. These contrasting forces within the mind tend to pull in opposite directions; the intellect pulling toward universality whereas sensibility pulls towards specificity and the body.

This tug of war requires using the unifying power of the imagination to actively mediate between these two mental energies. An imaginative synthesis arbitrates between these two opposite energies in an attempt to bring harmony and a good cognitive fit to mind. Freely playing between subjective sensibility and intellectual conceptualization, the imagination finds a suitable image to represent a commonly understood idea. This imaginative synthesis makes innerness visible and communicable.

Sometimes, as in Kiefer's work, aesthetic form illustrates the anxiety of long forgotten world events that show personal and cultural memories run deep. Throughout history, art has been a personal response to important events. Aesthetic form in an expressive painting is very different from taking a photograph because the image reveals an idea that goes far beyond mere documentation. Kiefer's paintings, as well as Kollwitz' work, recalls the horrors of two world wars that swept throughout much of Europe during the twentieth century. Aesthetic truth the culture would rather forget. But bringing these suppressed and often painful memories into form feels much like an act of atonement.

There is a pleasant tug of war between the materiality of the medium that contrasts with the starkness of its message, as in the painting *Aboriginal Cave Goddesses (1991).*

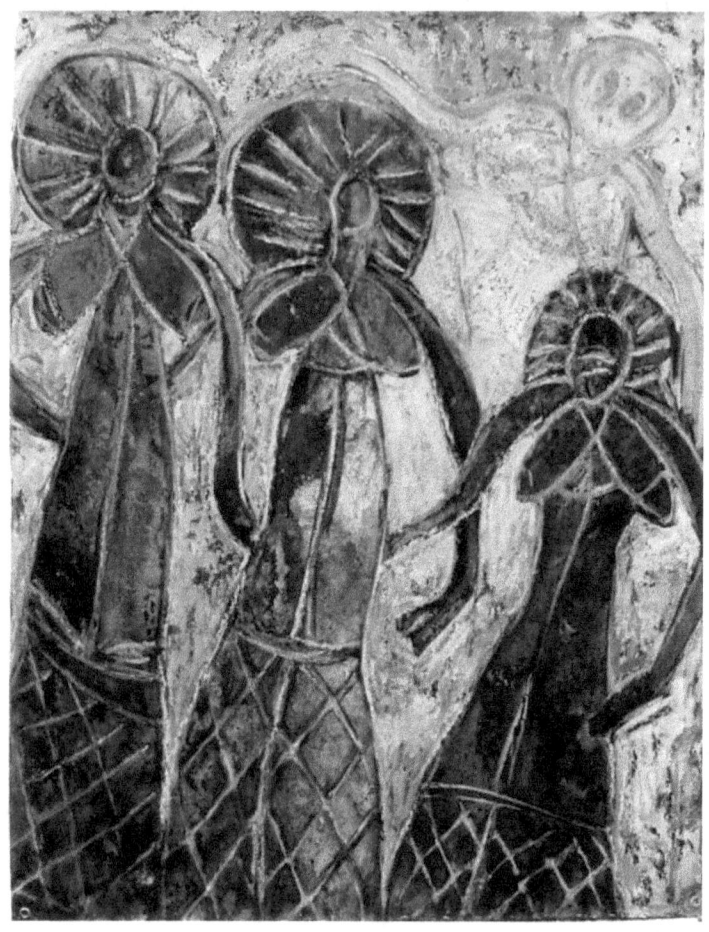

Aboriginal Cave Goddesses [1991]

This painting was inspired by prehistoric Australian wall paintings and intends to show the interconnectedness between past and present artistic form. Although having seen 1 photographs of this ancient rock art, these figures spontaneously sprung into mind from developments on the canvas during the creative process. As hands, eyes and mind harmoniously worked together, the image embodied many different levels of meaning that can be grasped by others if they take the time to think about its aesthetic form.

This image reveals a universal idea whose meaning is much broader than mere representation. It shows the implications of a conceptual truth that can finally be rationally reflected upon. When a particular visual image fits under a general concept or rule, the various mental capacities are operating effectively together. When aesthetic form represents a general idea, it satisfies the mind. This mental harmony has been described as a 'set of well-meshed gears that work smoothly together with little friction so the subsumption can proceed without difficulty'. Harmonious unity between distinctly different cognitive states makes the mind more than the sum of its parts.

Imaginative union between polar opposites energizes comprehension, enabling the mind to grasp the meaning of broader aesthetic and ethical values. This greater understanding inspires the imagination to further exhibit itself as fully as possible. Actively engaging the imagination serves to enhance this reciprocal relationship in determining the meaning of objective form. Furthermore, this imaginative synthesis is facilitated through the interplay between different mental abilities, allowing them to interact so they reciprocally enhance one another's activity. Free play between sensible intuition and the intellect allows the imagination to unite different cognitive states so we better understand our perception of experience and make valid judgments.

Sometimes the image may refer to deeply personal memories, as in the painting *Anticipation (1993)*. At the time, I was coming to terms with living alone, in a big house I didn't need and couldn't afford. I was thinking of selling and looking for a new place to live. It was a time for new beginnings.

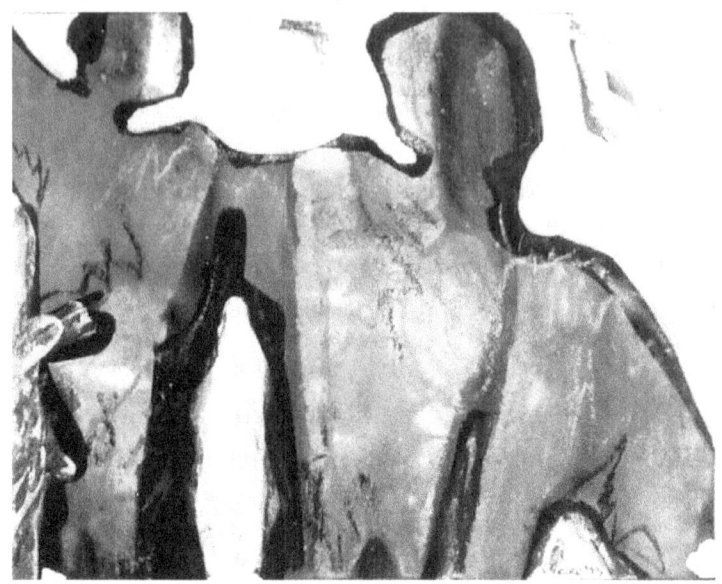

Anticipation (1993)

As paint was moved about, aesthetically meaningful form began to take shape on the canvas as well as in the mind. By making hidden emotions visible, the imagination seems to restructure lived experience. By bringing these suppressed yet intuitively recognized ideas into a fresh new context, a work of art makes the invisible visible and thereby understandable. Its development is driven by the creative act and art making process itself. Then aesthetic form usually articulates important personal truth that at the same time seems to reach back to cultural memories.

Aesthetic understanding provides a special kind of satisfaction that is different from the fulfillment of personal desires. Fully grasping and enjoying a work of art provides its own intrinsic reward, satisfying for its own sake. But aesthetic comprehension also reveals a wholeness of mind and its goal is internal and always authentic. The imagination brings sensory input under a general concept in much the same way a painter imposes order and aesthetic form on the chaos of colour and texture of the medium. Producing a general concept of an aesthetic idea into an innovative new art form balances these intuitive feelings with the intellect.

When distinct yet equally important cognitive ways of knowing are brought into form, different levels of interpretation and meaning can then be affectively as well as intelligently understood. If the imagination is free to play among inner thoughts and feelings, a visual representation of the unity of all experience is frequently embedded in the artwork itself. Meaningful aesthetic form demonstrates that people do not passively perceive their world, but actively engage their imagination to make the necessary cognitive links. But sometimes aesthetic form also shocks, as the imagination discovers an image that articulates a deeply suppressed emotional concept.

But if Kant is right and the mind gives structure to our reality, it is vital that these shadow memories are made conscious. Once these inner memories have been brought into visual form, they can provide meaningful insight into the commonality of the human condition. By making sensible stimuli visible, the complexity of meaning can then be rationalized on a personal, as well as cultural level. Conceptual ideas expressed in aesthetic form open the windows of perception and life can be viewed in a more global context. Delight and wonder at what has been revealed arises when the imagination brings harmony to the mind, which has tremendous transformative power.

Aesthetic delight is a particular and subjective pleasure, which is also a common and shared human value. When the mind is in relative harmony, it demonstrates the universal validity of aesthetic experience. Kant believed that this harmonious synthesis enlivens the mental faculties. Aesthetic understanding of meaningful form serves to rebalance and strengthen human cognition. Inspiring the mind to think and reason better. The free play of the imagination usually finds meaningful aesthetic form, which stimulates thinking beyond what can be spoken of in words.

DISINTERESTED CONTEMPLATION

Aesthetic delight can be found in the beauty of nature, in music or the rapture of dance, but it is the mind that actively shapes how we perceive this experience. These indescribable moments lift us from the deadening routine of our habitual lives. Aesthetic pleasure offered by the greatest works of art promise an experience of rapture and joy that continually renews the human spirit. But artistic creativity itself is also an intense aesthetic experience. Rapture cleanses the artist's thoughts and emotions about personal as well as world events by expressing them in artistic form.

Artistic creativity and sharing our artwork with others seems to be a common human activity that developed independently in various places across the globe. Most cultures celebrate and create art; some people write narrative, while others tell stories or make visual images from clay, stone or paint. Cross culturally and at different times, all over the earth archeologists have discovered aesthetically pleasing form; in paintings, sculpture and theatre plays. Everywhere people dance, sing and act out their cultural myths.

The apparent universality of aesthetic experience may explain why people are able to appreciate and understand the artwork made in other cultures, despite the different context, availability of materials and artistic adaptations. Although aesthetic response to a work of art is a universal phenomenon, artistic expression takes many different forms from one place to another. Contemporary artists are often inspired by the artwork of other cultures. Take for example, the painting *Cretan Goddess*. This painting was inspired by a archaeological photograph of an discovery on Crete. The image of an ancient goddess was carved into a stone wall. In stylized form, this image was juxtaposed on the canvas to express a new vision of an old story.

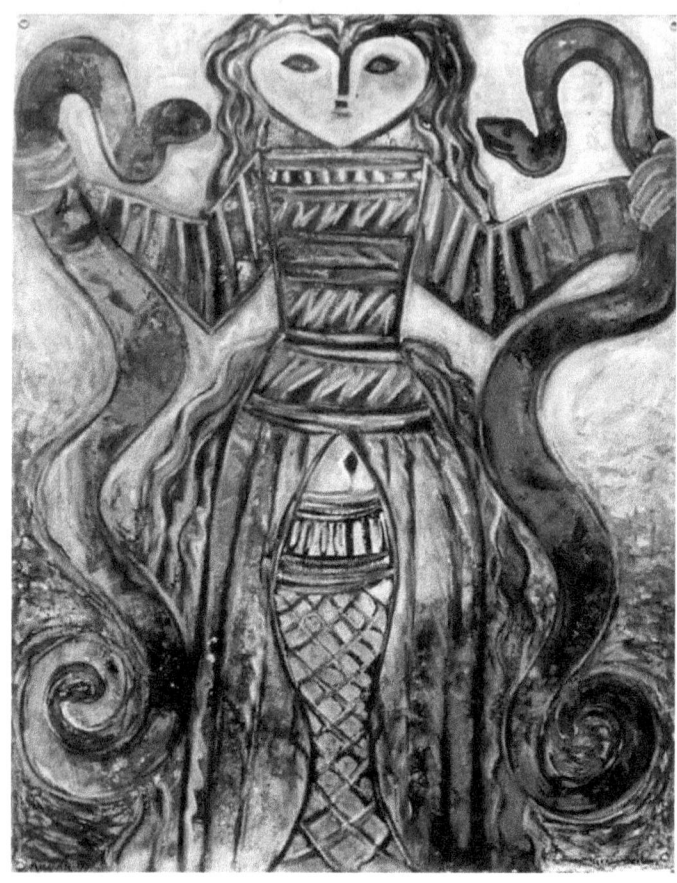

Cretan Goddess (1992)

The use of snakes and fish suggest not only Cretan mythology, but also Old Testament stories and their social implications. Snakes periodically shed their skin, and for that reason they have long been associated with spiritual rebirth, and the regeneration of nature. The fish form reminds me of the biblical image of Jesus, as 'fisher of men'. As well as the medieval legend of the Grail, and the mortally wounded fisher king. However, this is an extremely feminine figure with a heart shaped face, symbolizing love and protection. She stands firmly rooted, holding two massive snakes in her hands, similar to certain Athenian *Kore* statues. In the background the energetic blue half of the canvas suggests a body of water, perhaps representative of the ocean of knowledge. The sunlit sky may be understood as representing the light of reason.

Simply by attending to what an art object looks like, the imagination can make the necessary connections for grasping if only partially, the meaning of what has been expressed. Enjoy the work for itself, in an impartial manner, with aesthetic contemplation. Whereas Western culture puts the emphasis on disinterested contemplation, other societies perceive art in more pragmatic terms. Art as a source of aesthetic delight, which is valued for its own sake, stands in stark contrast to many other cultures where art expresses religious or political ideas. But in any case, we should approach a work of art imaginatively. Aesthetic judgment should not be influenced by personal feelings or desires.

Disinterested and sympathetic attention to a work of art provides the intellectual freedom from the mundane pressures of life to be reflectively contemplated upon. Whether it is a painting, a concert or a theatrical play, it seems *as if* for the time being, all worries and obligations are set aside to pay attention, and enjoy art for no other reason than for its own sake alone. Paying attention only to form in the artwork itself and contemplating it imaginatively by entering into the world of the artist frees the mind. Imaginative participation allows it the pleasure of weaving imaginings in a controlled manner. Making a disinterested aesthetic judgment is an intensely pleasurable experience because the imagination has been released to roam freely between intuitive sensibility and an intellectual concept.

When artistic form is disinterestedly enjoyed, it usually results in a powerful sense of cognitive delight that provides aesthetic understanding. Noticing the subtle details and complexity as well as its expressive qualities is what matters, not the issues of what monetary or moral value a work of art may have. Ulterior concerns should have no influence on viewers, as they surrender themselves to attending to the object's beauty, unity of form and the artwork's expressive intensity. Disinterested aesthetic enjoyment involves letting go and attending to understanding the meaning of the artwork's formal structure.

Sympathetic attention presupposes setting aside preconceived ideas and playing by the artwork's own rules, rather than importing our own. Attending with sincere empathy requires following the subtle prompting and implied visual metaphors that the active imagination discovers and makes explicit in artistic form. Disinterested attention to aesthetic form shows that the expressive purpose of an art object is more important than personal mental or physical states. There is a distinct feeling of objective pleasure in grasping the intent of an authentic work of art but it must be enjoyed for its own sake, and not for any instrumental value.

However, all interpretation of aesthetic form is ultimately subjective. Different social expectations; personal memories, cultural background and individual psychology will all come into play. However, the western conception of disinterested contemplation of aesthetic form is a relatively recent cultural trend. Sometimes, it seems a particular image fits perfectly and articulates something valuable that was already implicitly known to be true. For example, the painting *Sister (1998)*s depicts a cherished memory of childhood and the friendship between sisters.

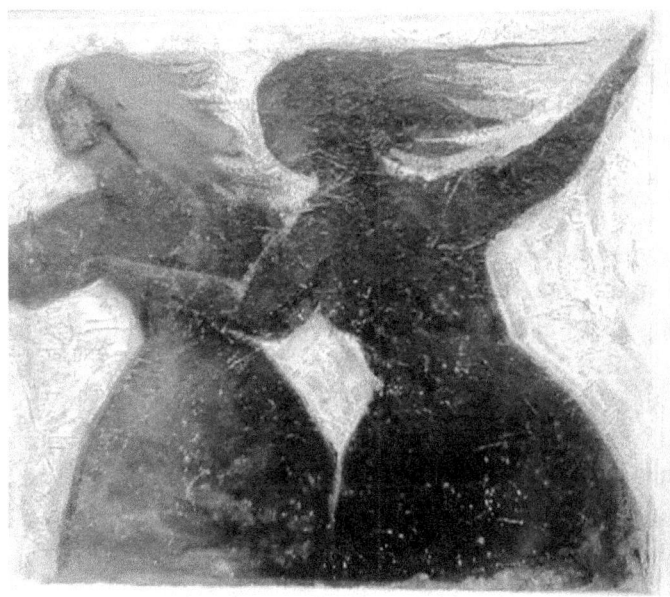

Sisters (1998)

This painting expresses in simplified form my inner thoughts and feelings about familial relationships, especially between siblings. Most people can easily respond to this image. Its simplicity speaks of the bond between sisters, yet there is also a tension in the gestures of these women. An expression of anxiety, even fear nudges my consciousness, expressing both personal and cultural issues. Although most viewers may not be aware of the specific details, aesthetic form seems to be able to speak in a commonly understood language that needs no explanation.

Prior to the eighteenth century the arts, including architecture served a more utilitarian purpose. One need only think of the magnificence of the Vatican in Rome, or the great European cathedrals to recall a time when art and architecture were used to teach spiritual reverence and moral principles to the illiterate masses. Europeans, who have no knowledge of Greek mythology or the meaning of West Coast native art, usually can appreciate the goodness of artistic form when they see an ancient statue of Zeus or a magnificent Haida blanket. But aesthetic appreciation may be limited by a lack of knowledge concerning the depth and value that an artwork articulates.

Therefore, a work of art should also be appreciated in context to where and when it was made and by whom. Even so, it is amazing that most people recognize and respond aesthetically to artwork made in other cultures, although its personal, cultural and historical significance may never be fully understood. It may be that cross-cultural recognition of significant form is an inborn part of human nature. Recognition of artistic form may relate to the human capacity for language. Aesthetic form speaks a language all its own that goes beyond mere words and text.

Although a casual viewer might not know the personal details and aesthetic reasons behind a work of art, on some level these different meanings may be grasped, if only in part. However, not every work of art is cross-culturally recognized, and some are not even recognized as art by all members of the same culture; Marcel Duchamp's ready-mades for example. Most artists, historians and philosophers today consider Duchamp's ready-made sculptures to be valuable works of art, however many lay people do not agree.

It is often the manner in which this artwork is displayed; in the context of art museums that raises it to the status of art. Aesthetic understanding of artistic form, including Duchamp's ready-mades, involves an attitude of empathy and a sincere effort to see beauty in patterns and in the work's expressive qualities. Distinguishing unique patterns is important because it allows the mind to create order from random sensory stimuli that is constantly impinging on human awareness.

A pattern that makes sensory perception visible delights not only the eye but also creates harmony in the mind. For example, a Turner painting of a beautiful sunset has been described as a series of sensory perceptions of nature that have entered the artist's awareness that the imagination brought into form. In the painting *Goldau*, Turner embodies his perception of a sunset on canvas and shares it with the world so others can imagine having seen the sun sink beneath the horizon, as he once saw it. In this landscape, the painter imposed a unique and subjective order on the chaos of random stimuli that impinged on his view of the setting sun.

Then his imagination created a sensuous and rational likeness, which is recognized as a good and true representation of the beauty of a sunset that speaks to everyone who appreciates its visual effect. This image can be interpreted on many different levels, if viewers impartially reflect on what its artistic form may mean. The imagination is inspired to find rational understanding in the beautiful pattern of a snowflake as well as in a painting whose aesthetic meaning the intellect alone would never find. Although expressive art usually has meaning, it may not always be immediately understood, as with the painting *Connected (1999)*.

I recall painting it and knowing that the three odd joiners between the figures had to be part of the image, although at the time I felt they detracted from the work. Without them, the title would make no sense but it's one of those paintings that remains somewhat of a mystery.

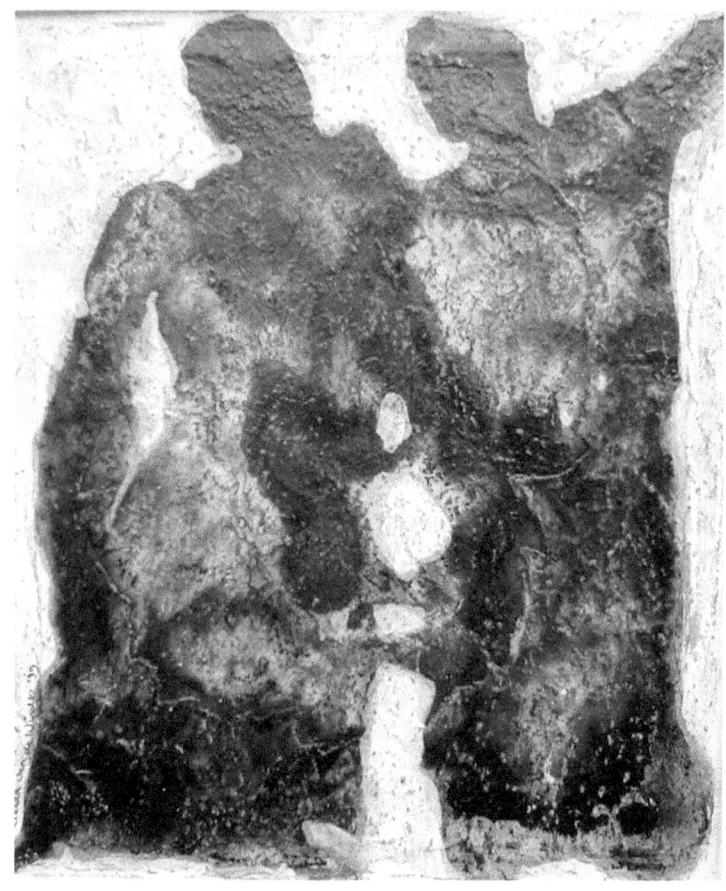

Connected (1999)

But this image does express an authentic aesthetic idea in a new way. The unusual colour and texture in this painting was the result of much experimentation of potential possibilities, as well as limitations of the medium. Building texture and colour from the application of different kinds of paint resulted in a unique textural surface. Enamel and acrylic mixed with oil and pastels. The figures, a male and a female, are intimately connected, at the hip. It's a visual pun on an old saying that some married people are 'joined at the hip'. A third form appears in the 'negative' space that both separates and holds the two figures together. This image is part of a series that explored personal relationships to gain greater understanding of the human condition.

Understanding the intent behind a visual image, of a sunset for example, inspires reason and aesthetic ideas that can only be alluded to in a work of art, and only partially understood. A unique artistic vision seems to become self evident, as the imagination connects the various cognitive elements to bring forth a new artistic form. Quiet contemplation is an aesthetic delight that opens viewers' eyes as well as their mind, in order to reach beyond the obvious. Unstudied reflection and free play of the productive imagination while reflecting on the beauty of an aesthetic object is, as Kant points out, is always new and one never gets tired of looking at it.

Disinterested aesthetic experience is a purposive act of mind, yet seems at the same time to be free from constraints and rules, as if form was created by nature itself. But a work of art is never a mere imitation of nature, nor does it follow a set of rules which can be taught. The natural quality of aesthetic form results from the imagination's freedom to discover a conceptual fit, rather than having a predetermined concept imposed on form. Only when a concept presents itself spontaneously to consciousness can its meaning be fully communicated. There are often many layers of possible interpretations concerning the meaning inherent in artistic form. A work of art expresses an aesthetic idea whose meaning may be interpreted in many different ways.

The pleasure of artistic creativity and aesthetic appreciation produces a feeling of harmonious unity between mental energies, when the mind spontaneously grasps the art form's meaning. In an attempt to express this idea in context with a general concept, aesthetic form sometimes surpasses the limits of personal knowledge. Evaluating the merits of a work of art requires that viewers activate their imagination in order to strike a balance between the aesthetic requirements of form and content. Disinterested attention to detail is required to grasp what this image means in context with the artist's intention.

A genuine work of art is always original and does not depend on the judgment of others for its production. Nor can the artist always describe how they came by an image only that it originated within the mind. Neither can the processes of artistic creativity be duplicated at a later date, nor can its meaning be fully articulated in any other way. Perhaps it is this mysterious prompting by the imagination that makes a work of art perennially interesting. But it may take years before deeper levels of meaning can be rationally understood as its message becomes clearer. '

The artist is also required to work disinterestedly during the art-making process. For a painter, aesthetic form is often a barometer of a particular psychological state that begins to manifest itself as the artwork progresses. Meaningful aesthetic form develops in context with corresponding thoughts and ideas about inner feelings that the imagination has brought into form. Intense concentration on colour, texture and form, in a painting as well as in nature, often leads to further reflections on the inherent value of the message embedded in aesthetic form. Even when it's abstract, like in the painting *Ancient Beginnings (1990)*, aesthetic form speaks eloquently through a wealth of concepts that the imagination finds within the psyche. These images enrich our perception of *Being* and being human. Only disinterested contemplation and actively engaging the imagination to play between intuition and conceptual understand can these abstract ideas sensuously embody.

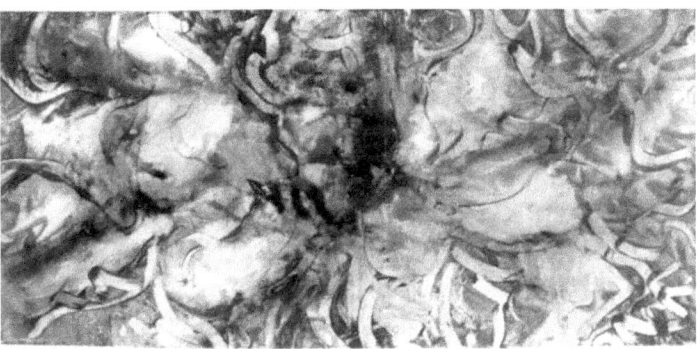

Ancient Beginnings (1990)

The imagination is capable of expressing these intellectual ideas, enabling the mental capacity to reason better about such abstract notions as peace and justice for all. Viewers who have a subjective disposition for aesthetic understanding often feel an expanded capacity of affection for all humanity. Therefore, understanding aesthetic form furthers the moral qualities of virtue, honour, and sympathetic friendliness towards others. Disinterestedly contemplation presupposes the awareness that common principles such as affection for humanity are the common ground of virtue and morality.

True virtue is acting according to these universal moral principles regardless of people's spontaneous impulse for self preservation. Appreciating aesthetic form in light of a general affection for humanity seems to be an innate quality of human consciousness. Ancient philosophy articulates this affection in the context of living a happy life within the community. These ancient ideas are expressed in myths that speak of personal and collective duties and obligations and were acted out in seasonal rituals that celebrate the cycles of nature. The ancients knew that strengthening aesthetic understanding was good and satisfying in itself.

Disinterestedly contemplating on the meaning of a work of art provides unity and wholeness that goes beyond the divisions that arise within the community from the struggle between morality and desire. Attempting to come to terms with the complex nature of meaningful artistic form has a long cultural history. Since prehistory, a work of art was displayed and aesthetically understood as a representation of the culture's sacred mythology. Art was considered to be part of society's magical heritage. It was celebrated in communal rituals, away from everyday life, within caves or forest groves. Many centuries later, artworks were increasingly displayed inside; in temples, cathedrals and churches.

By the seventeenth century, art had lost its social as well as sacred meaning. More and more, a work of art became a visual articulation of individual self-expression. Consequently, a new aesthetic language was necessary to adequately express what the artist saw around them. Painting in particular began to express how the individual artist perceived the world. With the invention of oil paint during the early Renaissance, painting increasingly began to dominate the European art world. As church patronage was replaced by wealthy merchants and the bourgeoisie, it drove up the demand for opulent portraits and pictures of the landscape. Paintings became highly desirable additions. A beautiful painting could show off new acquisitions, such as wives or land, and its dominance went unchallenged until the twentieth century.

VISUAL THINKING

Across time and place, great works of art have played an integral part in a culture's traditional heritage. A work of art brought the sacred myths and rituals into a commonly understood artistic representation. Works of art were used or performed during special communal rituals, not part of everyday life. Therefore these special gatherings usually happened in ancient forest groves, or in the bowels of a hidden cave within the earth. As time went on, these sacred rituals became increasingly institutionalized as more and more, artwork was moved inside temples, cathedrals and churches.

As demands for church paintings of the spiritual and divine diminished after the Middle Ages in Europe, paintings became the preferred visual expression of a new modern age. With the advent of the Renaissance, artists such as the Flemish masters created beautiful paintings in oil that showed the faces and opulence of a burgeoning capitalist society. Oil paintings in particular, were extraordinary in their ability to describe the secular wealth of the bourgeoisie. Master painters such as Rembrandt and Frans Hals revolutionized European painting with their interpretations of society on lushly painted canvas.

Many of these paintings were personal statements of aesthetic ideas that the artist's imagination had found within the mind. Although each artist approached their subjects differently, Rembrandt and Hals shared the ability to accurately express both the inner and outer character of their subjects. Their work was an inspiration to many others, including myself. For me, the unique materiality of paint provides many opportunities for creative self expression. Its liquidity creates a myriad of colour and form that contains valuable information that can be shared with others. For example, the idea behind the painting *Moon Dance (1990)* developed from the fluidity of the medium.

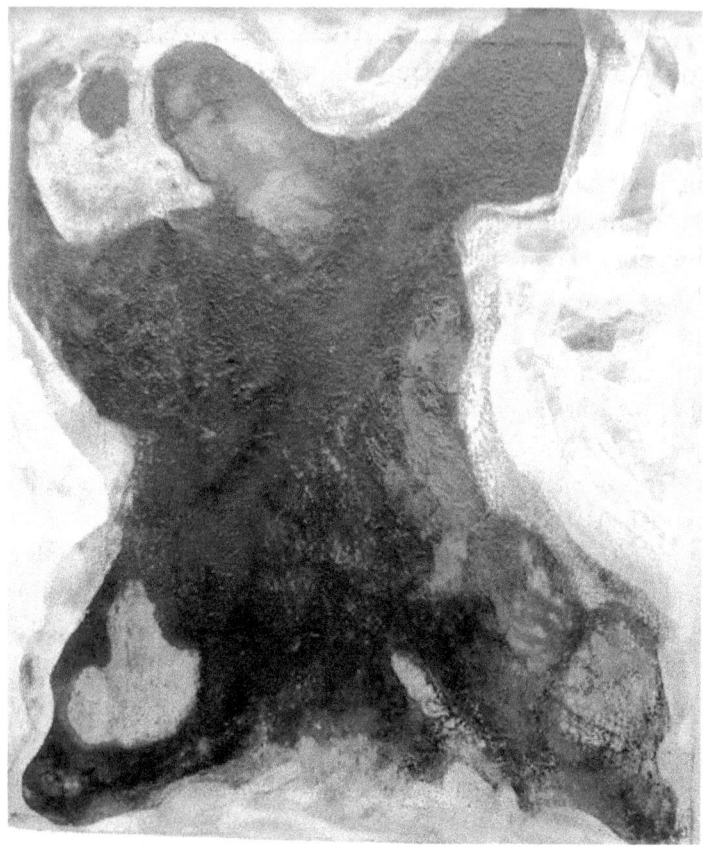

Moon Dance (1999)

This image depicts a dancer whose hands encircle a red full moon. Perhaps she is drawing down the power the harvest moon during a communal gathering. Although the artist has a special relationship with their work and may speak with authority about its aesthetic meaning, they may not always be capable of giving the best interpretation or critique of what is important or significant about it. A painting does not begin with a preconceived idea; often aesthetic form comes to mind once the initial application of paint has dried. Sometimes it takes much thought and quiet contemplation to see and bring forth the images. It may be true artists are sometimes poor critics of their own work, but only they know and truly understand its intrinsic meaning.

With the demise of the church and the advent of secularism, the production and exhibition of art became increasingly controlled by a complex system of art museums and galleries. This vast art network included not only museums and galleries but also many art schools and concert halls. This art world also encompassed various institutions for trading, commissioning and collecting art, as well as art history and restoration work. A thriving business sprung up around the production, exhibition and enjoyment of art that even includes the often baffling new art of the latest avant-garde.

The question of who decides whether a work is valued as 'art' or not depended on the acceptance of art experts and institutional art world. If an artwork was accepted by a gallery as well as art critics, it generally meant that the status of 'art' had been conferred on it. However, sometimes a full understanding of significant meaning behind the image seems to have little to do with this judgment. In the past, everyone in the culture knew what the artwork symbolized, but not anymore.

Since before the ancient Greeks, the arts have had the power to inspire awe and wonder at the sublime beauty of its aesthetic form. Traditionally, a work of art was linked to personal and cultural memory, as well as being a visual imitation of objects and nature. Especially painting as pictorial representation links art with imitation and representation, or to use a Greek term, *mimesis*. For Plato, painting was merely a second-hand simulation of a natural object and he dismissed art as being inferior to reality, a mere copy, and as such, always suspect. A tragic play or a mural were misleading, a deceitful facsimile from a true original. But this original was something that only existed in some transcendent world.

For the ancient Greeks, a work of art would always remain an inferior imitation of an ideal world, merely a dim shadow far removed from the objects in nature. For example, Plato describes the ideal form of a chair as existing in another realm, the wooden chair being only a copy. Therefore a painting of a chair is but a third-rate copy of a copy. However, Plato's conception of aesthetic form as an inferior imitation of experience is quite ineffective as a general account of art. Very little in a work of art has to do with imitation. It well known for example, that actors do not merely imitate their characters, they inhabit them.

Moreover, seeing a work of art as an inferior copy of a natural object does not begin to explain authentic aesthetic understanding of artistic form. For one thing, it negates the artist's imaginative search for creative goodness and authenticity. If the imagination has been able to balance sensible intuition with intellectual understanding, a work of art is never just an inferior copy of the world. Rather, it is a new and unique expression of an inner world and lived experience that the imagination unifies, as in the painting *Familie (1999)*.

The painting shows how the artist thinks and visually working aesthetic problems through to better understand personal issues. The title *Familie* translates from Dutch as 'family' and makes explicit reference to my cultural background. It represents a mother, daughter and three siblings. Two sisters and a boy unnaturally squeezed sideways in between. A dark field of withered flowers divides the mother and daughter from the others, suggesting a problematic fracture within the familial relationship.

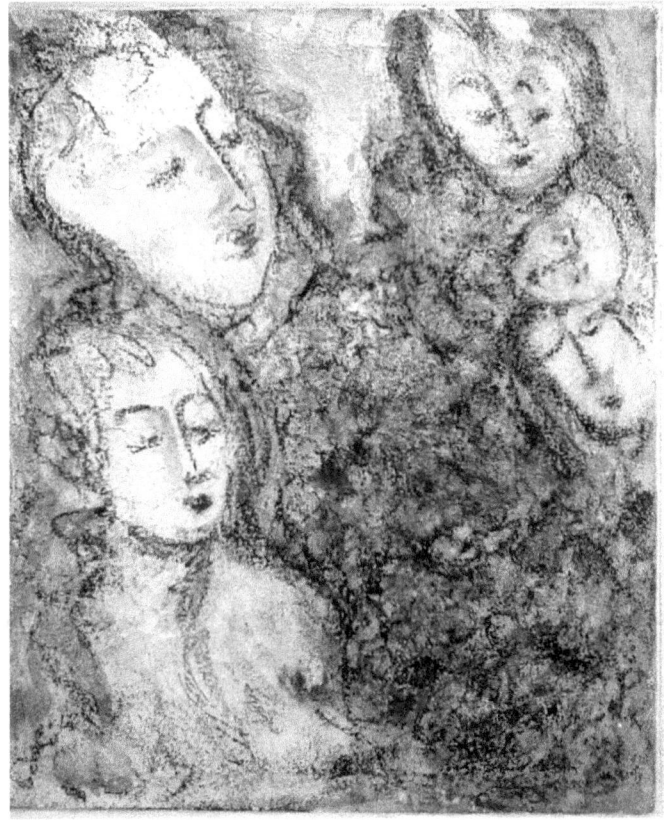

Familie (1999)

There is a lot of intense thought and feeling embodied in this little painting that still moves me. Perhaps because it so aptly describes a suppressed yet disturbing childhood situation, which nevertheless helped shape my perception of the world. Authentic artistic form has a special power to express a personal attitude, and often articulates much more than may have been consciously intended. But not all artworks can be experienced perceptually, nor aesthetically grasped through the senses.

John Cage's conceptual sculpture *4'33"* for example. This work of art consists of four minutes and thirty-three seconds of silence, which he describes as 'silent music' and an act of artistic anarchy. But is it art? Yes, of course it is art because the work successfully expresses an aesthetic idea, which is understandable. Four minutes and thirty-three seconds of nothingness makes a strong expressive artistic statement concerning the value of silence. Aesthetic understanding requires taking time to think about the many layered meaning that may be implied.

Cage asks viewers to approach this work with an empathetic open mind and an active imagination, so the mind can grasp what the art work's form is silently saying. Reflective disinterested attention to a work of art, a painted image for example, does not mean seeing only the splotches of colour on a two-dimensional surface. It also involves seeing the subtle variations of colour, texture and form. It is difficult, if not impossible for a painting to represent only the two-dimensional flat surface of the canvas.

Every nuance in colour and texture suggests the potential for artistic form in a three-dimensional space. After all, most people see something in something else and thus what they see is representational. It is one of the strengths of the painted image that the human mind is able to create three-dimensional form from splotches of colour and texture on a two-dimensional surface. But some would say that the advent of photography has made the art of painting obsolete. A photo, they say can represent form so much better. The issue of artistic representation may be irrelevant, but at what cost? What is lost if a painting lost its power to present aesthetic form?

Representational form in a painting is very different from a photograph. A painted image articulates inner thoughts and feelings about the artist's perception that goes far beyond mere documentation of the world. A painting articulates an in intensely personal view of things whose meaning is much broader than merely representing reality. Since the eighteenth century, a painting is no longer seen as a representation of reality, but as an individual, creative act of authentic self expression. Its aesthetic form an intuitive expression of intellectual concepts found within the mind.

But with this new aesthetic attitude, the language of art lost its common reference points both artists and viewers could traditionally draw upon to understand the work's deeper meaning. This change in aesthetic perception of art, not as imitating nature but as a unique product of self expression, reflects the culture where the work was made. There was a cognitive and perceptual shift by the end of the eighteenth century that bears witness to the fact that long-standing intellectual, spiritual and historical assumptions were being challenged and reinterpreted across Europe.

For centuries, Christianity's version of history and sacramental nature dominated the public domain. Humanity was a microcosm in a 'great chain of being'. But with the advent of the Renaissance, this entrenched and antiquated point of view began to change. Accordingly, artists were encouraged to seek an original vision of the world and express these ideas in a new aesthetic language. For example, the simplified form in the painting *Attitude (1999)* shows its postmodern minimal influence.

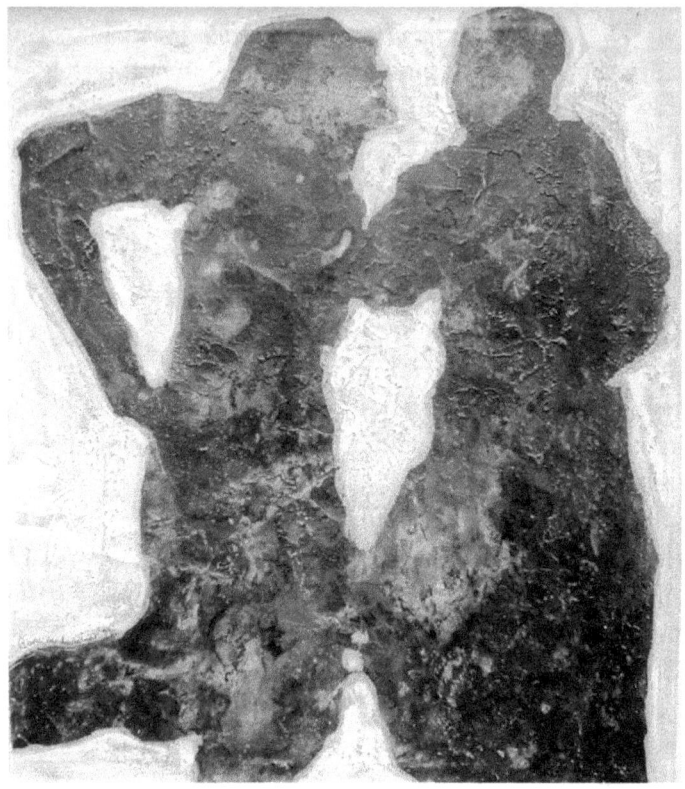

Attitude (1999)

Aesthetic form revealed itself in the colour and texture of the painted surface. Despite it's simplicity, the expression on the abstract faces tell a story that only the artist knows. Yet viewers can experience their own story if they take the time to enjoy this work. The lusciousness of the paint draws the eye in and follows the arm of the woman. Is she touching the tortured one or holding him up? What happened? Let the imagination guide you into the work.

This new aesthetic perspective, as the philosopher Monroe Beardsley observed, includes any perceptual or intentional object that is deliberately regarded from an aesthetic point of view. Modernist philosophy reflects a far broader view of what artistic form is supposed to represent. Beardsley includes looking, listening, reading, and similar acts of attention in this aesthetic perspective. Attention to the art work's formal properties, its shape and colour for example, arouses complex and valuable feelings and sensations.

Beardsley is absolutely right when he said that this aesthetic enjoyment is an experience worth having for its own sake alone. Aesthetic pleasure can be found in the particular sound of a musical score, which is especially satisfying to the ear. Or it can be found in the various elements of colour, texture or sounds that have the power to shape our thoughts and feelings and influence aesthetic response. The enjoyment of seeing the unity and harmony in a beautiful painting for Beardsley, relates to the intensity of aesthetic pleasure in the experience.

This intensity depends on whether a painting is contemplated under optimal circumstances. For Beardsley, viewing a work of art under optimal circumstances is what disinterested contemplation was for Kant. These aesthetic elements or qualities that are inherent in a work of art determine the comprehension of its complex meaning. Participants must be open to what is in the work because the inner thoughts and feelings of the artist are there, displayed for all to see as much as the texture and patches of colour.

Every element in a work of art speaks of the artist's search for self expression. The various aesthetic parts are intrinsically interconnected. They pull the work together so its intricate meaning can to some extent be articulated. Sometimes, like Cage's *4'33*, aesthetic ideas push society's conceptual boundaries.

But if the imagination is activated, people will experience aesthetic form in a whole new way. The unique expressive elements in a work of art articulate both conscious and unconscious qualities that an artist may have intentionally displayed.

Viewers are asked to make a conscious effort to respond sympathetically to these aesthetic elements by identifying with the speaker in the work. Aesthetic understanding requires paying attention, making a concerted effort to detach temporarily from the demands of the real world and allow the imagination to engage with artistic form. This detached contemplation allows the mind to imaginatively focus on the meaning of the 'picture-figure' image in a controlled manner.

However, some contemporary artists do not give viewers a 'picture-figure' image to contemplate, Claes Oldenburg for example. Oldenburg's *Invisible Sculpture* is located behind the Metropolitan Museum of Art. This ultra-abstract work is a site-specific installation that consists of digging a grave-size hole and refilled it again with earth. Oldenburg describes this art work as a conceptual 'underground sculpture'.

Viewers are asked to visualize the sculpture as loosened dirt from a particular section of Central Park. Once the hole was refilled, it could no longer be visibly perceived. However Oldenburg's conceptual sculpture is nonetheless part of the New York landscape. This work of art intentionally bypasses our perceptual sensibilities and its meaning can only be imaginatively understood by reflective and mindful contemplation. As in the painting *Dark Angel (1999)*, the angel a stark figure that appears to be readying for flight. Although her face is highly abstracted, we sense she's female. A red heart shape floats in the background. She may be a dark angel but she knows how to love.

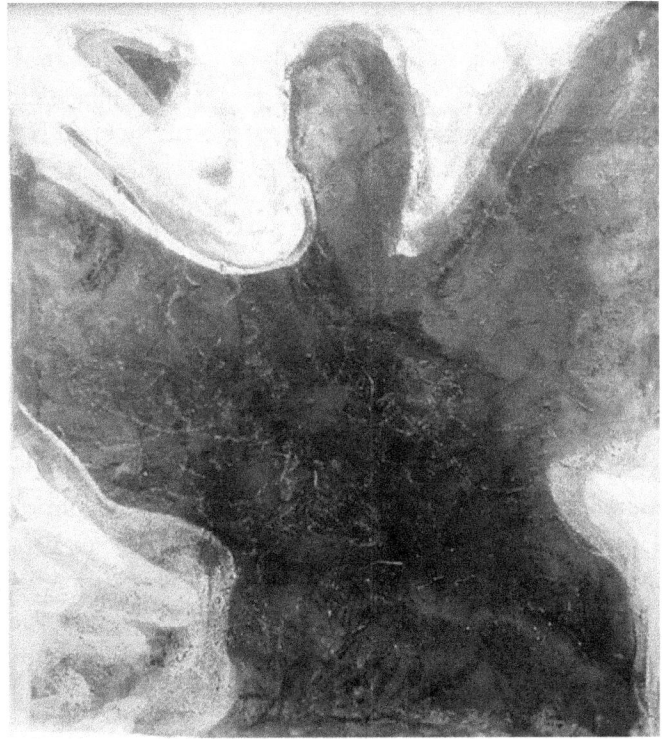

Dark Angel (1999)

I smile as these words appear on the page but it's true. It's aesthetic truth. The painting is at once minimalist but at the same time expressive, even abstract. Although not immediately obvious, there is always an interconnectedness to the past in a work of art. No one works in a vacuum and aesthetic form will always be to some extent culturally determined. Conceptual art was influenced by modernist movements such as Dada that challenged long held beliefs about what a work of art actually was.

Marcel Duchamp suggested that a work of art was not just a visual experience of the senses, but art could be anything at all. The American sculptor Claes Oldenburg pushes the boundaries of what art is by saying an underground sculpture that can not be seen, is as valid as one you can. Be that as it may, it appears that today anything is considered to be art if the artist intends the work to be viewed as such, even if the art itself can't actually be perceived. Sometimes aesthetic form articulates a personal revelation, giving viewers a sense that they already knew what the artist is trying to say.

There may be a push/pull effect on the senses; on the one hand viewers feel something has been revealed, yet on the other hand, people also sense that they already knew this revelation intuitively. Aesthetically feeling the 'rightness' of artistic form opens our consciousness, making us aware of new possibilities in life. A work of art is often valued for the way it makes people more aware by bringing a cherished idea or image of something only vaguely remembered into consciousness. Sometimes a particular form perfectly and *explicitly* articulates something valuable that was already *implicitly* known to be true.

If the imagination is able to unite both conscious and unconscious probings, the ideas expressed may be grasped on many different levels of experience. For example, viewers may perceive Turner's painting of a beautiful sunset as uniquely 'Turneresque' in response to the commonality of the painter's perception that coincides with their own world view. In an effort to restore cognitive order to what is perceived, people tend to project their personal experience onto an external image to comprehend its meaning. A work of art may impose a sense of order on their internal lives that is often overlooked.

What could be more important than bringing inner thoughts and feelings into aesthetic form? And what if not art is able to do this for society? However, understanding the intentions behind a work of art may change over time. Aesthetic perception may relate to personal and cultural morality, in art as well as in everyday reality. But aesthetic judgment always involves empathetic contemplation and recognizing an authentic attempt at self disclosure. This essential quality is embodied in the originality of aesthetic form itself. Originality and the authentic attempt at self expression are indispensable for evaluating an work of art.

Authenticity links artistic creativity to greater issues of ethics and morality. It demands originality, as well as imaginative thinking to bring inner thoughts and feelings into meaningful aesthetic form. The characteristics and materiality of a particular medium, paint for example, have changed little over the years. Much can be learned from the painters of the past. There is always a continuum in the artistic process that forms the foundation for the development of contemporary self expression. Often a work of art speaks for the individual as well as the community in a new aesthetic language. Original self disclosure always speaks in a way that has never been heard quite this way before. Therefore the language of art is always new and ever changing.

Sometimes the art making process also requires selectively breaking the rules of convention to fully bring a unique vision into form. But the successful artist needs to know the traditional norms and required skills of a particular discipline before they can bend or even break these rules successfully. The painting *Inspiration (1999)*, for example breaks a few rules, yet presents a compositional unity that works. It's a playful image that celebrates the joys of visual thinking.

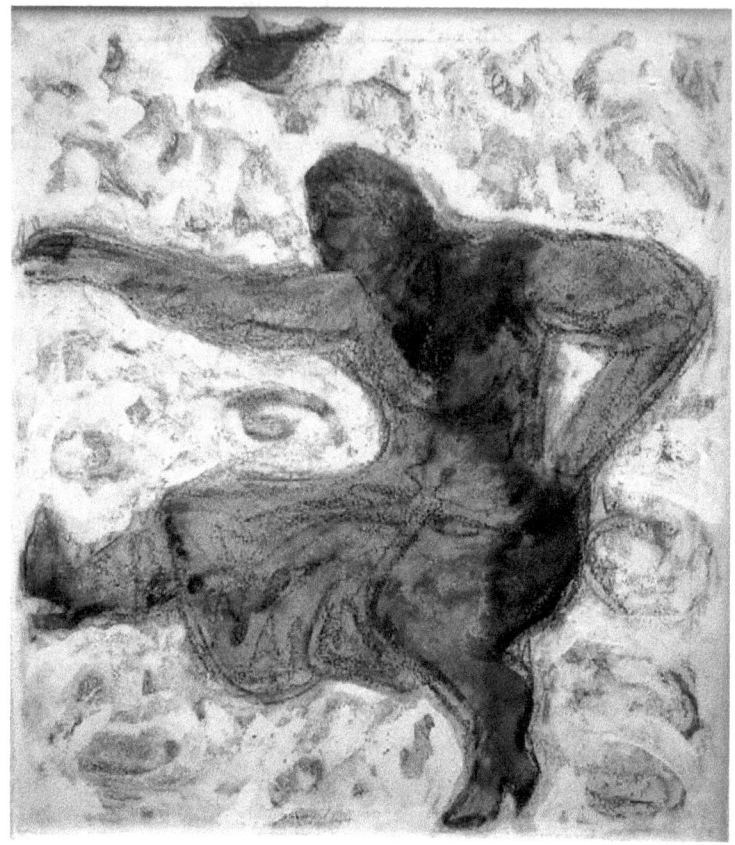

Inspiration (1999)

Dancing a jig, as the woman pursues what I would interpret as the bird of paradise, and may represent the artist's inspirational flight of fancy. Even the painted background joins in with the celebratory mood, as she dances her way through spirals and flowerlike forms. I still smile when looking at what this image expressed to me at the time it was painted.

Artistic form is often the result of much experimentation of both the potential possibilities as well as the limitations of a particular medium. For example, building texture and colour from the application of different kinds of paint results in a unique textural surface as different types of paint mixes on the canvas. As a painter plays with these interactions, a unique vision becomes self evident. The imagination connects these various cognitive energies to bring forth a unique aesthetic vision. This imaginative connectivity is the source of all authentic artistic creativity.

To some extent, the cognitive and affective decisions made during creative process remain visible in the finished work. With enough attention to structure and detail, complex ideas are communicated to the sympathetic viewer. Aesthetic form frequently embodies multiple possible interpretations that often reveal much more than the artist knew, or had consciously intended. A work of art may speak differently to the artist than to viewers. They may not have realized how much of their inner thoughts and feelings have been exposed to view.

Indeed, they may never have known that this or that quality shows in the work, whose significance can never be fully articulated. The intense sense of recognition, when the imagination discovers significant form is seldom forgotten. Even after many years, I can easily recall this pleasure of self discovery. These precious moments have been forever preserved in the art work itself. However, other people may have a different aesthetic response when they reflect on a painting. Perhaps they will recognize part of themselves the artist could not have known about or consciously intended to display.

The unique materiality of the paint itself provides many opportunities for creative thinking as form develops from the fluidity of the medium itself. Artistic form is never preconceived but grows as aesthetic ideas come to mind. Although the artist has a special relationship with the work and can often speak with authority about its meaning, they are not always capable of giving the best interpretation or critique of what is important or significant about it.

A work of art may be understood as a cognitive map of one's inner subjective world that has been brought into the public domain. Therefore, aesthetic form can never be entirely separated from language as such. The subjective intention to articulate self consciousness is an important source of valuable information both personally and for the society in which the artist lives. This discreet aesthetic language is grounded in the intuitive sensibility of the artistic personality that to some extent has been embedded in the artwork itself.

Sometimes it takes much thought and quiet contemplation to fully understand meaningful aesthetic form. But then, as in the painting *Butterfly Woman (2000)*, the meaning jumps out at once. This image shouts loud and clear in an aesthetic language that speaks of *joie de vivre*. The joy of living, celebrated in paint texture and form. This 'subtler' language in art speaks of complexity, personal and cultural that enriches its meaning. This image alludes to the button blankets of the coastal First Nations that has been interpreted in a whole new way. The spiral shape suggests Native American rituals as well as certain weather patterns in nature.

This image, like so many of the other paintings, may be interpreted on both a personal and cultural level. For me as the artist, I liked the distinct Native American reference in relation to a butterfly.

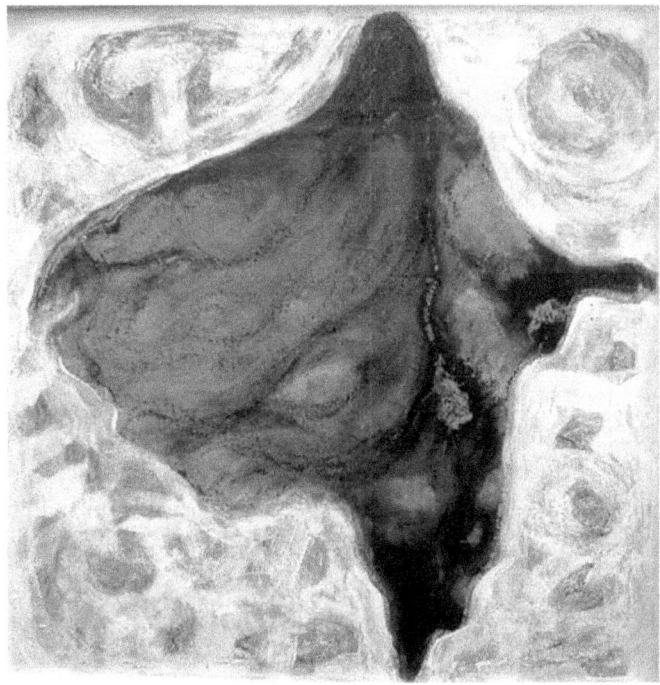

Butterfly Woman (2000)

The philosopher Richard Wollheim claims that Leonardo Da Vinci stood in front of a wall he was about to paint for days, in thoughtful contemplation, without once lifting his brush. Wollheim presumes this to be self evident of the artist's visual thinking process in formulating and articulation his aesthetic vision. It is reasonable to suppose that the thoughts occupying the painter's mind were on visualizing the painted surface. Perhaps Leonardo was arranging the images in his mind to articulate what he wanted to paint.

If what Wollheim says is true, the artwork had been created in the mind before da Vinci actually began to paint. I find it is difficult to believe that the painter was able to foresee precisely the exact images he was about to create. In truth, an artist is not able to fully anticipate the exact image of a picture because aesthetic form will manifests itself on a canvas or on a wall as the work progresses. Authentic artistic creativity is an imaginative journey of self discovery that must acknowledge the significance of the materiality and randomness of the art medium.

Authentic aesthetic form develops out of the problems and opportunities that are encountered during the creative process and the inherent unpredictability of the medium itself. Perhaps da Vinci needed to acquaint himself with the physicality of the wall itself. He said in one of his journals that a painter would be wise to study the water stains on a wall because these shapes are a rich source of aesthetic inspiration. Whatever went through the painter's mind as he stood there, the bulk of his visual thinking would have occurred during the painting process as his imagination played between concepts and innerness to bring forth meaningful form.

ART AND CULTURE

For a broader perspective of personal and cultural horizons, one needs to know the historical and philosophical traditions that underpin the making of art. Knowledge of the tradition of art history shows a work of art is always to some extent culturally determined. In the best of the arts, self expression and cultural meaning are harmoniously balanced. Yet there is often a palatable tension in a great work of art that seems to embody this pleasurable tension between self and other. That there is tension between these opposing demands has to be allowed, according to the philosopher Charles Taylor.

In addition, the materiality of a particular medium presents problems that are part of the expressiveness of the creative process, which is often resolved by visually thinking them through. The specific qualities of the medium are an intrinsic component of the finished work. For me, the painting process is seldom a struggle perhaps because, as an expressive painter, I do not decide in advance what will happen on the canvas, nor the exact colours that will be used. Nor do I consciously will or seek anything in particular. Visual thinking involves a lot of intense concentration on feelings that are deeply embedded in body memory and often have tremendous power to move us.

Sometimes aesthetic form is discovered that may aptly describe a suppressed yet disturbing childhood situation, which nevertheless helped shapes our perception of the world. But rather than a struggle, it seems that allowing the imagination to play freely between sensible intuition and the intellect it usually results in finding just the right form. For example, the painting *Desire (1999)* illustrates how, by giving the imagination free rein, it led to the discovery of these two figures within the paint itself. This image speaks poignantly of two human beings who are reaching out for each other in a gesture of deep yearning. There a pleasant yet urgent tension between the figures and background, as if this precarious balance and harmony might at any moment be shattered.

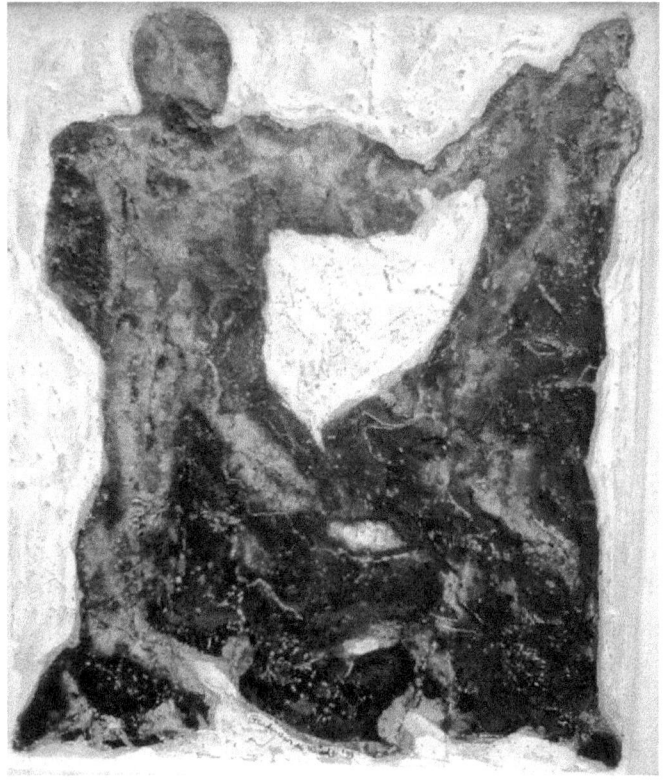

Desire (1999)

Upon reflection, perhaps the tension between these figures also implies that to some extent a cognitive struggle was required to bring these aesthetic ideas to fruition. But it was the materiality of the paint itself that brought these images of deeply hidden personal trauma into consciousness. Materiality is an integral part of the creative process.

For some, the materials used describe what has happened in their lives. Take Joseph Beuys' WWII memorial for example, this work is grounded in personal experience and humanist philosophy by his use of grey felt. He used felt for a specific reason. During the war, Beuys was shot down and wounded over the African desert and his badly burnt body was found by Bedouins. He recounts that the Bedouins covered his wounds with layers of felt, ultimately saving his life. But felt also makes reference to the material that has long been used in making military uniforms. Therefore his use of felt can be read on many different levels.

Being aware of the significance of using felt is vital for a finer grasp of his work. For Beuys, visual thinking involved setting his mind free to play between sensuousness intuition and conceptual form. As he manipulates the material, he may have asked himself, "Why grey felt? Why grey? Why felt?" Perhaps the answer would have been that felt muffles sound but the idea of felt may have made other suggestions to his imagination in its controlled free play. Grey felt was the material of the German field uniform; the uniform Beuys was wearing when his airplane was shot down. For Beuys, visually thinking through personal and aesthetic trauma opened up new ways of using his chosen medium more effectively.

Aesthetic form has a special power to express personal attitudes that sometimes articulates much more than the artist may have intended. Take Frans Hals' portrait of the Regents and Regentesses of Haarlem for example. Although Hals paints his subjects realistically and in full regalia, this portrait may also be seen as a telling testimony to his subtle sense of irony. At the time this work was painted, Hals was an old and destitute painter living off public charity. The painter seems to have overcome his subjective feelings to depict the people who held the purse strings to his marginalized existence more or less objectively.

It is this unforgettable contrast that is the 'drama' in this
painting, as Berger puts it that. Viewers may not know much
about the men and women Hals portrays, but the details in this
painting are self evident. Aesthetic form speaks eloquently of the
possible character of these people, if one chooses to look and
think about the expression on their faces. Berger suggests that
contemporary viewers study the evidence and judge for
themselves. The evidence is there in the details of the painting
itself for all to see.

Paying attention to the subtle details works a seduction on those
who take time to really look at a work of art with a sympathetic
eye. This painting confirms the innate character of a group of
people as they were perceived by the painter. Their austere, self
righteous faces provide adequate testimony of the poor old
painter, whose sense of irony is preserved in the image for all to
enjoy. His imaginative interpretation of the character of his
sitters works on the heart and mind and viewers accept the way
Hals saw these people.

People intuitively believe the truth of what the painter has
represented and this informs their aesthetic judgment. However,
it should be added that viewers do not accept the artist's
perspective innocently, but only in so far as it harmonizes with
their own way of perceiving the world. In general though,
imaginative form, especially in a painting, holds a special
fascination both for artist and viewer alike. Sometimes a painting
has a mysterious haunting quality. The painting *Endings (2000)*
shows what I mean. This haunting image lingers in the mind.
Form clearly illustrates an intense emotional event, which is
supported by its title. A close personal relationship has ended
and the man and woman walk away in despair.

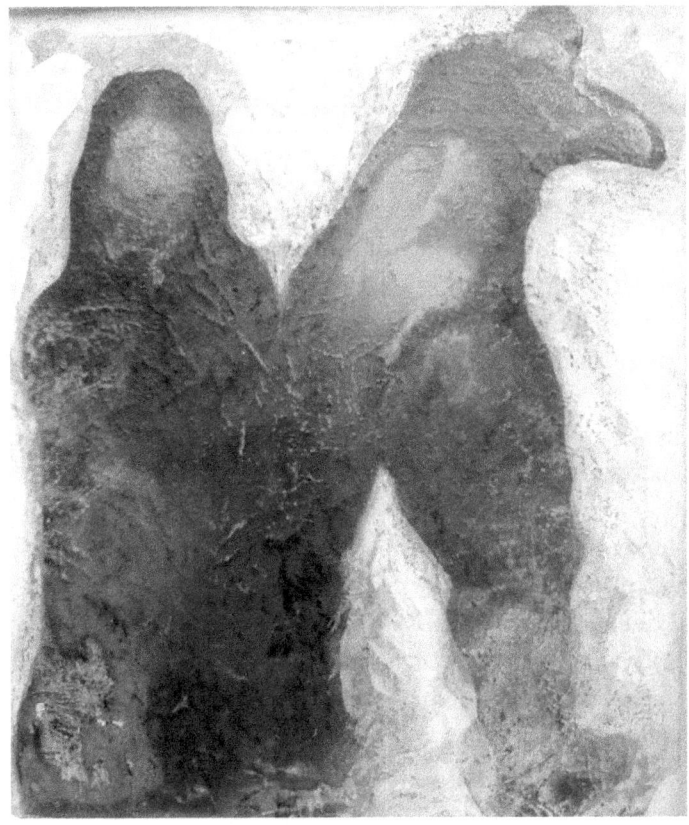

Endings (2000)

People intuitively grasp the intended meaning behind aesthetic form, as in the stern faces of Hals' regents and regentesses for instance. Perhaps they recognize these people because they represent social institutions that still exist today. They may also be comparing the character of these people with their own beliefs, their sense of morality and ethical values. Hals was one of the first painters in Europe to express a subjective perspective of an important social change in the western world. His paintings depict the new character of capitalism in the faces and figures of people whose personality may be easily recognize and thought about. It is precisely this feeling of familiarity that gives this particular painting its psychological and social urgency.

Whereas in the past, the fundamental purpose of art was to bring a sense of the divine into aesthetic form, over time art increasingly expressed a sense of the individual. This is especially true of European painting. Rather than portraying the holy family and important saints as in earlier art, paintings began to depict the wealth of the secular and social elite. Representation evolved from prescribed realism in wave after wave of artistic innovation until the nineteenth century when the invention of the camera forever changed how we perceive the function of art.

Painting was particularly affected. A photograph was much cheaper to make than a portrait. It could also more accurately record the appearance of people and things than a painting ever could. Consequently, the camera released painting from the demands of traditional depictions of secular and divine reality. The painter was now free to discover a new visual language and use their artwork to depict the visible as well as the invisible world. Hence the rapid evolution from realism to abstraction until Minimalism negates aesthetic form entirely.

Although Pablo Picasso's work became increasingly abstract, he adamantly maintained that his paintings always depict nature. Like many other painters, Picasso was particularly inspired to depict the female body. His portraits of women were fragmented and these Cubist images speak loud and clear of the intensity of his feelings. His paintings often contain a message that a particular image wants to articulate. But like most authentic works of art, the mysterious force behind perceived reality can only be hinted at and never be fully disclosed.

A work of art will always to some extent be autobiographical because it reflects the place, time and people in the artist's life. Take Marc Chagall's paintings, for example. Throughout his life, Chagall painted images that celebrate everything that he loved. In painting after painting, he depicts his marital happiness as well as memories of his childhood in Russia. We know a little about the artist's life so this horizon of significance determines how he perceived the world. These images also show how visual thinking about form brings hidden memories into consciousness. As specific feelings about personal experience become manifest, aesthetic ideas that its form contain may also spark a response in viewers.

A revolutionary new way of expressing the complexity of visual thinking was initiated by the French Impressionists. Painters from Renoir to Cezanne explore the transitory effects of light reflecting on the appearances of people and things. The Impressionists believed that the visible no longer presents itself simply to be seen. On the contrary, the visible is in continual flux and has become fugitive and difficult to pin down. A few years after the Impressionist revolution, the Expressionists progressively turned their gaze inward until the Cubists no longer perceived their world from a single perspective.

Although the painting *Remember (2000)* refers to a specific event, it articulates a feeling that is shared by most people. The image shook me because it brought an idea to mind that had long been suppressed. But there it was, on the canvas. For me, this was visual thinking at its best.

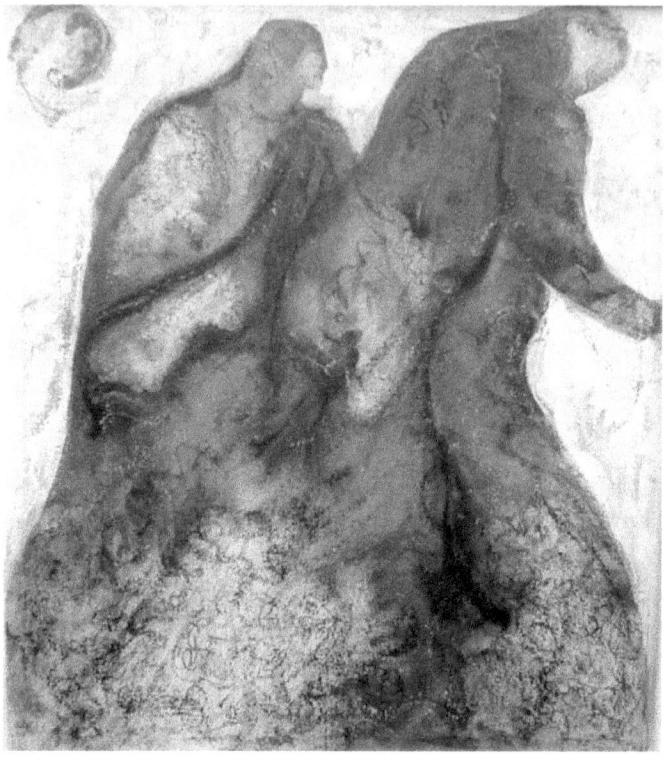

Remember? (2000)

With the advent of modernism, the relationship between artistic self expression and the quest to find one's place in the world becomes extremely intimate. Today, the painter is free to shape aesthetic form any which way they want but in the past, they were strictly controlled. Guilds established the norms and traditions that were to form the foundation for painting for centuries. The status quo was first challenged in France by the Impressionists and later by Cubism. Georges Braque and Picasso attempted to depict a true visual image of the complexity of perception by constantly changing their perspective of things. Creating aesthetic form became the paradigm mode by which the artist could come to self-definition. Painting with its fluidity and gestural qualities was particularly affected.

The canvas became an arena for physical and psychological exploration. The paintings of the Abstract Expressionist Jackson Pollock come to mind. Although his later paintings appear to be totally abstract, their titles reveal their connection to nature. In his negation to realistically depict nature, Pollock once exclaimed that he was nature. In his lonely search for aesthetic form, Pollock exemplifies the plight of the tragic artist. Western society tends to idealize the tragic artist as a great visionary hero who creates new personal and cultural values.

It was thought that artists, in their personal struggle to create meaningful works of art, are often better able to grasp the essence of the human condition. Perhaps it is true that shaping aesthetic form tends to provide one with a clearer definition of self. If nothing else, bringing inner thoughts and sensible intuition into a visible form provides a sense of the complexity and unity of human experience. Artists can't help but articulate subjective attitudes because all their personal experience shapes their work.

But it is a mistake to think that they are cut off from commenting on serious personal as well as social and political issues because it trivializes art. Everything that happens becomes part of the subject matter because a work of art reflects their thoughts and emotions. Picasso expressed his revulsion of the bombing of Guernica in a painting by the same name, and Goya's work makes a wry comment on the horrors of war. Their personal attitude and understanding of these events is there for all to see. For many, Goya's etchings and *Guernica* will always remain an eloquent personal and cultural outcry of their grief. Authentic aesthetic form has the power to speak across time and place about the tragedy of war that at the same time illuminates the commonality of the human condition.

Many historic works of art still engage the contemporary imagination and remain vital expressions of inner feelings and thoughts. The involuntary nature of the act of painting requires letting go of ego control, and not consciously seek to express something in particular but allowing form to freely and authentically reveal itself. For me, authentic artistic creativity shows that the active imagination has the power to bridge the abyss between personal and collective issues. This aesthetic unification of subject and object also reveals a greater human rationality and consciousness of self and others.

Artists search for the right words or musical notes or just right compositional line when suddenly a flash of intuition dawns that resolves the problem happily. It is a joyful feeling when the aesthetic pieces fall into place. Finding just the right form for an aesthetically pleasing composition happens in context with the materiality of the medium that has become intertwined with personal as well as a mythological self expression about the meaning of lived experience.

The painting *The Three Graces (2000)* illustrates how form seems to articulate a personal idea that originates in a collective mythological consciousness. As the title suggests, these three figures refer to an ancient Greek myth of three sisters, collectively called the Three Graces, three goddesses that personify joy, charm and beauty. This mythological concept is a recurring theme in the history of Western art. The three graces were the daughters of Zeus and Eurynome; on the left is Aglaia who represents splendour, Euphrosyne is in the middle, and she represents mirth and Thalia on the right, good cheer.

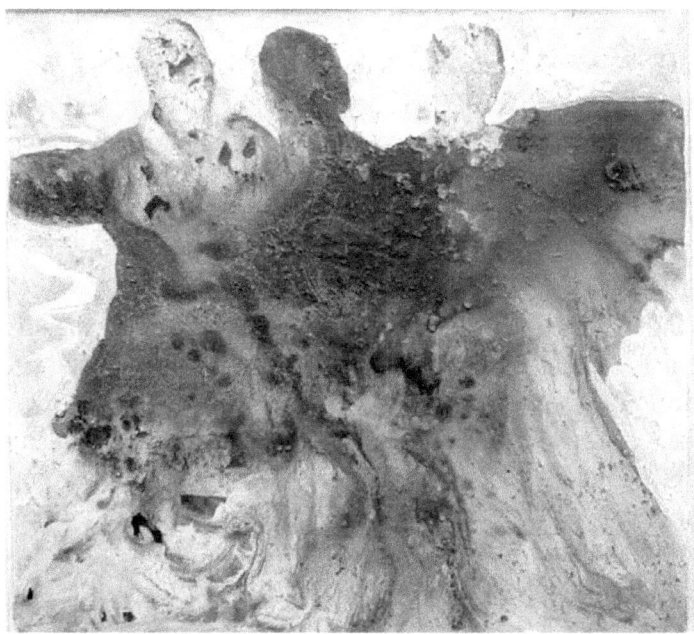

The Three Graces (2000)

Collectively they brought goodwill and joy to the people as well as the gods and goddesses on Mount Olympus. They presided over banquets and communal dances as well as other pleasurable social events. They also attend Eros and Aphrodite, the god and goddess of love and desire. Along with the Muses, the Three Graces have inspired artists and poets to create beautiful works of art for millennia. This image is a contemporary expression of an old mythos, whose idea turns up in later paintings. Aesthetic form depicts a long forgotten memory of a classical time of beauty and grace.

Often, aesthetic form plays with perception where the visible is no longer what confronts the eye alone. The Cubists were the first to realize that the human eye takes in the totality of possible views. Recognizing that our perspective constantly changes, they took this into consideration when painting their subjects. They began to move around the subject so their view was from different perspectives. This fractured the image and this increasingly splintered picture of people and things became more abstracted. But Cubists like Braque and Picasso maintained they were always true to nature and this subjective fragmentation was a realistic depiction of the way they saw the world.

The contemporary artist David Hockney also plays with the idea of visual fragmentation in his photo collages. With a nod to Cubism, he shows that a single snapshot is a limited statement because it represents only one moment in time. By taking multiple photographs from different angles and perspectives, Hockney tries to recreate how the eye roams across what it sees. He collects these various images and uses them in his work as a more accurate depiction of how we see the world.

While it may be true that photography more accurately shows the appearance of things than a painting does, no one can dispute the aesthetic power of the painted image. Take for example, Peter Paul Ruben's *Helene Fourment in a Fur Coat*. It depicts his young wife as she turns towards the spectator just as the fur slips from her shoulder. The painting looks as if the artist captured a moment in time but this image transcends time. In a superficial sense, her image is as instantaneous as a photograph but in a more profound sense, this magnificent painting contains both time and experience.

Unlike the immediacy of taking a photograph, a painting such as Rubens' takes considerably more time to make. The image is actually a composite of many separate moments. The painter captured consecutive stages in time, which have all been embedded in the details of the painted image. Therefore the painting displays the past, present and future all simultaneously. Today, we recognize Rubens as one of the great master painters who furthered the tradition of European oil painting. In visual images pregnant with meaningful aesthetic form, he celebrates the female form in luscious physicality.

The history of painting is associated with a few exceptional painters who produced extraordinary works of art that challenged the traditional norms and values of oil painting. However, the tradition of painting may have been somewhat distorted by a few great master painters who stood out from the masses. These extraordinary artists are acclaimed as the tradition's supreme representatives. These exuberant claims are made easier by the fact that after their death, the tradition of painting closed in around their work.

The truth is that most painters incorporated only minor technical innovations and the tradition of painting continued as though nothing of principle had been disturbed. From this misrepresentation of traditional painting, the myth of the great artist emerges as a larger than life hero, who wrestles with his angels and demons. In the end, this mythic artist is often consumed by the struggle to live with him or herself and with others in the world. However, there is a disturbing lack of women painters throughout the history of Western art, something postmodern artists have tried to rectify.

During the 1980s, there was a flurry of feminist art that celebrated the feminine traditions. For example, the painting *Dancing to a Different Drum (2000)* was inspired by traditional feminine led communal gatherings that celebrated the seasons, both in nature and in women's lives.

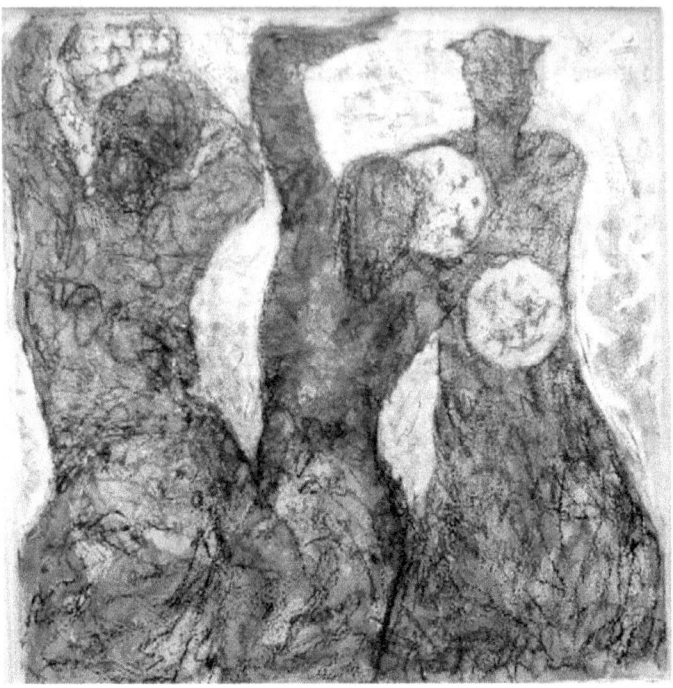

Dancing to a Different Drum (2000)

This painting depicts three women as they dance and drum in the time honoured way. Its form gives a sense that the women are dancing and drumming in unison, as a masked figure looks out at the viewer. I recall how these figures grew out of seemingly arbitrary marks made on the canvas to form a totally unified composition that only required bringing out from the medium itself. As intuition and intellect worked together, a previously unknown idea that the imagination had discovered was visually expressed and understood.

Of course, this image was also inspired by literature and films of the day but the figures themselves came directly from interacting with colour and paint itself. I think it is important to stress that there was no preconceived idea of what this painting would articulate prior to its conception. For me, this painting expresses a personal and collective need for a new world mythology to replace the loss of a grand narrative to explain the mystery of human existence in a new aesthetic language. Perhaps the contemporary alienation from loved ones in Western culture can be overcome if people remember that all human perception, including the perception of divinity, resides in the mind.

Berger compares the idea of the stereotypical artist as a kind of Jacob wrestling with an angel. Gauguin, van Gogh and many others are classic examples of tormented artists who struggled with inner and outer demons while creating great works of art. It seems as if these artists struggled not just with life but also with the very language of art. But for other artists, the creative process is seldom a struggle because they do not decide in advance what will go on the canvas, nor the exact colours that will be used. Neither do these expressive artists consciously will or seek anything in particular.

Rather than a fight with the medium, the expressive artist allows their imagination to play freely between intuitive sensibilities and intellectual understanding. This creative synthesis usually results in finding just the right aesthetic form. Working with nature, rather than against it, the painter accepts guidance from this imaginative free play. This causes a mysterious tension as if the precarious balance and harmony between subject and object might at any moment be shattered. Upon reflection, perhaps this inexplicable tension implies the necessity of cognitive unity to bring these aesthetic ideas into form.

But it is prudent to remember that the popular conception of the heroic artist is relatively recent, occurring mainly in western culture and there only since the early Renaissance. Between the fifteenth and nineteenth centuries, European painting clearly shows that a cultural shift occurred in western ideology that coincides with the advent of capitalism. During the Renaissance, oil paintings were increasingly in demand as visual expressions of new cultural attitudes concerning the acquisition of property and purchasing power of new capital.

The aesthetically pleasing materiality of oil paint is uniquely able to express the new wealth in Europe, which many believe could not have found expression in any other visual art form. Original oil paintings of this period bear witness to the birth of the new age of capitalism in the glorious details of people and objects. These images paint a picture of the owner's wealth and status like no other art form had been able to accomplish before. Oil paintings became the favourite way to show the acquisition and abundance of buyable and desirable objects of the time.

Traditional painting has a long history of drawing on publicly shared aesthetic understanding that was based on the divine. Even secular subjects were perceived as being intensely meaningful in a social context. The popularity of paintings during the Renaissance did to appearances what capital had done to social relations; reducing everything to the equality of objects. Everything was exchangeable because everything became a commodity.

Even at the best of times, it has never been easy to live the life of an artist. And it is true that some artists struggled not just with life but also with the very language of art. The painting *Lamentations (2002)* expresses the sometimes overwhelming loneliness of the solitary artist who struggles just to get by. But there are always exceptions to the rule.

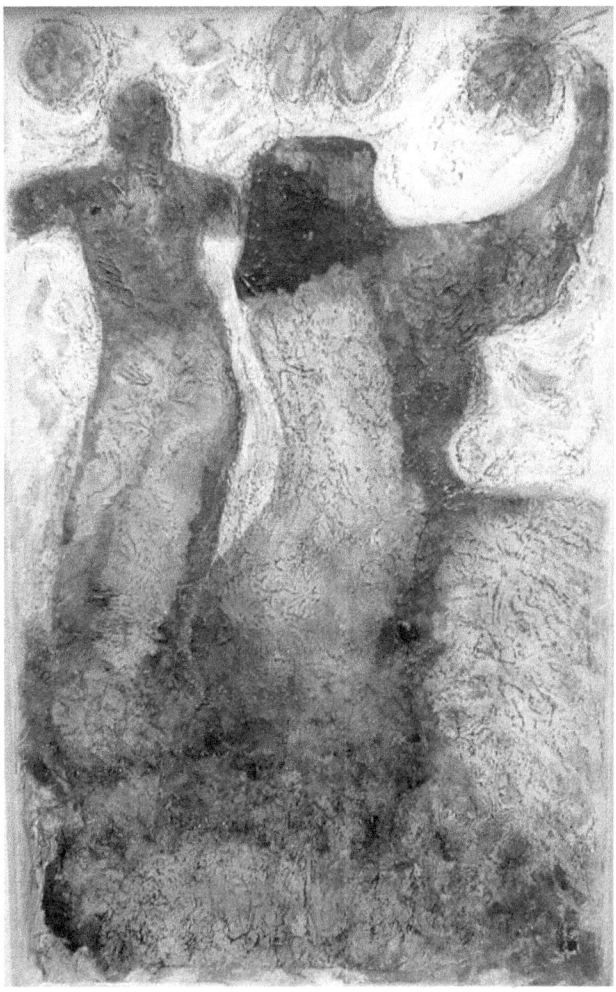

Lamentations (2002)

The magnificent paintings of Vermeer, Rembrandt, El Greco and Turner, to mention only a few, contradict the assertion that reality can be measured by its materiality. But if the viewer studies these paintings in relation to the tradition of painting as a whole, they will discover that these artists were exceptions of a very special kind. Many paintings of the period merely reflect the rise of a new capitalist middle class in Europe. The bourgeoisie, more often than not only desired a painting as an expensive acquisition that confirmed their social status and depicted their possessions and wealth. However, some early Dutch landscapes painted during the seventeenth century by Ruysdael and Hobbema didn't seem to serve as expensive statements of capitalist wealth and possessions.

Neither did these paintings express a common cultural understanding of divinity, nor did they serve a particular social purpose. They painted Dutch towns and the countryside, which was considered to be an independent artistic activity. The result was that many landscape painters starved or gave up painting entirely. But many were extraordinary innovators, and their work greatly influenced the tradition of painting. The paintings by Ruysdael and Hobbema are exceptional in terms of redefining artistic vision. In addition, Rembrandt, Turner and Constable discovered how to use light by sketching and painting the subtle and often ineffable nuances in the landscape.

These innovations led progressively away from the substantial and tangible towards the indeterminate and intangible that points to the later paintings of Monet and the French Impressionists. An original painting has a special sense of immediacy, making it ever contemporary. Its tactile testimony concerning a historical moment is literally there before the viewer's eyes, closing the distance between the act of looking and the time required to paint the work. In its sense of immediacy, an original painting contains the silent proof of the painter's perception as well as their thoughts and emotions.

Authentic self expression clearly shows that aesthetic form cannot be separated from the painted surface but are intimately connected. Imaginative fusion between form and context shows they are entwined and interdependent. Both form and content are equally necessary for aesthetic understanding of the art work's essential meaning. Aesthetic form often suggests a long forgotten story, one that most people can readily comprehend and perhaps even relate to. Its meaning needs no words or text, not even a title to explain the subtle message behind its artistic form

The painter's imagination has found form in the plasticity of the materiality of paint to adequately express the intensity of an aesthetic idea. But art is never a mere illustration of this idea. The object is not to illustrate an aesthetic idea, on the contrary. If the prompting of the imagination has been followed, the illustration *becomes* the idea. The nineteenth century Symbolist painters explored the notion that a painting could articulate much more than the artist's subjective response to nature. They believed that freeing the imagination releases the mental power to create order from the objects in nature within the act of painting itself.

The artist allows forms in nature to speak directly to the paint. Rather than dictate aesthetic form, the painter allows form to freely and authentically manifest itself in the art medium. Authentic artistic creativity reveals that the imagination has the power to bridge the abyss between personal and collective issues. This unification of subject and object reveals a greater human rationality and awareness of self and others. Visual thinking has been permanently embedded for all to see, as in the painting *The Mothers (2003)*. In the gestures and brush strokes that permeate the materiality of the painted surface; something a mere reproduction can never show. Imaginative form has a special mysterious power that fascinates both the artist and viewers alike. Perhaps this mystery lingers in the work because aesthetic form illustrates a intensely emotional subject. Like motherhood and all that it suggests.

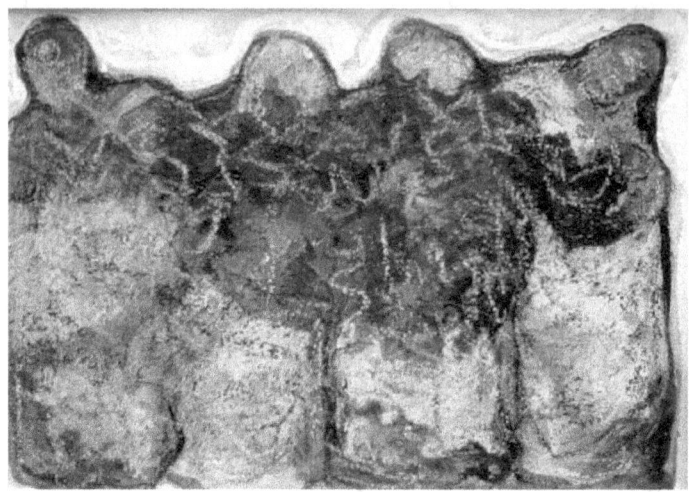

The Mothers (2003)

The involuntary nature of the act of painting requires letting go of ego control and not consciously seeking to express something in particular. Caspar David Friedrich for example, paints the landscape in order to express a personal vision that goes far beyond mere perception of the objects he saw in the landscape. The artist's paintings speak of the ineffable and spiritual in nature as well as within himself. His work is not based on any accepted conventions of traditional oil painting but originates from innerness .

THE MALAISE OF MODERNITY

After the Second World War, another cultural shift in visual thinking occurred as a group of New York artists known as the Abstract Expressionists continue the European enquiry into the nature of aesthetic form. Artists such as Willem de Kooning, Barnett Newman, Hans Hoffman, Mark Rothko and Jackson Pollock used painting as an intense and expressive physical act. But the creative innovations of Action painting would ultimately lead to the nihilist perspective of Minimalism. With the advent of globalization, postmodern Minimalism was an abrupt reaction against the optimism of modernity.

Postmodernists reject the idea of a unifying cosmic order that had traditionally informed society. Minimalist painters denied that aesthetic form, however abstracted, should be linked to nature and denounced the need for artistic self expression in art all together. For Minimalists, the two dimensional structure of a painting's flat surface was incompatible with depicting the illusion of three dimensional space. It seems as if nothing was sacred, as philosophers such as Jacques Derrida, Jean-Francois Lyotard and others deconstructed the very meaning of language and art.

In response, many postmodern artists made works of art that are difficult, if not impossible to understand. On the positive side, postmodernism did acknowledge the relevance of many different voices, giving minorities a chance to articulate their unique perspective of the world. However, there are too many voices all clamouring to be heard, and too few people are listening. The deconstruction of experience has led to a general sense of malaise in today's society that certain artists attempt to address. The painting *Holding up the World (2000)* for example, alludes to this idea.

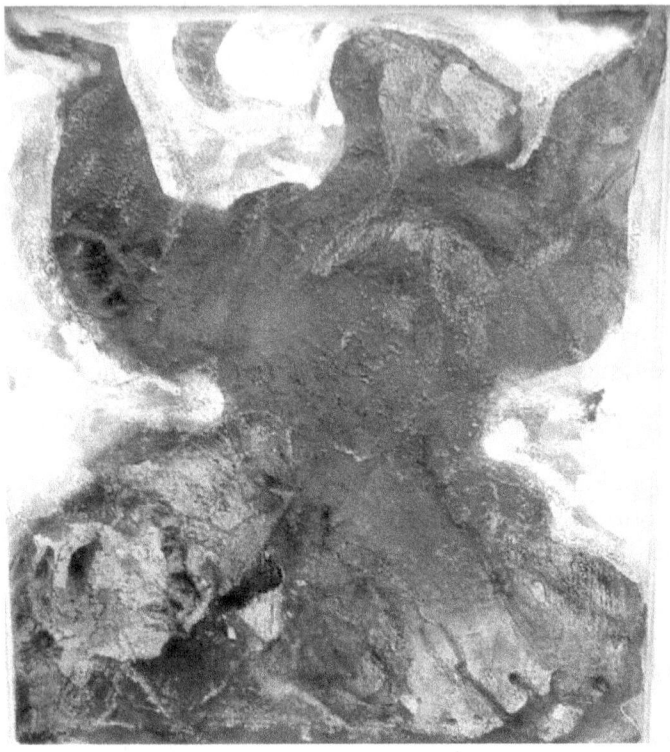

Holding up the World (2000)

My work is often inspired by both personal and world events. By expressing my anxiety in aesthetic form, I try to make sense of what happens around me. Other artists such as Alselm Kiefer, Judy Chicago and Tracy Emin, also use art making to express their concerns about many social issues left unspoken by their society. Their art articulates a new aesthetic language that is intended to function as a pedagogical tool. Each in their own way, critiques the traditional view of western culture; its history, art and philosophy.

There is a tendency in postmodernism to reject traditional grand narratives of an all powerful god that includes a negation of all authority figures. This cognitive reversal has shaken the very foundations of human thought, affecting not only religion but also science and morality. Losing faith in the underlying unity of experience resulted in a general feeling of malaise in today's society. Although this posthuman view threatens to destroy humanity's very existence, perhaps losing the traditional moral and spiritual foundations was the price western culture had to pay for the search for individual freedom and a greater sense of self consciousness.

It may have been a necessary step in humanity's cognitive evolution to question the authority of a unifying grand narrative to advance the idea of liberty and personal fulfilment. This cultural transformation has its roots in ancient Greece and Plato's allegory of the cave, if this story is interpreted as a metaphor for humanity's quest for individual consciousness. The search for self fulfilment and individualism reappeared during the Renaissance, finding full expression in Kant's philosophy of mind. His philosophy transformed western thinking by stating that all perceptual understanding originates in the mind, and does not come from outside the body.

Kant's philosophy fits perfectly with the modernist view of individualism, where man was considered to be the centre of the universe and the divine was to be found in the mind alone. Restructuring Plato's allegory of the cave for a new age., Kant believed that once having seen the sun, people were now free to live in the light of reason, rather than merely watching dark shadows on the cave wall. But this quest for self consciousness has become endemic. Losing the cultural and spiritual ground of a grand narrative has become problematic for postmodern society.

The quest for self fulfilment has encouraged self absorption and the alienation of posthumanism, with all that this name implies. The individualistic search for self consciousness has resulted in selfish isolationism. The loss of general communal guidance and rules has eroded respect for law and order. It appears many people have lost sight of their social obligations, as well as the rights of others in the community. In addition, contemporary life is often transitory because an economically globalized culture has to be extremely mobile.

But greater mobility and personal freedom also brought new knowledge about different ways of living from a variety of cultures around the world. For example, some societies are more feminine centred, engaging in ritualistic music and dance as part of their seasonal celebrations. Because postmodernity encouraged the expression of many voices, a great variety of art, literature and film has become available to the general public during the latter part of the twentieth century. In addition, artists and philosophers were free to express these alternative perspectives of the sacred and secular world in their work.

Consequently, in an effort to reclaim a lost part of their history, the age old idea of the feminine divine was enthusiastically reinvented by many women in the west. Some believed that there is a tremendous personal and collective need for a new mythology. The world needs a new story to replace the loss of a unifying grand narrative. A fresh explanation capable of explaining the mystery of *Being* and being human anew would require a quantum leap in consciousness. These ideas were the inspiration for the painting *Quantum Leap (2001)*. The image of a young woman leaping across the canvas, for me says it all. Despite its minimalist execution, this canvas hums with activity.

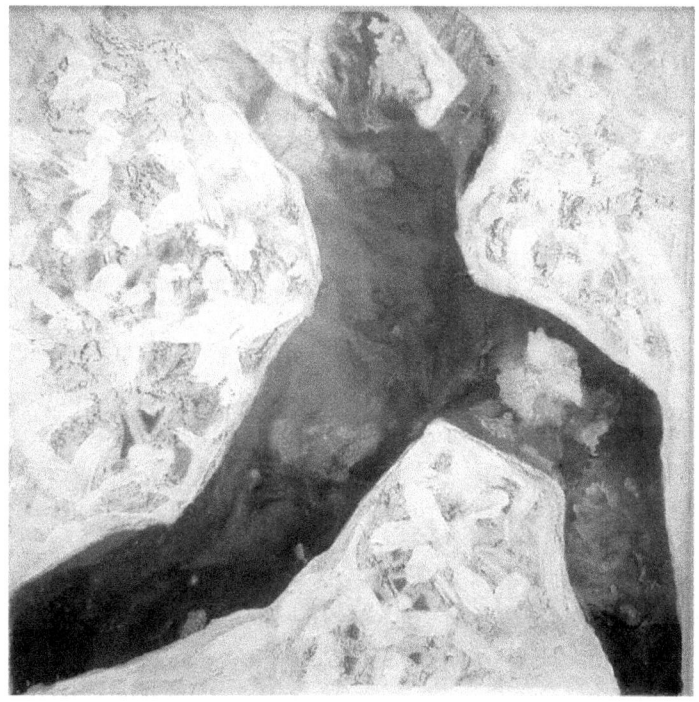

Quantum Leap (2001)

The woman is leaping over some unseen hurdle, and by doing so, she has been liberated. The title alludes to quantum mechanics and reaching beyond the horizons of consciousness to a greater understanding of what it means to be human. Its aesthetic form articulates a more hopeful outlook for our ability to bridge personal and cultural differences. Prior to modernity, people were born, lived and died in the same place. Their entire life was spent among an unchanging group of people and most did what was expected of them. There were clear rules in place regarding what was considered right and wrong that everyone understood.

Cultural values, as well as social norms and rules were traditionally passed on to the next generation by elders in the community. However, in today's global society, people seldom stay in one place long enough to feel connected to others. Often, children or parents are forced to move far away from home to find work, leaving the security of family and friends behind. In this mobile world, consumerism and greed have all but replaced the cultural foundations and religious traditions that sustained humanity for millennia. It has become abundantly clear that for many, the Almighty Dollar has taken the place of an Almighty God.

Although there is a terrible price to pay for this compulsive search for self gratification, some still believe that the modernist notion of individuation was the crowning glory of western culture and art. Charles Taylor argues that the search for greater individuation was a necessary and valuable human development. However, the down side of this compulsive search for self consciousness has been out of control consumerism. It is lamentable that the horrendous power of today's greed and self-gratification has invaded the cultural ideology of almost everyone on the entire planet.

John Berger laments the unnecessary pain increasingly suffered across the planet. The result of selfish greed and personal detachment from others has created a posthuman culture of isolated people who live in a world of pain that no drug can cure. There is a general complacency and erosion of democratic values today. The fundamental decisions that affect the disenfranchised are made unilaterally and without any open consultation or public participation. However, even if given the chance to participate and vote, most people would rather abstain.

Most people keep to themselves and don't bother getting involved in their community. This extreme autonomy of the individual has left many people desensitized to the misery of others, whether they are the next door neighbours or the horde of starving millions in Africa or Afghanistan. It seems a shame that most westerners don't exercise their democratic right to vote at election time. Nor do people care about the personal and cultural values of the politicians who represent them and make decisions on their behalf. The majority just want to be left alone, so they can play the latest computer games after a long day at the office.

Taylor refers to this erosion of individual responsibility as 'soft despotism', which describes a culture where most people have given up an active role in how society is to be administered. He claims that the western world has become a culture of narcissism and paradoxically, this has led to a loss of individual freedom. When the majority fails to exercise their hard won democratic rights during elections, people have effectively given away their power. In addition, a labyrinth of government bureaucracy has usurped many gains in personal civil liberties, while the system actively discourages individual participation. Lacking the will for change, people continue their treks to the mall in gas guzzling SUVs and continue to live in an increasingly violent and often ruthless world.

Everyone looks out only for themselves, while social safety nets for the less fortunate are rapidly disappearing. With the natural abundance in the province of British Columbia, for example, it is unconscionable that the mentally ill are abandoned to live on the streets and in the gutters of the less affluent areas in Vancouver. The painting *The Circle (2001)* suggests a different society.

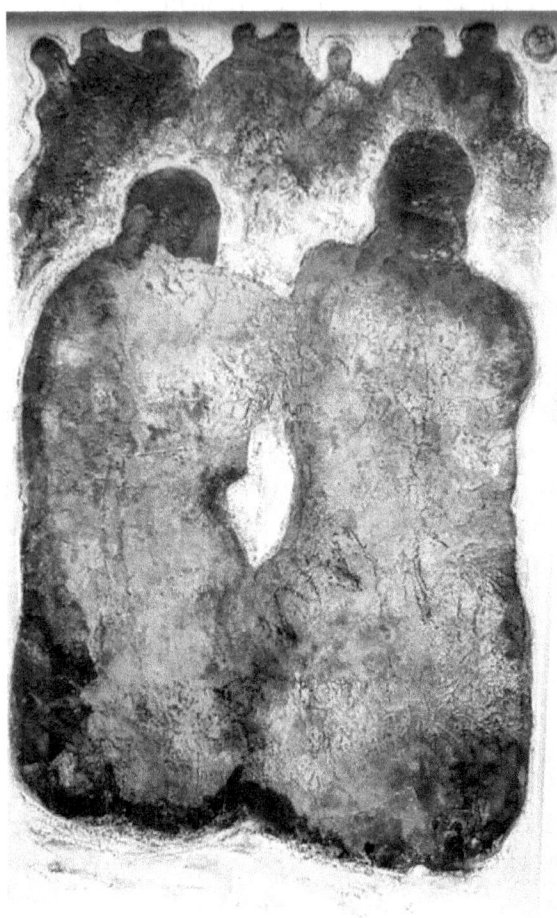

The Circle (2001)

The image depicts a circle of women. Two central figures have their back to the viewer and it feels as if we have accidentally walked into a private celebration or perhaps a tribunal, where the fate of the women will be determined by the group. The full moon in the background adds to the solemnity of the occasion and refers to the ultimate power of the age-old council of women who made important decisions for the community. Expressive form has taken on a meaning of its own and aesthetic understanding should not necessitate further articulation. The intended meaning has to some extent, been embedded in the painted image itself. I recall as these figures grew from the fluidity of the paint that their significance became increasingly clear. Although the title clarified its meaning, form itself will determine how viewers interpret what they see. An image of the past, of a council of women totally engaged in bringing unity to the group.

Berger believes that this acute disengagement today with others lies at the base of our culture's ideological pitilessness. Horrified that humanism, so proudly thought to underlie western civilization, turned out to fit with a desire for committing obscene atrocities; at home and abroad. But perhaps these atrocities are only possible because western culture has exemplified the virtues of a form of humanism that believes instrumental reason to be superior to intuitive sensibility. This unnatural disparity between thinking and feeling may be the source of the general sense of malaise and disenchantment in today's world.

However, sharing aesthetic experience can bridge this sense of alienation. As if to counter this moral nihilism, some artists today strive to articulate the difficult task of personal individuation in context with their society. They use art to gain a broader perspective and better understanding of personal and cultural history. Shaping aesthetic form facilitates the ability to use emotional wisdom to open the mind to the complexity of human experience. A work of art can tap into inner thoughts and feelings about our lives that involve every aspect of a person.

Artistic creativity and the imagination facilitate the interplay between the physicality of the body, the intellect as well as the senses and emotions. In the process, aesthetic experience develops our social and spiritual wellbeing in a dance between different ways of knowing that leads to a deeper understanding of *Being* and being human. This cognitive interplay reconnects a personal link to the roots of our shared humanity and realization that the intellect must be balanced by intuitive sensibility.

Participation in the arts opens the window of perception to beauty and the diversity in others and in nature. This renews respect for the environment and the natural rhythms of life. Opening the eyes to a new way of seeing requires an interdisciplinary vision to reconnect the various fields of knowledge that have been institutionally kept apart. An interdisciplinary perspective is not only a prerequisite for aesthetic experience but it also relates to political thinking on a global scale.

Seeing unity in aesthetic form can be applied to other areas in our daily lives. A work of art shares valuable knowledge with the community since time began. Engagement with art facilitates a more fluid way of thinking that allows people to see the interconnectedness of various disciplines. In reality, the separate disciplines such as economics, politics, media studies, public health, ecology, national defence, criminology and education are all interconnected and affect one another.

Some artists creatively question the status quo while making new associations between different areas of knowledge. Take the painting *The Gathering II* (1992) for example, inspired by the button blankets of the First Nations people.

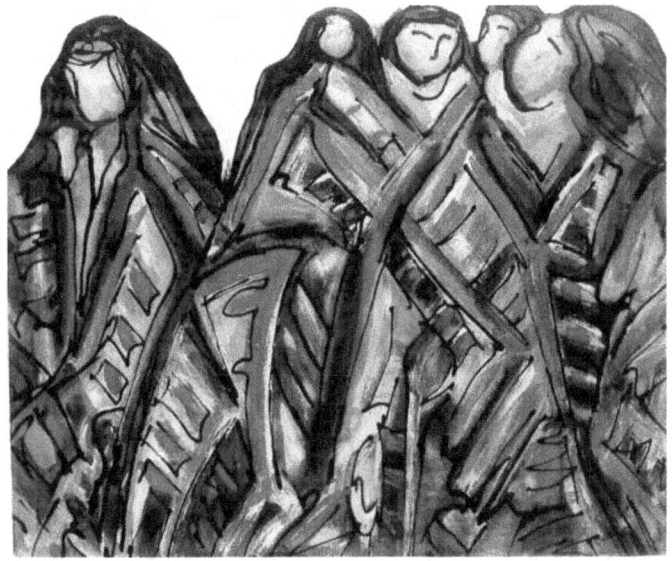

The Gathering II (1992)

Understanding a work of art requires expanding our awareness to see the unnecessary suffering taking place in the world. This painting speaks to the plight of First Nations people in Canada who live in abysmal conditions. It acknowledges the rich cultural history of these people and makes a silent comment on the colonial past. This is the starting point, according to Berger but in order to grasp the pervasiveness of the problem requires an interdisciplinary vision.

Artists have always been the visionaries of a culture. Artistic creativity involves taking risks in exposing the emotional inner world to others, yet doing so is crucial for sharing emotional truth. Activating the imagination allows the mind to make the creative connections between the various areas of knowledge. Artistic creativity helps to ignite the imagination through innovative experimentation in a particular medium. Freedom to playfully explore aesthetic ideas that well up within the mind is essential in order to make and appreciate a work of art.

Aesthetic form comes from the heart as well as the mind and an imaginative synthesis between sensibility and intellectual concepts often leads to new and valuable insights that can be shared with others. Sometimes art can turn cognitive corners so much more rapidly than policy. But a work of art also serves as a reminder that the past cannot be altered. What is done is done. It is only in the present moment that we can change the world and learn from our mistakes. As the past retreats into memory and the future withholds its presence, people can live aesthetically in the moment and that is where art can help.

The creative imagination understands on an emotional and intellectual level that a new manifestation for the future of humanity can be created from the past. Aesthetic experience offers a worthy ideal for a happy life that looks to the future as a time when beauty, pleasure and freedom will again become the domain of art and culture. Artists and philosophers know that this model of culture is the source of all harmony of beings that belong together. Although the quest for individual autonomy and greater self consciousness has led to the malaise of postmodern society, Taylor argues for the moral ideal behind the concept of individualism.

The drive for individuation reflects the human need for self fulfillment and greater level of consciousness. This requires being true to one self, and living an authentic life. Living authentically in the moment not only involves balancing inner body wisdom and the intellect but it also requires living in harmony with others. This holistic balance begins with the individual and radiates out into the family, then the community and the environment and into every society across the globe.

This universal truth of *Being* and being human underpin all cultural difference and extends to every living being on this planet, no less for one than the other. There is a darker side to the limited focus on the self and the egotistical drive for individualism. Focusing only on the self narrows and flattens the context that gives life meaning. This loss of contextual significance in contemporary life has led to apathy. People lack passion and the ability to perceive the beauty that surrounds them, preferring to live empty lives in a seemingly barren and disenchanted world.

This extreme focus on self gratification, global consumerism and greed has created a materialistic philosophy that Donald Kuspit describes as the harsh tyranny of postmodern culture. It is astonishing that in a new millennium, humankind faces the same material problems it always has, with some new ones thrown in for good measure. Poverty, disease, famine and war are still issues today, just as before but along with these problems, environmental pollution and natural and manmade disasters have contributed to the displacement of millions of people.

It seems to me that living without the secure foundations of a grand narrative or a sense of the divine has left a void begging to be filled. Taylor wryly observes that it is easy enough to conclude that the decline of the classical order leaves only the self and its powers to celebrate. But the inevitable slide to subjectivism and its blend of authenticity with self-determining freedom is all too readily released.

Every person understands the meaning of sorrow and joy, and everyone recognizes beauty. It is only in the personal expressions of these universal truths that people encounter difference, as in the painting *Requiem (2002)*.

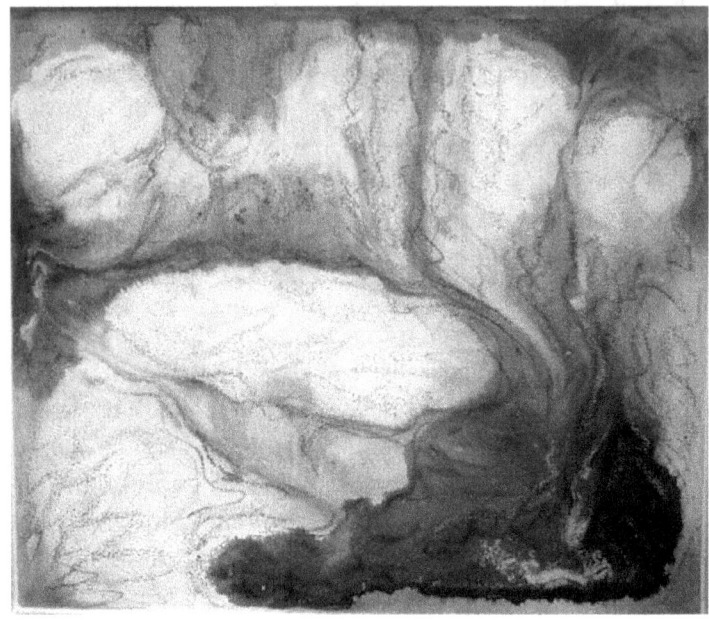

Requiem (2002)

Despite its highly abstracted form, the sense of profound sorrow leaps out at the viewer. As the title implies, this painting is a personal expression of intense despair concerning the fragmentation of today's society, where family and friends often live far apart. This painting brings to mind a sense of indescribable loss at the separation and loss of loved ones that still has the power to affect me. For me, this image clearly shows a woman on her knees, clutching her face as if in great distress. Bent over, she seems to be crying. This idea is reinforced by the puddle of paint emulating from her face.

The shapes above her body are meant to represent various thought forms that suggest different aspects of fragmentation of family and friends in contemporary life. Contemporary biological and nuclear warfare aside, it seems most people lack a sense of

fairness and respect for others and social justice and equality
for everyone is rapidly eroding. As different cultures clash over
ideological differences, the chasm between east and west
becomes ever greater, as each side demonizes the other.
Demonizing others makes people appear less than human, but it
also precludes any possibility of mutual respect. Overcoming this
chasm between different ideologies requires that people engage
in a reciprocal dialogue to find the fundamental similarities of
human nature.

But artists who live an authentic life can model a more ideal
existence for others by expressing the essential truth of what
being human entails. With a little humour and good will, people
can argue about ideas but don't have to kill each other over
different points of view. A respectful exchange of ideas reveals
that despite personal and cultural differences, humanity is
intimately connected. Turning the contemporary discipline of
science upside down, quantum physics has shown that
everything in the universe is connected to everything else.

Similar to Kant's response to the new physics of his day,
quantum mechanics has changed how contemporary people view
the world. Quantum theory explains the world as consisting of
ever smaller particles, all interacting unpredictably with each
other. In response, artists began to explore the unpredictability
factor. As in Kant's day, this new scientific thinking has the
power to change how artists and philosophers perceive and
understand human experience. This change of thinking in terms
of quantum physics extends across all artistic and academic
disciplines.

Therefore, there is a profound need in today's culture for a new
interdisciplinary vision, which is capable of explaining what is
actually happening in the world. This new global vision requires
an open dialogue between the various disciplines and fields of

knowledge that academic and political institutions have kept separate. A fresh new interdisciplinary perspective is an essential precondition of thinking politically and comprehending the unity of human existence. Although cultural tensions, the politics of self-interest, consumerism and the clash between different ideologies create constant conflict, people have a lot in common if given the opportunity to freely express themselves.

Universal principles provide the necessary ground for initiating a respectful and reciprocal dialogue. An open exchange of ideas concerning personal and cultural differences may facilitate a meeting of minds. In addition, sharing aesthetic experience with others provides a safe place for a mutual exchange of ideas between different artistic expressions of what it means to be human. Aesthetic experience strengthens social ties among different people in a society and renews their connection to the earth that sustains them. It can do the same for engaging different cultures. When a progressive society gives all of its members the freedom to discover the self in relation to others, and supports everyone equally in their search for inner truth, a solidly grounded global community is created.

POSTMODERN DECONSTRUCTION

Although a mutual exchange of words is a necessary prerequisite for a harmonious existence, for the philosopher Jacques Derrida deconstructing language meant that words and text are independent of the author's intentions. Meaning is solely determined by whether the words speakers use accurately reflect their intended meaning. For Derrida, language can only record what is in a text. The name and ideas of the author have no substantial value in themselves.

It may be true that once expressed, language takes on a different meaning, however the speaker's intensions should always be considered. But in the end, an utterance must be able to stand on its own. Therefore, it is crucial to use language very carefully, making sure to choose words that clearly articulate the author's experience. Once an utterance is made, words takes on a life of their own and the intentions of the speaker may become irrelevant. An expressive work of art is no exception.

For Derrida, the artist as speaker is irrelevant to the viewer's interpretation of the work they created. Aesthetic form must speak for itself. Understanding a painting for example, should not necessitate further explanation because the ideas are embedded in the painted image itself. Although titles may help clarify its intended meaning, aesthetic form ultimately determines how viewers interpret what they see. But the complexity of ideas behind artistic form goes beyond mere words and text.

Consequently, the viewer must use their imagination to comprehend the depth of what the artist has tried to express. Take the painting *Annunciation (2002)* for example. This image is a particular favorite of mine because the message it contains is one of gentle optimism and hope. Artistic form, reinforced by the title, illustrates a well known story about the visitation of Mary found in the bible. The archangel Gabriel appears to her, bringing 'tidings of great joy'.

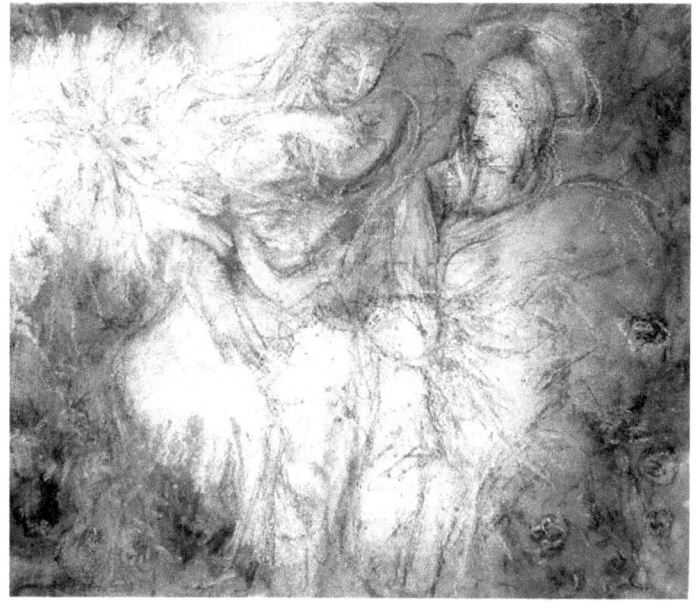

Annunciation (2002)

However, here the angel comes in female form, and appears to be waving a magic wand, much like the fairy godmother who transformed Cinderella in a Grimm's fairytale. The figure on the right represents Mary, who casts her eyes down modestly as the angel swings her wand, while she articulates her message. The star-like form hovering above Mary's head reminds me of the divine flame of the Holy Spirit that appeared over the heads of the apostles at Pentecost.

There is also a suggestion of a halo to indicate not only the woman's holiness, but also the tremendous significance of the occasion. In the foreground, flower-like forms float sporadically within an ethereal bluish-green, giving a surreal sensibility to the figures in this painting. The rose forms also make reference to Marian iconography. In medieval times, roses were commonly understood to be associated with her image. Once these figures became visible, there was no denying what they referred to. These forms were embedded in the paint and only required a little 'pulling out' with colour and line to be understood.

For me, this painting presented a powerful message that resonated within body memory and needed no words to be understood. Its message, intensely personal, could then be shared with others. I don't agree with the poststructuralists who claim that as soon as the utterance is made, it no longer belong to the speaker. For them, this also applies to aesthetic form. Once innerness has been made public, it no longer belongs to the artist alone.

For Derrida, language is used in a system of difference that determines the meaning of the utterance, be it in words, text or aesthetic form. He rejects the structuralist view of closure to the meaning of an utterance. Once an idea has been expressed, it becomes part of the public domain of a language. What has been said now belongs to the world. Everyone can freely express their individuality and communicate who they are and what they think in the words and text of a commonly understood language. But this requires carefully choosing the right words or aesthetic form for effective communication to make private thoughts and feelings understandable.

But there is a problematic single-mindedness to the deconstructionist idea of the indeterminate nature of language. For one thing, this view negates the dialogical aspect of an utterance that enhances the meaning of words and text. For another, Derrida seems to forget that personal and cultural limitations may restrict a speaker's ability to effectively communicate the determinate meaning so others are able to understand. This view also negates people's sense of autonomy and personal power to learn a new language game that may not necessarily require words or text. There are certain ideas that cannot be articulated in words and text alone.

If the intention of the author is of little consequence once an utterance is made, it follows that once a work of art is finished and made public, the artist's intentions are also irrelevant. A work of art must speak for itself in an aesthetic language of form that may only be partially communicable. But usually aesthetic form speaks more effectively than words in articulating the complex meaning of personal thoughts and feelings. Authentic artistic self expression frequently results in a fresh and original statement that also articulates new ideas about important social values. However, far from being irrelevant to the meaning of aesthetic form, the artist's intentions are manifested in the art work. Its meaning is inscribed in a language most people can understand.

Often mere words and text are not enough for meaningful self expression. Not everything knowable can be articulated in propositional form. There are cognitive limits that are not easily defined and there are limitations to words and text. Sometimes, appropriate words cannot be found by using pre-existing and outdated models. Communication may require inventing a new language game to better articulate a personal aesthetic vision. Take the painting *Eureka* for instance. Although the title helps, this image requires no explanation to be understood. The word *eureka* originated in ancient Greece and translates as the celebratory exclamation "I've found it"! The word itself is attributed to Archimedes who exclaimed *'eureka'* when he discovered the answer to a scientific problem he had been thinking about.

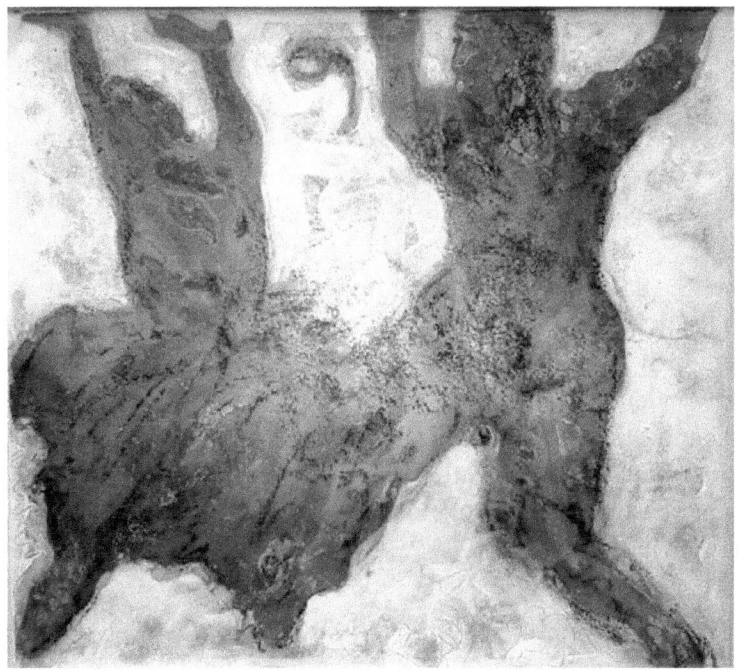

Eureka (2002)

This painting celebrates a discovery of a more personal nature, as a man and woman rejoice together in sheer ecstasy. The unity of design and composition expresses a harmonious balance between masculine and feminine energies, yet these dancing figures appear as if ready to jump off the canvas, shattering this fragile equilibrium. Even the spiral between the two figures seems to echo ecstasy, as they dance together in joyful abandon. A closer look at the background affirms this happy mood, which is reinforced by the heart shapes scratched into the wet paint.

This image demonstrates that in the act of painting, it is possible to reach beyond the merely narrative and historical to express a very contemporary perception of human relationships in terms of ancient and enduring aesthetic ideas. In this painting, the mind reached beyond cultural narratives and historical mythology, in order to express the joy of personal relationships. By synthesizing traditional and mythological, modern and rational, the work achieves a puzzling and provocative mixture of elements that inspired me to reconsider my assumptions and formulate a new vision of lived experience.

But the deconstructionists were right that the final authority lies with the utterance itself and artists are never the absolute authority of the work's determinate meaning. But the artist may have additional knowledge of a uniquely personal nature that expands the interpretation of its intended meaning. Knowing more about what was in the artist's mind offers a richer aesthetic experience because a work of art is a personal statement of what is seen in society.

Since the eighteenth century, artists are no longer defined by their skill to imitate objects in nature. Painting in particular becomes increasingly equated with original and authentic self disclosure. The crucial cornerstone for deconstructionist philosophy is synthesis of the modernist principle of artistic originality with the postmodern notion of 'many voices' who all want to be heard. Today, everyone is called to live life authentically, and not in imitation of anyone else. Being true to one self is a new and important concept that stresses people must not miss one moment of life. Living fully and honestly as whom they really are.

This idea of self determination and being true to personal potentiality and originality underpins the core issue of the ideal of authenticity, but it is often an intense struggle. The challenge of deconstruction reflects the malaise of modernity during a time when long held cultural values were rapidly eroding and the connection to people as well as nature was all but broken. This polarization of today's malaise is three-fold; people are divided *within* themselves, they are divided *between* themselves, and they are divided *from* nature and the earth.

Most people have lost contact with the natural rhythms of the earth and the traditions of the ancestors, leading to a general melancholy of the soul and disenchantment with life. The need to be heard and be recognized by others requires an honest disclosure of personal identity through open dialogue, while respecting the need for recognition in others. Although today every person is free to express their own original and complex vision, all too often there are too many voices and not enough listeners.

Meaningful communication starts with a discussion between two reasonable people with different horizons of significance who attempt to find commonalities in their thoughts and feelings. Recognizing the uniqueness of each individual expression of personal truth demands a reciprocal relationship of trust. It also requires the ability to share common points of reference in a mutually understood language. When we communicate effectively, we realize each person is an integral part of a cultural whole. By extending this commonality to others, people learn to articulate their personal experience. Sharing unique insights in a dignified and respectful dialogue allows everyone's voice to be heard. Take the painting *River of Life (2002)* for example. This image makes innerness visible, and thereby understandable in context with a collective past. But at the same time, these figures also map out a possible future with a more optimistic outlook.

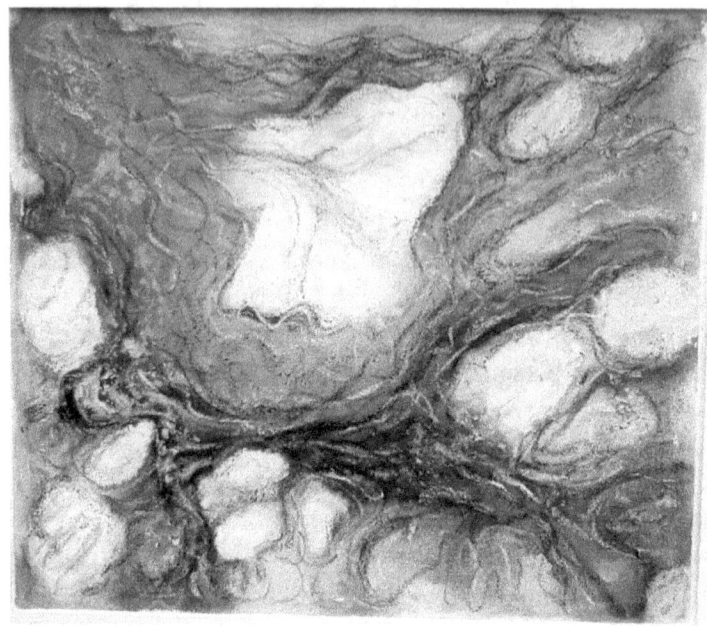

River of Life (2002)

These two figures, although highly stylized, suggest a man and a woman who have taken the plunge, so to speak, into the river of life. The stream runs rapidly along, dispersing among many threatening boulders, but the figures seem unafraid, even ecstatic as their hands embrace the running water. For me, artistic form is always discovered in colour and the paint itself. This painting clearly articulates metaphorically both the place where I lived at the time it was painted, as well as the beginning of a new personal relationship.

The imagination had found exactly the right form to give expression of a personal truth whose meaning is intuitively recognized and understood. Aesthetic form speaks of personal truth that may at the same time reflect the common needs of others. Each person has the right to freely exchange ideas with others who matter, in a familiar language that has self determining freedom interwoven with authentic self disclosure. In a larger context, this is also true of the language of art. Personal identity can be discovered in the authentic expression of self by another person in the subtle language of art, but titles are also important.

Words and text make shared assumptions publicly available as a reference point for all members of a linguistic group. Everyone can draw upon commonly understood words and text that provide insight into the aesthetic ideas behind an image. For many centuries, artists have shared certain basic assumptions about the ability of art to express the divine as well as the secular and preserved these ideas within aesthetic form. However today, many artists no longer have a common aesthetic language to drawn upon for inspiration. It seems as if each person is required to articulate anew the nature of their world for which there are no adequate representation. Consequently, the artist must choose authentic aesthetic form from a 'forest of symbols'.

But for some, the inner search for the self is not their main concern. Instead these artists explore a greater order of something beyond the self that speaks of the essential nature of the human predicament. For them, a work of art connects the present to the past. The link between the living and dead reveals our human frailty as well as the power of transfiguration that is present in aesthetic form. Some contemporary artists also search for a new aesthetic language as a personal response to socially relevant issues. They are concerned with human relationships and their place in the world in context with the natural order of things. Their art expresses a deep need to belong to society and honour their obligations to a larger order, rather than to a subjective self.

Kiefer for example, creates art that speaks to the malaise of a post-war generation. Forced to face the breakdown of universal values after the tragedies of the Second World War, Kiefer and his generation reach into the past for aesthetic form powerful enough to express his culture's melancholy. Kiefer studied informally with Joseph Beuys at a time when Beuys was synthesizing complex aesthetic ideas into conceptual and performance art under the influence of *Arte Povera* and primitivism. Described as a unique voice in the dialogue between art and life, Beuys thought that aesthetic form contained all the elements that matter to humanity; be they psychological, spiritual, historical or scientific.

It is from Beuys that Kiefer learns about artistic integrity in shaping authentic aesthetic form. Beuys creates aesthetic form that refers to his war experience. For both these artists, artistic creativity becomes the means for gaining greater awareness about life in context of making a work of art. The despair depicted in Kiefer's paintings express the fears and insecurities of a post-war generation concerned with the legacy of Germany's past. Born after the war, this generation felt threatened by a future devoid of cultural ideals and tradition. As a result, many people lost confidence in the traditional humanist ideals they inherited from the Enlightenment.

Like other postmodern artists, Kiefer borrows liberally from such diverse sources as the Old Testament, Nordic mythology and North American shamanism. I have done the same. Take for example, the painting *Aboriginal Goddess (1988)*, which was inspired by an Australian cave painting of an ancient goddess.

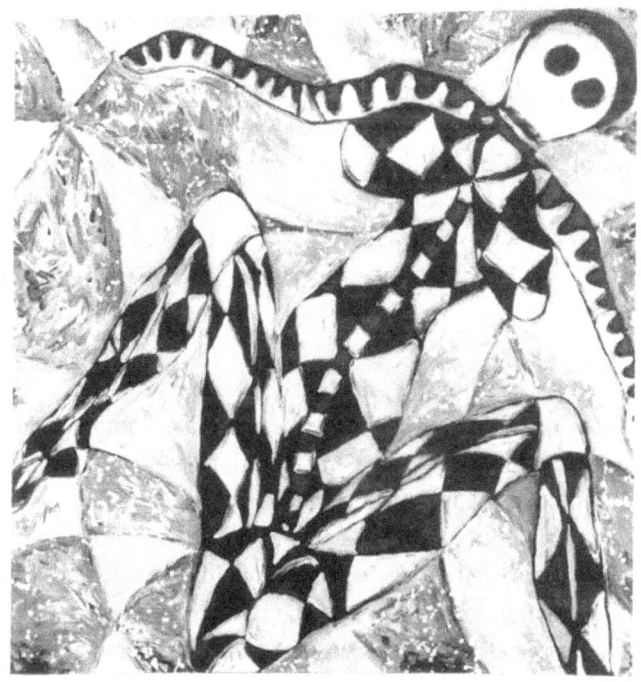

Aboriginal Goddess (1988)

For aboriginals, these paintings were not just made for religious purposes, but for also for healing. Artists left their mark on these walls to connect to the ancestors and pay tribute to the goddess. Like other artists, I made use of a variety of metaphors and mythologies and borrow freely from multiple cultures in order to create intensely personal representations. Kiefer also amalgamates a variety of cultural narratives and reworks them into an innovative aesthetic statement about world events. His imagination draws freely from western philosophy and the history of art, uniting these elements in artwork that expresses these historical ideas in contemporary terms

The nature of these paintings is intertextual, in the sense that the artist freely mixes complex ideas and different materials on huge canvases that contain many conflicting cognitive and affective associations. In the act of painting, Kiefer mixes elements from the Exodus out of Egypt with ancient ideas about the celestial hierarchy of Dionysius the Areopagite and gestures of the German military. His work demonstrates that it is possible to stretch beyond mere narrative to express a very contemporary perception of current events. And then express this understanding in terms of ancient and enduring ideas.

The imagination reaches beyond cultural narrative and digs deep into ancient mythology to find meaningful aesthetic form. Synthesizing the traditional and modern, these paintings achieves a puzzling and provocative aesthetic statement. The complex personal and cultural reference points inherent in much of Kiefer's work are intended to stimulate reflective thinking. He is a philosophical painter who creates art that intends to provoke further questions concerning people's most basic assumptions. In massive paintings of the German landscape, he inspires viewers to reconsider their long held beliefs and formulate their vision anew.

Although postmodern painting is referentially grounded in modernism, artists often mix abstract and representational elements that are detached from the object, making the intended meaning sometimes difficult to fully understand. Artistic creativity today can be an extremely complex process. A painter may alternate different types of paint on the canvas while the imagination explores associative ideas concerning western culture's artistic and historical heritage. Contemporary art tends to rework modernist assumptions to raise important questions concerning the essential nature of representation.

Consequently, a work of art may push the conceptual limits of aesthetic perception and rational understanding. As they express their curiosity, artists pose questions about what is real and what is simulated. Kiefer for example, uses the art-making process as a metaphor for the chaos of the times. By creatively employing mythical, historical and cosmological grand narratives to shift people's understanding of the past, he seeks to clarify important issues that were left unresolved within modernism. His paintings attempt to shed light on questions that relate directly to the postmodern world.

The power of these images reveals that the cultural narratives of the past still exert power over people's thinking. His tragic outlook and cosmological themes raise important questions about technology and the postmodern moment. It is not uncommon for artists to appropriate images from a wide variety of sources, including art history and philosophy. Kiefer mines ancient and modern cosmologies and mythologies as well as popular icons of the grand narratives of the past in search of aesthetic form. Understanding the complexity of possible interpretations arouses many thoughts and feelings concerning the mysterious source of aesthetic form in context with collective memories of mythological and historical events.

For most artists today, everything is fair game in making a work of art that can challenge people's complacency and limited world view. When the imagination finds exactly the right form to give expression to an inner concept, its meaning is intuitively grasped. Then art speaks of a personal truth that may at the same time reflect the common needs of others. Aesthetic form, by making inner feelings visible, becomes understandable in context with the collective past. At the same time, a work of art maps out a possible future with a more optimistic outlook. Painters may use the canvas as an arena to play out their post-modernist vision. Multiple levels of intense meaning may generate curiosity about one's own feelings concerning certain events. For example,

the painting *Survivors 2003),* expressed my concern of events
happening across the globe.

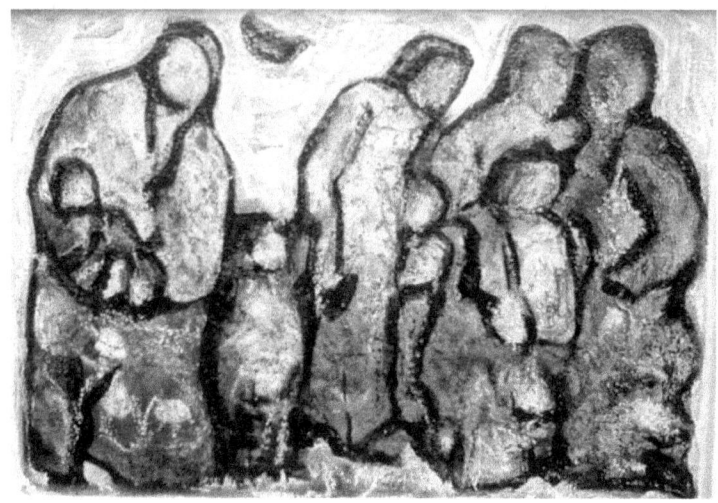

Survivors (2003)

Its title was inspired by the daily news. The figures represent the
millions of displaced refugees in the world that have been left
homeless because of famine or war. These pathetic people are the
lucky ones, they are survivors, but a sense of disillusionment
hangs heavy among the women and children. The painting's
starkness is reminiscent of Kollwitz. And like Kiefer, this image
articulates a sense of losing faith; in god and a unifying grand
narrative. It asks a fundamental question concerning the nature
of human existence, on earth and in the cosmos.

Contemporary art often reflects a more complex and developed
perspective of personal and collective history. Essential to this
expanded view is the idea that tragic action exposes many
different perspectives of reality that interconnect, but do not
coincide. Many of Kiefer's paintings reflect this multi-

dimensional point of view. He intentionally plays with the tension that exists between these different planes of aesthetic understanding. Take the painting *Midgard,* for example that plays with multiple perspectives of the landscape. This image simultaneously refers to Teutonic mythology as well as historical events and the land itself, as perceived from different perspectives.

On the one hand, the view appears to be close to the earth, yet at the same time one seems to hover above it. This push pull of perspectives creates a pleasurable tension and this ambiguity gives the painting a mysterious sense of existential disconnection and separation from the land. The tragedy and malaise of contemporary society is intimately connected to this collective sense of separation from the natural world. Not only have people lost their connection to the land but they have also lost faith in a unifying mythology to explain the meaning of life in metaphorical terms.

Some artists seek to advance art's pedagogical function in the sense that fundamental knowledge of *Being* and being human is passed on to the next generation in aesthetically pleasing art. Kiefer, for example used the icons of grand narratives to clearly express this loss and the need for a new mythology whose concepts and narrative most people can readily understand and believe in. His work shows that ancient ideas and mythological stories still have instrumental value for contemporary society. By making explicit reference to the past and traditional cultural values, the painting *The Naming (2003)* also challenges the nihilism of outdated modernist thought.

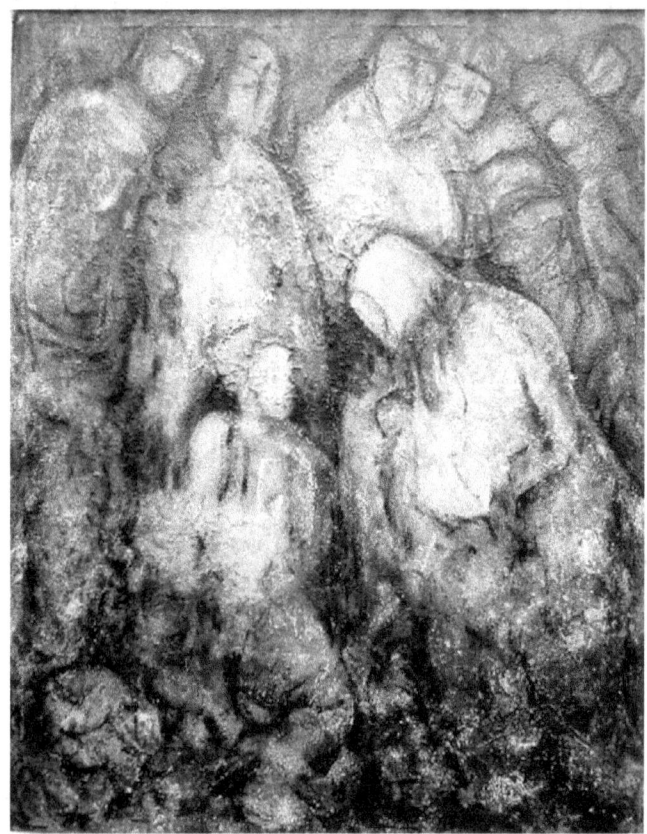

The Naming (2003)

This painting questions the dominant role assigned to words and text in a language and the tendency to acknowledge science and rationality as the only legitimate form of knowledge and reliable basis for action. This image raises intelligent questions about the nature and mystery of the world, the cosmos and humanity's place in it. It asks viewers to reflect on traditional values as well as appreciating old cognitive maps in a contemporary context. Contemplation on possible meanings generates curiosity about certain world events.

Artistic form has the power to provide a fresh perspective of the complexity yet commonality of human nature. Art opens the mind to new possibilities and this often requires imagining beyond what is consciously known. An imaginative synthesis is absolutely crucial to be able to grasp the new cognitive maps that are necessary to navigate contemporary reality. With postmodern art, there is no ultimate and determinate right meaning of what aesthetic form represents. Kiefer even uses words and text in some of his paintings to articulate a powerful aesthetic statement that speaks to the complex relationship between art, history and the natural world.

And he is not alone. Judy Chicago, Tracey Amin and many others also use words and text as a visual artistic statement. However, interpreting and understanding the inherently multi-layered meaning of text as art is somewhat ambiguous and subject to change. Art reflects life and by making inner shadows visible, aesthetic experience interacts with the words. The text in these images may go a long way towards healing the malaise in today's disenchanted world. This is the pedagogical task of postmodern art.

CONTEMPORARY FEMINIST ART

The nature of contemporary art may be complex and its intended the meaning often intentionally multi-layered. *The Dinner Party* by the American artist Judy Chicago, for example, one of the most significant works of art of the twentieth century. In this monumental interdisciplinary installation, Chicago articulates many complex personal, art historical and cultural interpretations of meaning. *The Dinner Party* is a collaborative project that took shape between 1974 and 1979. For the first three years, Chicago worked alone but then a group of women volunteered to help.

By the time *The Dinner Party* was finally finished, it had cost $250,000 and involved more than four hundred volunteers. This epic work represents another cultural shift in visual thinking as it challenged the mainstream perspective of history, art and philosophy. The multi-faceted nature of this work speaks of an alternative feminine interpretation of western history; one seen in context of actual human experience. Chicago's vision is both revolutionary and profound. Using her work to promote social change by honouring women's history and demanding respect for what women have accomplished.

Her deliberate feminist strategy was to reclaim 'women work' as being valuable and worthy of a celebratory dinner party. Up until recently, the historical record neglected the artwork made by women, considering it 'busy work' rather than art. Today we know better. Art takes on many faces and even women can paint. But I do agree that when women express innerness, aesthetic form often takes on a different aspect. Rather than a fight on canvas, a female painter may incorporate more sensuous and flowing form. Take for example, the painting *Lohengrin (2003)*. Its fluid movement across the canvas gives the image a dreamlike quality. Vegetative forms seem to grow around a cocooned woman, asleep with a swan at her feet. This image draws on an old story of my European heritage and the title sprung up in my mind as I worked. Even though I knew the title, I was unfamiliar with this story until I researched it later. Meaningful form simply grew out of the unsentimental manipulation of the materiality of the paint.

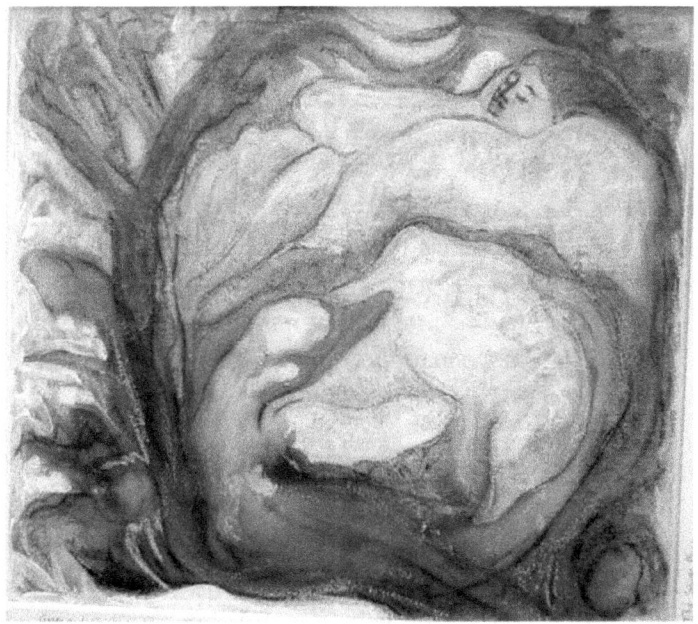

Lohengrin (2003)

This image brings to mind an old Flemish fairy tale about the Swan King, much like the Arthurian legends of the Grail. The story begins with the queen of Brabant, whose castle in Antwerp had been besieged by an evil knight. She calls on Lohengrin, the Swan Knight, to rescue her and protect her city. Lohengrin quickly arrives in a boat pulled by a magic swan, and defeats the evil knight, and they live happily ever after. This surreal dreamlike quality gives this painting a sense of romance, somewhat like a bed-time story told to children.

By using the forms that were created by colour and texture, the imagination is free to make the necessary cognitive and affective connections. This painting articulates a powerful personal and cultural narrative that speaks to the complex relationship between art, cultural history and nature. This depiction of an old narrative was initially inspired by the head of a swan, which was clearly visible in the chaos of colour and paint. From there, the image grew to incorporate a woman securely tucked into billowing blankets. Nature is represented by a tree that grows across the bottom of the canvas, and climbs along the entire left side of the painting. The swan looks lovingly on, as Elsa dreams of her knight who would come to her rescue. Often, a work of art has both personal and cultural connotations that may be grasped if one takes the time to look and think about it.

Take Chicago's *The Dinner Party* for example. This monumental exhibit first opened at the San Francisco Museum of Modern Art in March, 1979. By the time it closed, more than one hundred thousand people had seen it. After its premiere, the exhibit left on a nine-year international tour that began in the US and then travelled to six countries on three continents. From Canada it travelled to major cities in Europe and ended in Australia.

The exhibit opened at sixteen different venues, and in every city, there were long line ups and record breaking attendance. But despite its popularity, this heroic work of art was not well received by the established art world. Critics described it as 'bad' art or 'kitsch'. They did not understand that Chicago and her collaborators had created a new visual language that challenged European history in terms of women's accomplishments. After many years of intense criticism of both the work and the artist,

This great work of art clearly has stood the test of time and its brilliance has not diminished. This moving exhibit still retains the power to elicit an emotional response from viewers, provoking much contemplative thought and intense feelings. The installation consists of a massive triangular table, with thirty-nine place-settings for mythical and historical women, dating from prehistory to the present day. This three-sided table rests on a floor made of nine hundred and ninety-nine tiles; each inscribed in honour of a notable woman.

Chicago intentionally seats the women in three groups of thirteen, perhaps as a reference to the thirteen people at the Last Supper, all of which had been men. Traditionally, the numbers three and thirteen have enormous significance for women across the globe. Among other things, the number three refers to the phases of a woman's life as maiden, mother and crone. The number thirteen suggests the days in the monthly phases of the waxing and waning moon as well as a woman's monthly menstrual cycle.

The sheer size of this work is impressive. The triangular table alone measures forty-eight feet on each side. In addition, the depictions on the thirty-nine place settings are powerful visual statements in themselves. Each image celebrates the valuable contributions these women have made to western culture. Each lush and lovingly made setting, sits on an exquisitely beautiful embroidered runner that compliments the elaborately hand-painted porcelain plates. In the spirit of *The Dinner Party*, the painting *Commitment (2003)* also pays tribute to the protective feminine principle, honouring woman as a vehicle of life.

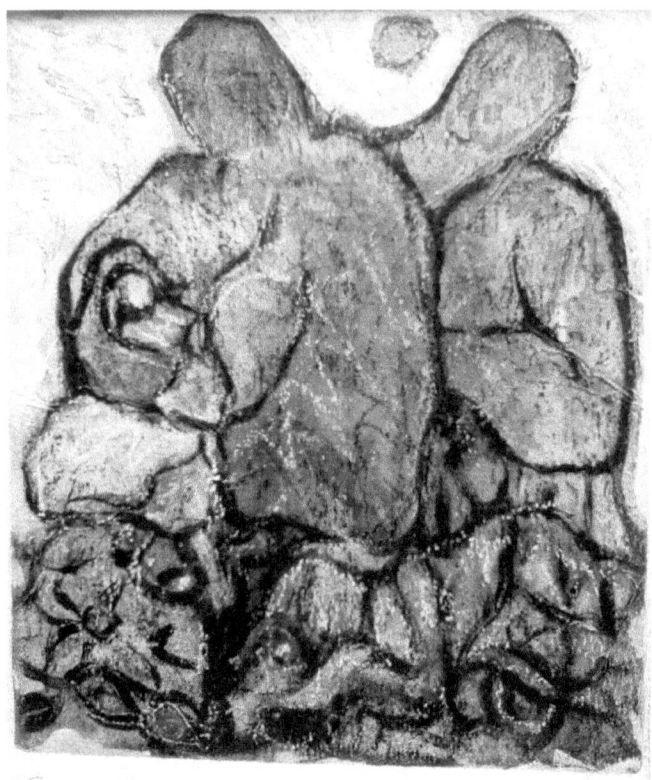

Commitment (2003)

Heavily outlined, the figures are reminiscent of medieval stained glass windows of mother and child that can be seen in the great cathedrals of Europe. The overall feeling this image projects is one of a close knit family, of a mother holding her child while father looks on in awe. The sun hanging between the two main figures suggests the light of the sun's life giving energy. The chalice-shaped sky reminds me of the shape between Mary Magdalene and Jesus, in Leonardo da Vinci's *Last Supper*.

The iconic character of this image is meant to celebrate the protective feminine energy, as well as the family as the bedrock of society where a child's education about the world begins. A mother's central role in shaping the foundation of family life has all too often been taken for granted in contemporary culture, something Chicago tries hard to redress. In groups of thirteen, the women at *The Dinner Party* face each other across this immense triangular space. Chicago used a non-hierarchal structure when she seats the women in chronological order as cherished guests at a banquet held in their honour.

One enters the installation through a corridor hung with banners that invoke biblical text that articulate the momentousness of this event. The entire space of the room intended to induce a visionary aesthetic experience. Viewers are asked to reflect on and appreciate the physical beauty of sumptuous detail and the inherent message the artwork so eloquently expresses. By honouring women as the vehicle of life, *The Dinner Party* pays tribute to the protective feminine principle. Chicago emphasized that women not only play a central role in caring for family but were also the foundation for the culture. She explains that *The Dinner Party* takes viewers on a tour of western culture, a tour that bypasses what we have been taught to think of as mainstream.

But despite its monumentality, she acknowledged *The Dinner Party* was merely a limited representation of a small portion of feminine history. So much has been repressed over the years, but this great work of art will be a powerful inspiration for women artists and philosophers for generations to come. It may be true that the historical record is severely skewed because history is written by those in power. In the annals of the West, the less powerful have been marginalized and all but forgotten. With the advent of postmodernism however, these voices are beginning to be heard. But Chicago admits that to rectify this historical oversight would require an entirely new world-view, one that acknowledges the history of both the powerful and powerless people in the world.

The Dinner Party is a monumental tribute to the contributions that women have made in philosophy and the arts over the centuries. This work was also intended to be a powerful pedagogical tool to teach women about their long forgotten heritage. Chicago play on nostalgia to express an authentic mythology of the feminine experience that echoes Kiefer's concern over the loss of a grand narrative. The artist and her associates believe that our culture needs a feminine perspective to formulate an objective and holistic view of reality. The human experience is not just about the mighty and who won the war.

History also involves mothers and fathers and children who live and die on the land. Human experience is also about collaboration, taking care of each other in order to survive and live well. But this more feminine perspective on history is all too often negated. Similar to Kiefer's reflection on the character of European history, Chicago and her collaborators seek to address a glaring omission in the historical record. A true account of history would acknowledge the interconnectedness of humanity.

Somewhat like the painting *Before the Fall (2003)* that presents a perspective on childhood that everyone can relate to. This painting may be seen as a self portrait when I was a child. Wearing a new dress, pure-white with light blue smocked embroidery that mother had worked hard to make it and I was about to ruin by falling into the canal. Like Chicago's use of embroidery, this painting celebrates feminine creativity and motherhood. I still have happy memories of that beautiful dress so lovingly made by hand. In the all too few hours my mother had to relax, she still thought of her children. This painting froze a moment in time. The imagination brought a childhood memory into form that speaks loud and clear.

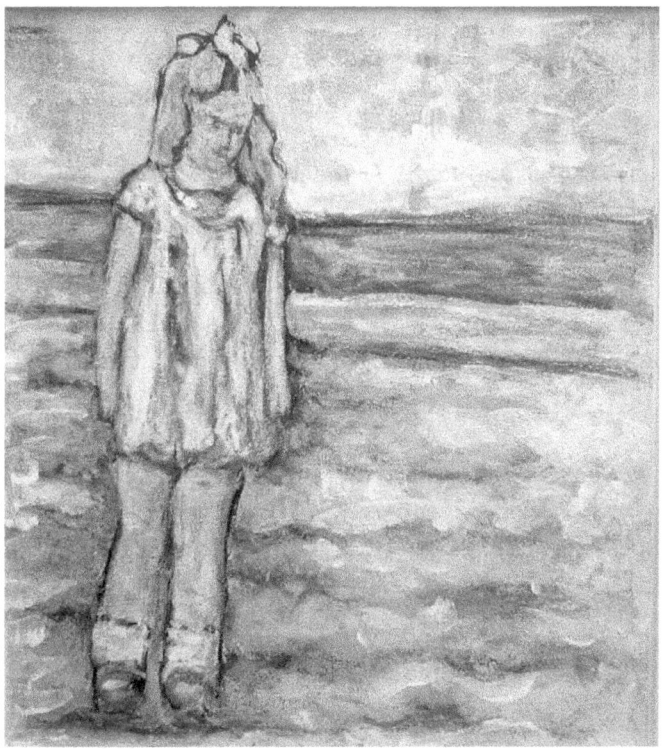

Before the Fall (2003)

Chicago did the same by creating aesthetic form that reworked the feminine heritage in art as well as philosophy. At *The Dinner Party*, each woman is symbolically represented by a place-setting made especially for her. Each is unique and different from the others. Their seating arrangement has been sequentially arranged. Beginning with the mythological primordial goddess of prehistory and ending with the twentieth century American modernist painter, Georgia O'Keefe. The overall concept focused on bringing the value of the feminine character that is missing in traditional art historical and philosophical discourse to people's attention.

The women invited to the table span from the classical to the late twentieth century. In this way, viewers are invited to think about the laudable achievements these women made to western society. Chicago and her co-workers have created this work as a staunch reminder of a missing part in the collective cultural memory. Using symbolic form, the first wing represents the ancient goddesses and the second, female saints of the Christian era. The third portion of the table seats women of the 'age of revolutions', paying final respect to such modernist artists and thinkers as Georgia O'Keefe, Virginia Woolf and the philosopher Hannah Arendt.

Initially, *The Dinner Party* pays tribute to the prehistoric fertility goddess figurines, also known as 'Venuses' that have been found in the excavations of ancient civilizations across Europe. These figurines were usually small amulets of faceless females with voluptuous bellies, round breasts and an enormous buttock. These miniscule sculptures are thought to represent the prehistoric mother goddess, of creation as well as death and regeneration. The goddess was known under many different names, depending on the place where her artifacts have been found.

The ancient concept of a great mother goddess seems to have been a cultural development in many different parts of the world. Chicago also pays tribute to Ishtar, the great Babylonian goddess as the personification of the planet Venus in her double aspect of morning and evening star. Her counterpart is the Semitic goddess Astarte who is mentioned in the Old Testament as Ashtoreth and the ancient Greeks called Aphrodite. In Mesopotamia, Babylon and elsewhere, the goddess Ishtar was worshipped for millennia. She was the protective feminine divine and infinitely powerful giver and taker of life.

In antiquity, the goddess was worshipped in highly developed cultures like Babylon that had extensive knowledge of writing, mathematics and astronomy. These matriarchal societies developed sophisticated legal codes, built irrigation canals and left behind great works of art, made by people who had a good eye for aesthetic form. The figures seem, in retrospect, to be almost contemporary. Wall paintings in particular show a strong sense of design and high degree of skill. It would be no surprise if these paintings were made by women. After all, the first painter was a woman if Pliny's story of Dibutades is to be believed.

The Corinthian maiden invented the art of painting when she traced her lover's profile on the wall to remember him by. The painting *Coming to Meet (2003)* also refers to an absent lover. At the time it was painted, I was in love with someone who lived on the other side of the world. This image celebrates the reunion, which had been planned for the summer. We would soon meet again and my heart opened yet again to being in love. Everything about this painting expresses joy and the figures, despite being abstracted, are clearly identifiable as to whom they are.

This image also pays tribute to the cycles in life, good times and also that separation from loved ones is part of it all. The waxing and waning fortunes of life signal birth, death and rebirth. In ancient times, this eternal cycle of return was celebrated in seasonal rituals that honoured *Being* and being alive. Like *The Dinner Party* that pays special tribute to the primordial goddess as the first named deity. By doing so, Chicago acknowledged the potency of our foremothers who laid the groundwork for the development of a complex civilization.

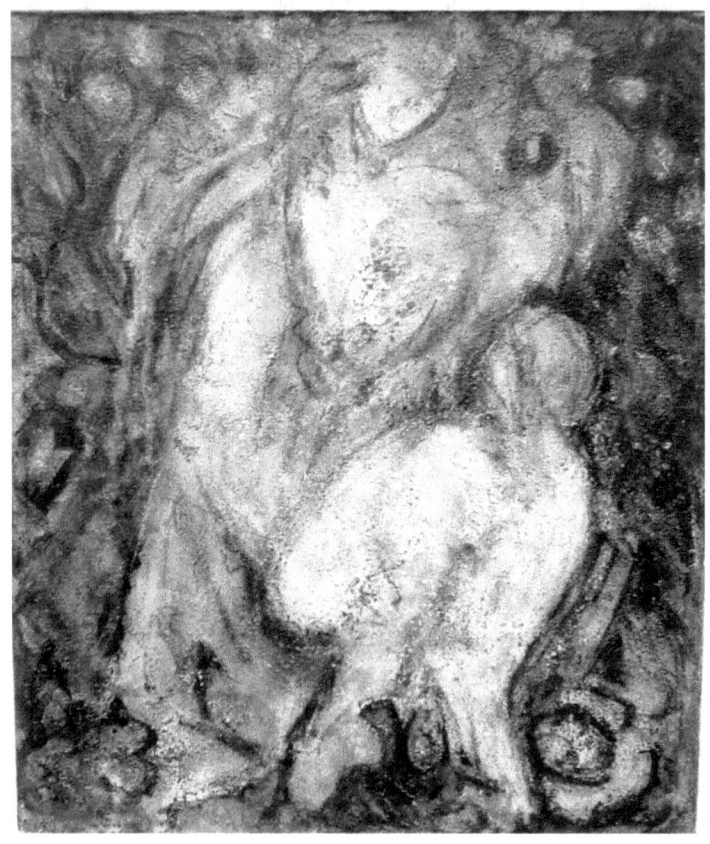

Coming to Meet (2003)

As the Supreme *Being* of feminine centered religion, the goddess
was worshipped by everyone, even after the status of women
began to decline. Archeological and literary evidence
demonstrate that the Hebrew equivalent of Ishtar was still
worshipped in Israel between 1150 B.C.E. and 586 B.C.E., when
the temples of Yahweh and Ashtoreth stood side by side in
Jerusalem. But over time, the belief in a benevolent mother
goddess changed from venerating the divine feminine to
worshipping an all-powerful father god. However, remnants of

Ishtar/Ashtoreth's memory can be found in the early Christian notion of Sophia, as the abstract symbol of the highest form of feminine wisdom. It was only later that Sophia was transformed into a purely spiritual dimension, rather than an active feminine power in society and religion.

Chicago argues that the ethereal concept of Sophia developed in the centuries after Christ with the early Gnostic religions. Sophia as the goddess of wisdom was the active thought of god who created the world. But the vital life force of the feminine divinity of old had already lost much of her original power and Sophia was more spirit than a substantial being. The table setting for Hildegard von Bingen is auspiciously placed in the center of the second wing where she faces Ishtar and Sophia.

Saint Hildegard was an influential twelfth century abbess who was a visionary artist, talented musician and well respected as a formidable political and religious figure of her time. She was also an eminent scholar, scientist, botanist, and a leading medical woman, as well as a prolific poet and composer. This wing also seats the great seventeenth century Italian painter, Artemisia Gentileschi. Gentileschi was taught to paint by her father during a time when women for the most part were denied access to education and apprenticeships. During her career, Gentileschi became a well established artist who traveled extensively, painting great historical and religious works as well many portraits. She also gained admission to the Academy of Design in Florence, a feat that was extremely unusual in her day.

The last wing pays homage to a diverse collection of twentieth century artists and philosophers. Emily Carr, Sonia Delaunay, Frida Kahlo, Kathe Kollwitz, Berthe Morisot, Gabriele Minter, Louise Nevelson, Suzanne Valadon, Isadora Duncan, and Martha Graham have all been represented. *The Dinner Party* also pays tribute to the great modernist philosophers Hannah Arendt,

Mary Esther Harding, Suzanne Langer and Simone Weil. This work articulates Chicago's uniquely personal perception of the western historical record.

Chicago and her collaborators use traditional feminine art-making practices such as quilting, embroidery and porcelain painting to create a stunning visual statement. The exquisite detail, design and finely crafted needlework that is used in *The Dinner Party* is a visual delight in itself. But these sensuous details tell a story that also broadens our perceptual understanding of the historical marginalization of women that goes far beyond what the artist may have intended as an educational imperative.

Something Chicago refers to with *The Dinner Party's* celebration of feminine traditional arts. Beautiful embroidered runners as a luscious visual celebration of each one of these women's accomplishments. However the reverse of these placemats tell a different story. On Mary Wollstonecraft's runner, the front contains delicately embroidered eighteenth century birds and flowers but the back is starkly appliquéd with the image of the author on her deathbed giving birth to Mary Shelley. By making innerness visible, Chicago has indeed given contemporary viewers a glimpse of our shared cultural heritage. Something that the painting *Eostre: Sunna Wakes (2003)* also refers to.

This painting was inspired by the early European mythic origins of Easter as a shared seasonal and religious celebration of spring. Eostre is the great mother goddess of Northern Europe, who was worshipped by the Saxons at the spring equinox. She represents both the dawn and new beginnings as well as being the goddess of fertility.

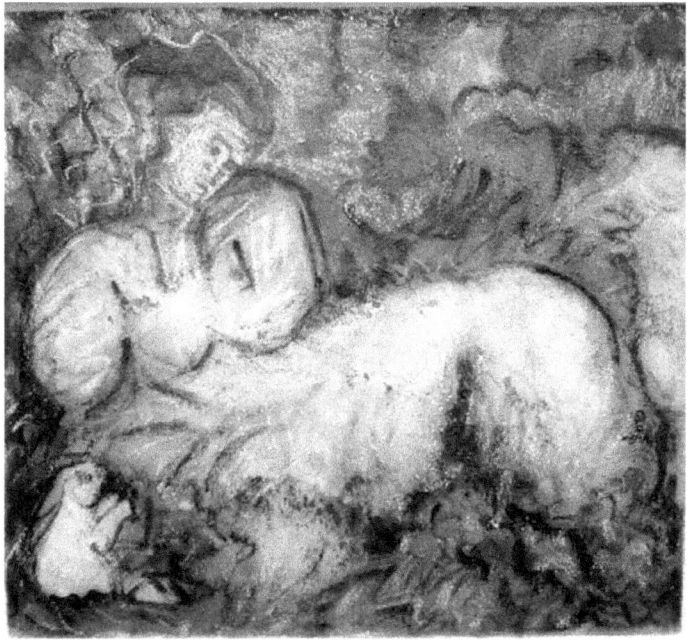

Eostre: Sunna Wakes (2003)

Eostre is the old Saxon word for springtime. Celtic in origin but Eostre was worshipped throughout Europe. She was known by many names including Ostare, Eostra, Eastra and Eastur. Sunna refers to a Scandinavian goddess, also known as Sunne or Frau Sonne, who represents the sun. With the return of spring, people celebrated the return of summer and longer days of sunlight. This image may be understood as a visual metaphor. The sun goddess wakes from her winter slumber. The rabbit at her side confirms its meaning: fertility and regeneration, of the earth, as well as the people. Traditionally, springtime was the time to reseed the earth. It was also a time when fresh sprouts of the summer crop appear above ground and animals and children were born. The solstice is a time of year when the light and the darkness are in balance. Something still celebrated today in many towns all over Europe. Traditional *paasvuurs* are lit on the second day of Easter and some still believe that jumping over the dying embers assures fertility.

Chicago intentionally used traditional feminine handwork and painting on china to provide viewer with artistic form that speaks of a shared cultural heritage across time and place. Her critical observations suggest that there is an urgent need for rebalancing masculine and feminine energies. By paying sincere respect to all mothers, daughters and grandmothers, this great work of art silently articulates the complexity of its meaning for generations to come. *The Dinner Party* represents a new aesthetic language that effectively expresses an alternative view of the value of woman's work that has for the most part been ignored by western culture.

The haunting installations of the UK artist Tracey Emin in many ways resemble Chicago's *Dinner Party*. Emin also uses traditional feminine handicrafts, combining embroidery and quilt-making to make powerful visual aesthetic statements. In many ways, her work can be interpreted as unifying visual art with literature. She freely uses words and text in her art to express her inner thoughts and feelings about contemporary issues. Emin uses language to express her subjective and very private memories about traumatic events in her life that at the same time are intended to be socially relevant aesthetic statements.

When language appears in the midst of visual art, we assume that the words and text are just illustrative. However, Emin challenges us to think of writing as visual art and visual art as text. Sometimes this artist intends to shock, yet we intuitively sense the authenticity of her struggle for greater self consciousness and aesthetic understanding of half hidden memories. The work takes on a literary character that challenges the limits of language.

Constantly reinventing herself, Emin edits her often extremely personal articulations of inner wisdom for all to see. Her work also speaks of shared human values; of pleasure and pain in sometimes disturbingly graphic images that the imagination found in the shadows of her psyche. In many cases, Emin's art depicts her personal memory of often horrendous life events, which at the same time also reflect the experience of contemporary life in general. Exposing innerness requires brutal honesty yet aesthetic form only hints at what is subconsciously known.

A work of art can say so much but aesthetic understanding requires activating the imagination and letting the mind wander through aesthetic form in order to discover the subtle meaning behind the image. Sometimes authentic self expression presents an entirely new conception of an idea that artists and philosophers have wrestled with for centuries. Take the painting *Enlightenment (1992)* for example. This image seems to present a paradox; a puzzle perhaps. What does it mean?

Reflective viewers will grasp that this painting is an authentic and sincere attempt to articulate the inner search for whom the artist really is. The answer to these questions lies in its aesthetic form as a reflection of inner wisdom that lies hidden in our genetic memory.

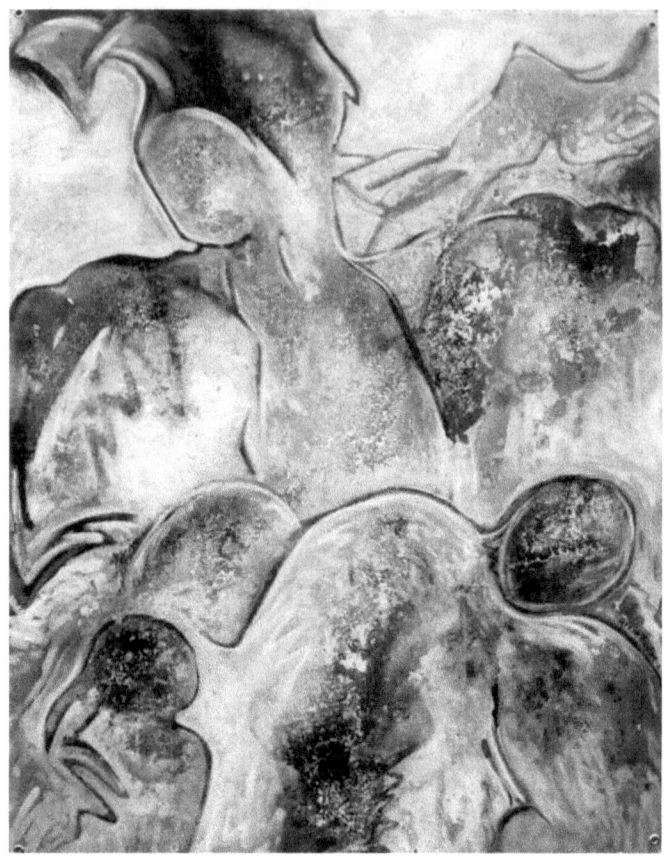

Enlightenment (1992)

But sometimes, a work of art can be something of a paradox. Like Emin; on the one hand, she exposes herself to public view yet on the other; she remains in control. The artist remains the mediator between articulating personal experience and trying to understand it in relation to the cultural record. Similar to Chicago, she is a great story teller. She also uses traditional feminine handicrafts such as appliqué and embroidery and unifies them both literally and metaphorically with words and text. For example, *Don't Sell Me Your Fucking Fear* is her caustic reply to the tragic events in New York City on September 11, 2001. Similar to Kiefer and Chicago, Emin intends to articulate a fresh new perspective of contemporary western culture, where nothing seems to be sacred and everything is for sale.

Although Emin intends to shock us with her disturbing visual utterances, she also wants to present an authentic reflection of social issues such as consumerism and selfish greed in contemporary life. Her work gives viewers a unique postmodernist perspective because the artist associates the meaning of events in her life in context with contemporary culture in general. Like Kiefer and Chicago, Emin attempts to transform the often tragic events of her life into meaningful art that provokes much contemplative reflection. These postmodern artists express an expanded awareness in relation to the culture in which they live. Their art reminds us of our obligation to others in aesthetic form that goes far beyond the search for personal self expression.

THE ENLIGHTENED EYE

The cultural shift in consciousness that began in the early Renaissance found expression in Kantian philosophy of mind and many works of art reflect this change in visual thinking. Artists were no longer anonymous entity but individuals on a personal quest for individuation and greater autonomy. Eventually, this led to the Impressionists, Expressionists and Cubists who challenged the western tradition of art. After the invention of photography, painters were free from demands for realistic depictions of people and nature. In response, artists began to explore the abstract qualities of paint. Texture, pattern and colour on a flat two-dimensional surface.

Rather than being a mere realistic depiction of something, the canvas became an heroic arena for artistic creativity and defining self awareness. Increasingly, painting as well as literature becomes more abstract and eventually led to the deconstruction of both language and art. Postmodern artists and philosophers challenged tradition in search of new answers to perennial questions concerning the relationship between the individual and society. As a result, a new language game was required; a new aesthetic philosophy to adequately express these concerns in a 'subtler' language that goes beyond the inner search for self expression.

This change in aesthetic thinking culminates in postmodern nihilism and conceptual art that questions how people think about what they see. Some artists were mainly concerned with making art that speaks to ethics and morality and that required a broader perspective and an enlightened eye. Aesthetic understanding also requires an imaginative flight of fancy that takes the viewer beyond the horizons of everyday experience. It requires raising one's consciousness, something the painting

Free at Last I (1988) tries to express. Carousel horses, symbolic of freedom, dash into a vibrant sunset. But that's just the beginning. Let your imagination guide you and enjoy. There's more to this painting than meets the eye.

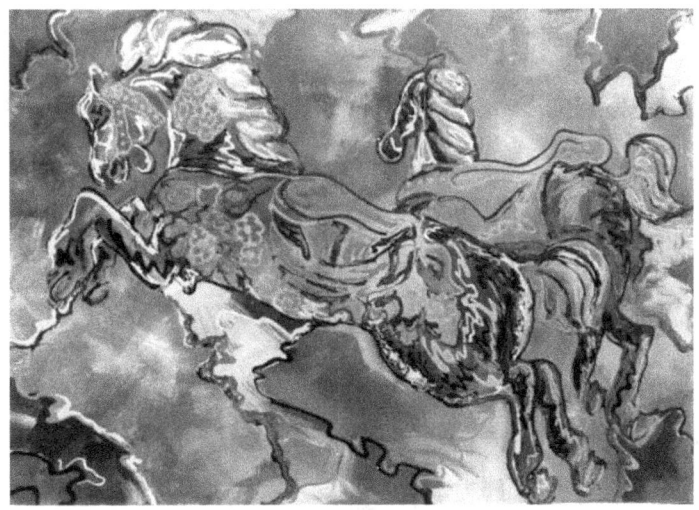

Free at Last I (1988)

Postmodern artists search for authentic aesthetic expression that articulate exactly what they want to say in a way that others can understand. But they know that once a statement is made, their intention may no longer be relevant. Whatever has been expressed must stand on its own. While artists like Emin and Chicago retain the modernist intensity of art making as a quest for individuation, their vision extends beyond the personal to a greater awareness of themselves in context with society. But sometimes aesthetic form may not be enough and words and text are necessary to fully express what one really thinks or feels.

With the advent of today's information age, previously suppressed knowledge has become readily available, giving artists a chance to explore ancient mythologies and grand narratives for personal expression and meaningful aesthetic form. Feminists like Chicago and others reach into the past for a half-remembered mythology of a great mother goddess. They may use their art to critique certain discrepancies in the culture's historical records. For them, a work of art not only expresses a greater self awareness, but it is also intended as a powerful pedagogical tool to present an alternative perspective of Western history.

Today, there are unprecedented opportunities to learn about different ways of life and cultural rituals from all over the world. Twentieth century computer technology has opened up new information channels and the internet makes previously unknown information publicly available on a global scale. A wealth of images is now available to almost anyone on the planet. The world-wide web has woven humanity together so little that happens in the world remains hidden for long. This global perspective further expands aesthetic thinking. Focus is shifting from a modernist obsession with the self to a renewed sense of community' a cultural transformation where every voice can be heard.

In his treatise *The Postmodern Condition,* the French philosopher Jean-Francois Lyotard foreshadowed the advent of computerization and technological miniaturization. Written during the 1980's before the 'computer age', Lyotard warned that these changes in technology would greatly affect global culture. These periodic changes have been the stepping stones of humanity's evolution throughout the ages. With profound sensitivity, he describes modernism and postmodernism as being part of a natural cycle of renewal and decay.

Lyotard explains postmodernism as a period of slackening and an end to experimentation, in art as well as philosophy that would revolutionize every aspect of life. However, he rejects the modernist expectation that industrialization and changes in technology will help make us happy. It is true that technological advances have merely resulted in people living increasingly inauthentic lives. Consequently, a sense of malaise and disenchantment has taken root in today's society.

Although Lyotard's insightful assessment of the state of knowledge presents a bleak outlook of the future, the appendix offers humanity a semblance of hope. Here, he proposes that aesthetic enjoyment and understanding the sublime in art as well as in nature may be the saving factor for the disenchantment of postmodern society. As he deconstructs the laws of nature, Lyotard was aware that infinite human experimentation, in the arts as well as in technology, shows that the world is in a constant state of flux between decay and regeneration.

For Lyotard and others, deconstructing the past is a necessary part of the natural cycle of personal and cultural renewal. Modernity, in whatever age it appears, cannot exist without a shattering of belief. But this constant demand for the new and different has led to sensationalism and ever greater extremes, not only in the arts but also in technology and the media. As a result, it has become increasingly difficult to configure and distinguish worthwhile aesthetic form from the excess and diversity of daily information.

People today expect to be confronted by aesthetic form that expands their awareness of the world, be it in a painting, sculpture or dance. The painting *Illumination (2003)* refers to this expansion of consciousness that will hopefully lead to an illumination of greater truth.

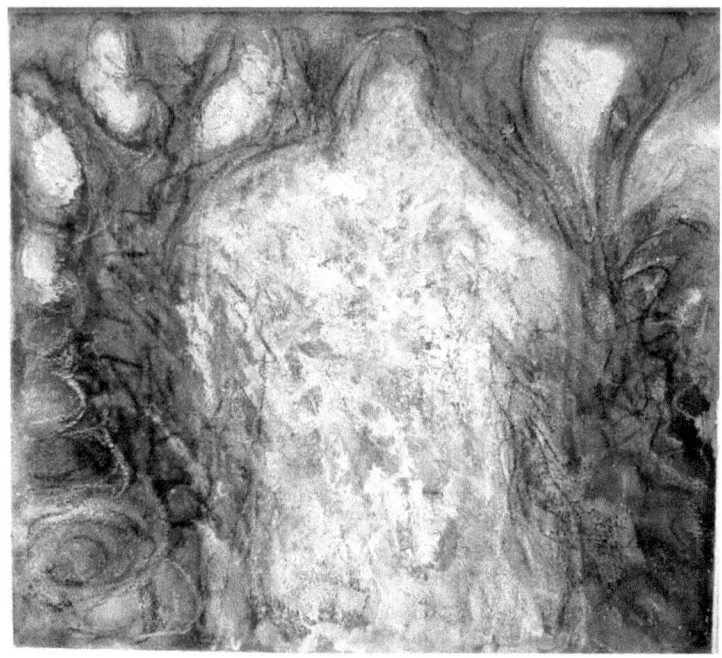

Illumination (2003)

The British philosopher Paul Crowther suggests that the deconstructive nature of postmodernity is part of a broader play of constantly changing codes and signifying practices in the ever-accelerating demand for the new and unexpected. But despite the continual impingement on the senses, enjoying meaningful artistic form remains a constant point of reference. Some contemporary art attempts to bridge the gap between past achievements and today's pluralistic sensibility. Artists today have unlimited freedom to assimilate and appropriate ideas from many different cultures.

Borrowing from earlier times and places, some draw their inspiration from the mythical past while others make no particular reference to any specific world mythology or for that matter, to the history of art. Sometimes expressing the interconnectedness between an aesthetic idea and the potential for artistic form may demand the invention of a fresh new aesthetic language. The jubilation at discovering a new language game, as Lyotard points out, results from the invention of new rules in the game, be they pictorial, artistic, or any other. This requires keeping an open mind and freeing the imagination to discover a unique image that articulates the inherent meaning behind perennially recurring events.

Contemplative appreciation initiates a dialogue between aesthetic form and the viewer if they sincerely try to grasp the complexity of what has been expressed. But it may also be helpful to know the artist's background and life events to fully comprehend a work of art. Having additional information that only the artist can provide, is invaluable in grasping the depth of aesthetic form. Often a work of art can be understood on many different levels. On the one hand, the image may be understood as a social critique of the culture, but on the other, it may show the timeless bond between artist and viewer that even time and space is unable to break.

The essence of authentic self expression in shaping aesthetic form is sometimes profoundly self-referential, yet it can at the same time embody and communicate a more general meaning for others. Understanding the depth and different types of meaning requires use the imagination to empathize with the speaker. Developing an empathetic imagination enables aesthetic enjoyment in context with intellectual concepts that the work may bring to mind. Aesthetic experience requires an enlightened eye that looks with a certain degree of detachment at art in context with the time and place where it was made. Aesthetic appreciation is an affirmative response to fundamental concepts that have been made accessible in the sensuousness and materiality of the medium itself.

However, aesthetic sensitivity may take time to develop. Therefore it is important that engagement with the arts begins in a child's early years. There is an energetic harmony of mind when we aesthetically understand what is being communicated in a work of art that grows over time. The momentary unity between two distinctly different mental movements results in a pleasant cognitive tension. It feels good when the imagination reaches beyond what it knows and understands potentially new and valuable ideas.

Imaginatively going beyond cognitive limitations reveals that the human capacity for reason is far greater than what was previously thought. The empathetic viewer, who spends a little time thinking about the inherent meaning of the image depicted, may grasp the urgency of its message that the artwork articulates. Aesthetic form seems to originate in collectively shared memories of ancient myth and traditional grand narratives. There is reason to believe that these aesthetic ideas reside in the shadows of the psyche and can be made visible in the creative act of shaping aesthetic form.

For many artists, bringing these mental images into aesthetic form is an imaginative attempt to gain a better perspective of life's events. The essence of authentic self expression in shaping artistic form is often profoundly self-referential, yet it can at the same time embody a more general cultural meaning and communicates it for others. As in the painting *Creation (2003)* that clearly shows a very personal view of the creative process in terms of giving birth.

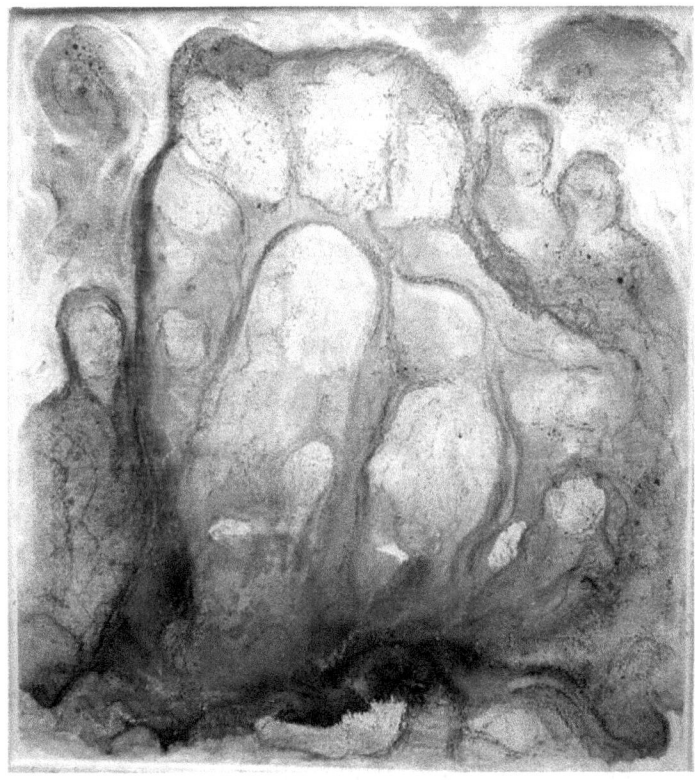

Creation (2003)

As the title implies, this painting is a response to Michelangelo's interpretation of creation on the Sistine Chapel ceiling. He depicts the moment of creation as a Zeus-like god reaching from a brain-shaped cloud to touch Adam's hand. Rather than the traditional version of an old bearded man giving life to Adam, this painting counters this erroneous idea by depicting a crouching female, surrounded by her three children. This painting illustrates the value of having additional knowledge that only the artist can provide. This image may be interpreted as an imaginary family portrait because these three children are clearly my own. Although the figures are highly stylized, I easily recognize my son to the right of the mother, and my two daughters to her left. The children seem to materialize as if from her body, perhaps articulating a more realistic view of creation.

Although this painting depicts actual people, none of these figures were consciously preconceived. Instead these figures developed slowly as one after another spontaneously came to mind as the hands and eyes imaginatively worked the materiality of the paint. I like the many levels of interpretation this painting embodies. On the one hand, it can be read as a social critique of Western culture's perpetuation of a distorted view of creation that subjugates the feminine. But more importantly, this image confirms the enduring love and commitment between a mother and her children, a bond even time and space was unable to break.

Painting from the imagination offers both artist and viewer a greater insight of the human condition in an image that articulates an inner vision of possible worlds. Once an image has come into form, the intellectual and emotional concepts it evokes can be contemplated upon and understood. A work of art may speak of the human predicament. Perhaps it refers to the millions of people who are refugees from poverty, hunger and war. Unfortunately, the displacement of people is no longer a rare event in today's globalized society. *Diasporas* occur almost daily and all over the world.

But in the end, it is up to viewers to imagine the meaning of the art work's utterance. Since time began, art has had the power to draw people into the rhythm and drama expressed in the materiality of the media. Contemporary audiences intuitively grasp an authentic attempt to express the complex paradoxical nature of what it means to be human in today's materialistic culture. Viewers appear to be fascinated by a painting's depiction of mythical ideas and they intuitively respond to its inherent message that speaks of the commonality of the human condition.

Kandinsky describes this intuitive response to mythical ideas and consequential comprehension as a corresponding vibration in the human soul. The human need for expressing primordial ideas will remain forever embedded in the artwork itself. The need for expressing mythological ideas will to some extent be intuitively understood by many generations of art lovers to come. However, apart from a work of art's aesthetic considerations, its enduring value will depend on the depth of allegorical meaning that the artist was able to bring to the surface of consciousness.

In any event, the art making process is a creative act that brings an expressive idea forth into aesthetic form, which is able to articulate a greater consciousness of *Being* and being human. In addition, a great work of art evokes a sense of the unity of human experience. However this notion of collective unity has been challenged. Although minimalist postmodernism rejects the idea of a unifying grand narrative, the implied drama in certain contemporary paintings suggests a baroque interpretation, one of gods and goddesses cavorting as in a Greek myth.

Some paintings have an undeniable theatrical sense of movement and rhythm whose lyrical pattern suggests that the artist may have visualized aesthetic form in musical terms. The empathetic viewer who spends a little time thinking about the meaning behind the painting *The Promised Land (2004)* may grasp the urgency of the message this image articulates. The restlessness and dynamic movement of the figures confirm that this depicts a personal and cultural transformation. Behind the main two figures, more human forms seem to fade into the background. These half formed shadows may suggest severed relationships in the artist's social fabric.

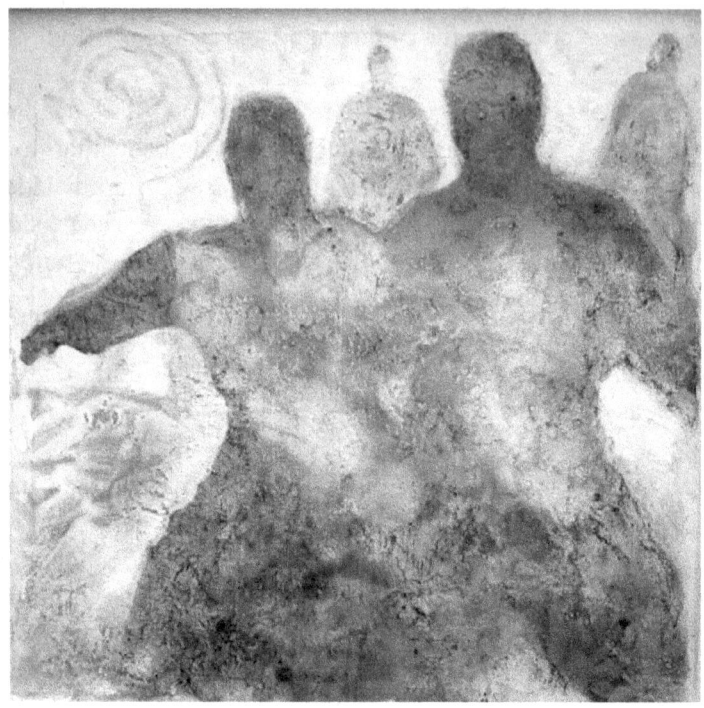

The Promised Land (2004)

To counteract the pathos of personal and cultural loss embodied in this image, a spiral in the background offers hope. In addition, two figures dash arm in arm towards an unknown future. They are still refugees but they are heading towards the light. This too is a recurring theme in my work. These sensuous rhythms are intended to take the viewer outside themselves so they too may see beyond the limitations of personal horizons. But this calls for an enlightened eye to penetrate beyond the merely representational. The enlightened eye recognizes an authentic expression of inner truth that may only be partially remembered.

Aesthetic understanding is not necessarily found in what a person is seeing but it is more about what is been awakened inside. Even the artist may not immediately know where an image comes from or what it means. Sometimes a work of art is a shock to the intellect that releases the imagination, moving the mind to search for a new concept that communicates a previously unknown idea. Active imaginative engagement in making and appreciating art develops the ability to reach for richer and more productive aesthetic form to express ideas that are not available to consciousness in any other way.

Extending the mind beyond its cognitive limits also facilitates a greater appreciation of living a more humane life; humane as in consciously striving to embody only the very best human qualities. Cultivating the classical virtues of mercy, tolerance and compassion while living a civilized and happy life and extending this right to others. Artistic creativity and aesthetic enjoyment creates a place for silence where the imagination is free to roam between intuition and conceptual understanding. When the imagination is released, it is more able to bridge the gap between the illusion of difference between self and others. After this deception is bridges, the mind can more clearly comprehend the underlying commonalities of existence.

It was Kant who first made the connection between aesthetic understanding and morality. He proposed that aesthetic experience enlivened people's psyche, thereby igniting nobler thoughts and feelings so the mind could grasp new insight into morality and general social values. The idea that aesthetic understanding enables the mind to perceive a potentially greater rationality is important. The incessant noise of pluralist voices in contemporary society need to be balanced by ample opportunities for aesthetic experience and reflection, in the arts as well as in nature. It makes people aware that they are far more than what they appear to be on the surface of things.

Aesthetic form may be understood on many different levels but an image of inner truth is always self referential and somewhat autobiographical. Discovering authentic artistic form within the shadows of emotional body memory reveals that a higher power presides over human consciousness. At times, aesthetic form provides a greater comprehension of morality in context with general social issues. This meta-awareness shows there are moral principles behind aesthetic understanding that link ethics to aesthetics..

As the philosopher Ludwig Wittgenstein famously said, ethics and aesthetics are one and the same. This view of morality demonstrates people are free to act within the constraints of reason. People are only free to the extent that their actions do not infringe upon others. Free to do as they want without hurting others. Appreciating the significance of this simple aesthetic idea reveals that this moral law exerts a powerful and attractive force on human consciousness. Take for example the painting *Because of Eve (1986)*. Looking at this painting many years later, I now see the suppressed anger beneath the surface. In the woman's gesture and face.

That was me; married, respectable, with all the time in the world to work at my art while my husband paid the bills. But I paid too. Playing the housewife and housekeeping when I had to. I remember staring into the kitchen window one evening as I was doing dishes. After I had cooked a meal and readied the house for my husband's return.

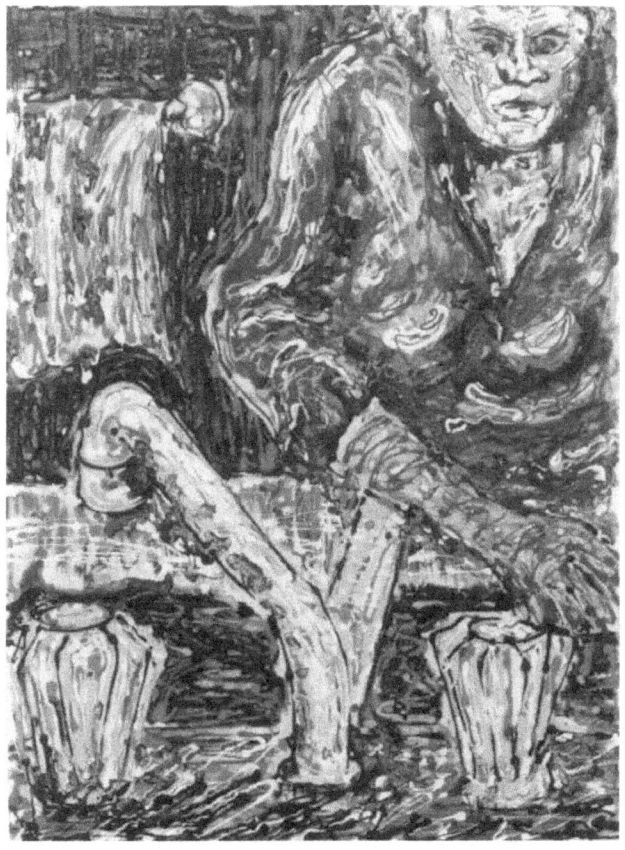

Because of Eve (1986)

And this is what I saw; a haggard woman hanging over a kitchen sink. I was 37 years young, at my prime, and eager to learn. Fresh out of art school, I applied to my art making as a job. While trying to come to grips with what making art was all about. Somehow I knew artistic creativity was much more than making a pretty picture. The creative act revealed me to myself. As this image shows, aesthetic form speaks the raw truth.

As free rational and moral beings, humanity is indeed supersensible, capable of self determination and positive change in the world. Everyone has the capacity to be a moral and reasonable person who has the power to act well and make good judgments about the validity of contemporary norms and values. Philosophical reflection demonstrates that it is reason itself that underwrites personal freedom. Self-determining personal freedom is a moral issue because it can only be achieved through social interaction within a mutual open dialogue with others.

Freedom to articulate self awareness as well as the right to be heard requires a social agreement between speakers to play by the rules of a commonly understood language game. Communicating self awareness through an aesthetic language is a creative act of self determining freedom. It asks others to imagine a different perspective of reality. Using allegory, metaphor or aesthetic form facilitates the imaginative ability of others to project their self awareness into the meaning of the syntax of an utterance.

This calls for mutual trust that a particular language game is true to the speaker's intended meaning. The philosopher Colin Lyas, points out that these social agreements need not be universal and can even be altered as a person's life changes. He acknowledges that these social contracts are to some extent affected by the past as well as the future, but points out that they are all that underpins language. Social agreements that people make in sharing a language game may not be global but it does require that people set aside their personal biases.

Contemporary language games involve complex ethical negotiations between speakers and listeners. Understanding requires an enlightened eye as well as a well developed sense of empathy. A new language game asks people to listen, if not disinterestedly, then with empathy in a sincere attempt to grasp what is been communicated. A strong sense of ethics and morality must guide a respectful dialogue between different people.

Authentic artistic form plays a visual language game of self disclosure by metaphorically articulating a collectively shared personal concept. When the imagination is free to make the cognitive connections, aesthetic form may reach back to primordial and ancient creation myths and at the same time, extend our perception into the future of contemporary science and technology. No matter what form a work of art takes, mutual self disclosure demonstrates the value of tolerance of different voices in today's society.

The implied drama in certain contemporary paintings is intended to take viewers outside themselves, so they too may see beyond the limitations of personal horizons. However, this calls for going beyond the merely representational to express an unknown aesthetic truth which is only partially remembered. For example, the painting *Solution (2004)* articulates a personal vision of possible worlds. This image offers a broader understanding of tolerance.

Although its title suggests an optimistic outlook, the image itself seems to have a foreboding quality, perhaps because the figures have been darkly outlined against a bleak greyish sky. To support this interpretation, there is a huge blue moon hovering above the seemingly fleeing figures. This painting speaks of the human predicament of the millions of people today, who are refugees from poverty and war.

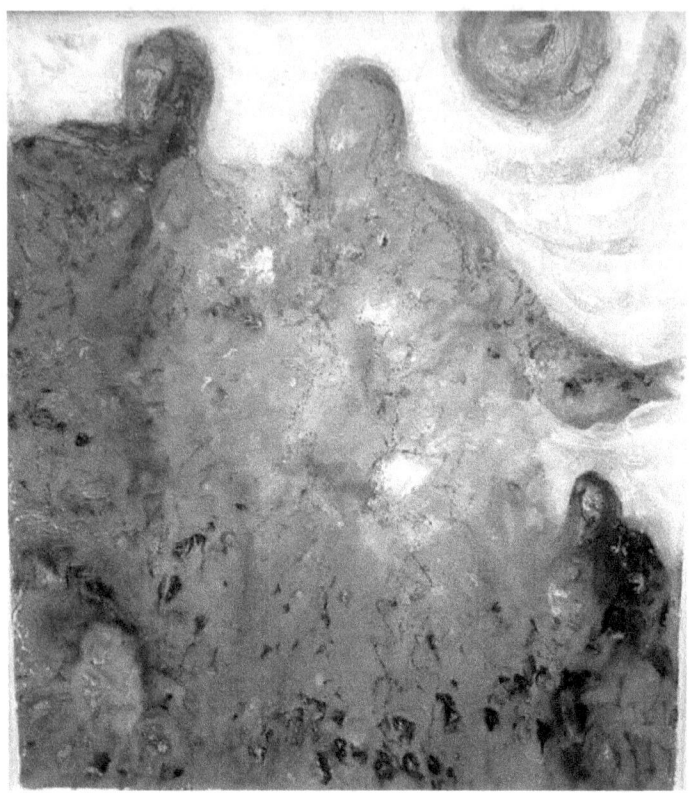

Solutions ([2004)

Although reference was made earlier to the connotations associated with the blue moon, no mention was made of the obvious. Blue moons are a rare natural event. Ancient people associated a blue moon with coming disaster. It is also a scientific fact that a blue moon may be caused by smoke or particles of dust in the earth's atmosphere, especially after a forest fire or volcanic eruption. Folklore has it that the Krakatoa eruption of1883 in Indonesia was the reason the moon was blue for nearly two years. It seems this catastrophic meaning fits better with the aesthetic sense of this painting; however the title suggests that this narrative may yet have a happy ending.

However, in the end, it is up to the viewer to imagine the meaning behind the image. Artistic form seems to have the power to draw viewers into the rhythm and drama expressed in the materiality of paint, understanding its meaning in context with a story these figures seem to articulate. Many of these paintings attempt to express the complex paradoxical nature of what it means to be human in today's culture in an original and pleasing aesthetic form.

Although individuals may not always agree with the moral principles of others, in general postmodernist thought supports the notion that there are multiple ways of interpreting an utterance. But ultimately, there is no one true and certain language because the comprehension will always be limited. Elliott Eisner concludes that at best, belief is about as good as it gets. While it is true that there is tremendous diversity among cultures and people speak many different languages, the syntax of a 'subtler' language of art can communicate a collective vision of the world in ethical as well as aesthetic terms.

The complex nature of communication not withstanding, the function of all language, and the language of art is no exception, is to express and share the significant meaning of an intellectual concept in aesthetic terms. However, aesthetic form never simply articulates a literal meaning nor is it strictly a vehicle of social ideologies. The commonality of aesthetic understanding demonstrates that the language of art has validity in its own right. Although art may have a useful or a social function, aesthetic form should first of all be appreciated for its own sake.

The process of aesthetic comprehension begins with an enlightened eye that perceives through all the senses. What should be of concern is the relationship between structure and form in context with how the art work was shaped. Aesthetic awareness provides fleeting impressions of what people seem to intuitively know. Although these illusive sensible intuitions are non-conceptual, they do have certain general characteristics that the imagination uses to find a suitable intellectual concept. Understanding is complete when the imagination finds a word or a image within the mind that can accurately articulate this general concept.

The imagination brings these intellectual ideas into form. For me, these ideas take shape as a visual image begins to emerge from the medium. Aesthetic understanding involves imaginatively making order out of the chaos of the multiple sensible impressions perceived in the medium. Although form may be modified as the artwork develops, titles that come to mind often indicate complex personal associations. But the meaning of a painting may be intentionally ambiguous and multi-faceted.

Disinterested engagement with aesthetic form strengthens our natural ability to imaginatively perceive the moral and social value of what may have been disclosed in the work. In a Wittgensteinian sense, ethics and aesthetics may not be the same but they are definitely two sides of the same coin. The fundamental nature of aesthetic perception is a visual dialogue with structure and form that the art work takes. As the work progresses, often a title or a phrase will come to mind. As in the painting *Boogie Woogie (1992)*, its title plays with art historical concepts. Mondriaan's interpretation of New York City comes to mind. My interpretation is more organic but that may be because I am a woman and see things more in an organic way. I strongly believe that there are two very different ways of seeing the world; one linear, the other fluid. Both are equally valid.

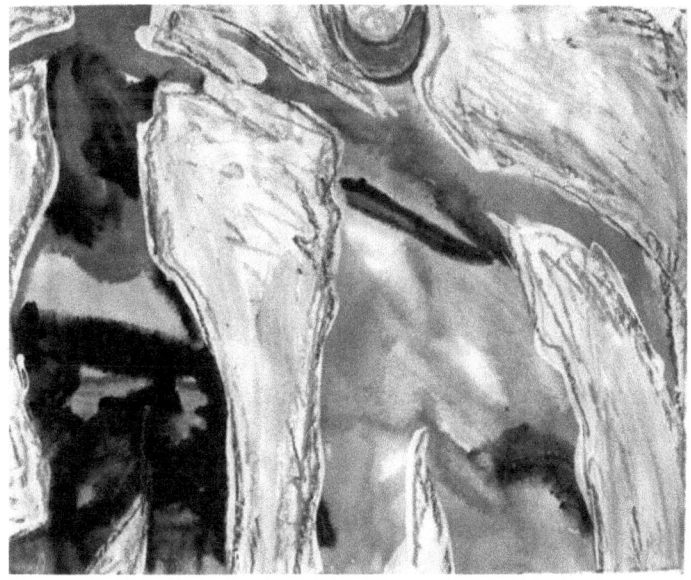

Boogie Woogie (1992)

Rather than passively looking on, aesthetic appreciation requires an empathetic response. And to contemplate the work with empathy for the revelation of *Being* and what is involved in being in the world. And most important, seeing rather than merely looking, and that necessitates developing an enlightened eye and a new aesthetic language.

A NEW AESTHETIC LANGUAGE

Ideally, artistic creativity is a personal quest for enlightenment in aesthetic form that also has relevance for the community. This expanded sense of self awareness is encoded within the medium of the artwork itself. Making personal vision public has value and greatly benefits others who recognize the articulation as inner truth. But the artwork also embodies the personal choices the artist has makes while shaping an aesthetic idea. When artistic form has been successfully brought forth from the sensuousness of the medium, it reaffirms our intellectual power to make good ethical and aesthetic choices.

It is fascinating how the sensuousness of shaping form can articulate aesthetic and ethical judgments. Picasso's painting *Guernica* comes to mind, perhaps because the meaning behind this image shouts out his indignation at the horrendous consequences of war. Without a word, this painting states what could not have been said in any other way. It's fractures image and the tortured forms say it all and we know instantly what it means. Human perception is complex. We never just look at one particular thing. The eyes are constantly moving and in a constant state of flux. Taking in many different impressions that arouse curiosity, while continually making connections between seeing and understanding the objective world.

Berger describes looking as an act of choice. As a result of this act, what people see is brought within their reach. Active perception, particularly when engaged with aesthetic form, involves a passionate response to something outside one's self, which is nonetheless recognized intuitively as being part of our own inner life. Aesthetic comprehension involves the mental capacity to engage in a sympathetic interchange with the artwork and its creator. This requires temporarily setting aside personal interests and taking the necessary time for reflective contemplation, as in the painting *Opposition (2004)*. What is the artist trying to say? Is that her, standing in opposition to four others. Do they represent the family or are these forms symbolic of other ideas? And what does this image say to me personally and collectively?

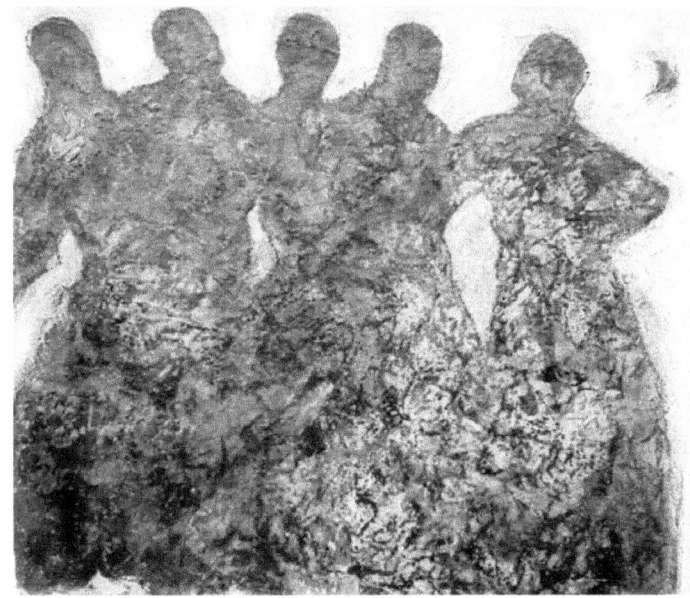

Opposition (2004)

The viewer is asked to reflect on the image and think about what it may mean. A crescent moon gives a hint. The power of an aesthetic experience lies in the ability to project one's self into a visual language that has the power to open the heart, as well as mind. This is no surprise, considering that the arts have always been crucial as a means to gain greater understanding of the human predicament.

A work of art opens the viewer's perception to a different perspective and interpretation of reality that has the potential to expand their cognitive horizons. Perhaps this is so because aesthetic experience offers the chance to imagine an alternative possibility of what could be. In addition, aesthetic understanding develops greater tolerance if not respect for difference, and the value and diversity of artistic expression within a multicultural society. The variety of authentic artistic creativity stimulates the imagination to seek meaning beyond a fixed perspective of the world.

Art made in other cultures is accepted and enjoyed, both for its similarity and difference. A work of art takes participants beyond the familiar. But regardless of where an artwork is made, the language of art speaks through its natural rhythms and gestures that articulate shared human values that cannot be fully expressed in any other way. Aesthetic experience requires trusting the subtle suggestions that the imagination presents. Allowing the body and mind to follow its promptings in the act of conceptualizing form as it unfolds within the medium.

Therefore, the creative act is usually a fluid process. Aesthetic form itself is flexible, shifting and changing in order to provide clues for the artist in shaping the material. Rather than as a means to an end, with authentic artistic creativity ends follow means. One acts and then the act itself suggests further actions so ends that did not precede the act follow. An intuitive aesthetic response to aesthetic form, no matter from what culture or tradition it comes from, requires imaginatively adopting a sympathetic attitude. In contemplative reflection and thoughtful attention to a work of art, viewers with an enlightened eye know when they see a new vision of self in relation to others.

This aesthetic experience may counter the forming of negative stereotypical generalizations that serve only to polarize between *them* and *us*. Living well together in today's multicultural society requires knowledge and appreciation of the valuable contributions made by many different people. Living harmoniously in a multi-cultural community necessitates that the need for cultivating ethical and aesthetic judgments. Postmodern thought respects everyone's freedom to choose their own way of life and their right for personal self expression. Respecting cultural difference is important, as is an honest effort to make good personal choices for the sake of others.

It may also require a willingness to hold back certain habits if they offend others within the community. Cultivating greater tolerance of diversity, both personal and cultural, will redefine what a happy life in a contemporary democracy is all about. Active engagement in the arts, our own and that of others and enjoying the variety of aesthetic expression, goes a long way towards creating a community that respects diversity and the vitality of many world views. After all, most cultures across time and place have had a predisposition to express themselves through rhythm and song as well as visual art.

Art making seems to have been a shared human activity since time began. Sharing aesthetic experience satisfies a common human need for friends, family and love. Most cultures across the globe honour the idea of passing along their artistic legacy to future generations. The greatest art expresses the very best that our ancestors wanted to preserve. A work of art is the legacy left to humanity by those who came here before. We need only remember. Sharing aesthetic understanding develops a sense of empathy for the lived experience of others. Art can reconcile sorrow and joy because it displays the innerness of those who came before, as in the painting *Mimesis (2004)*. This image plays a visual language game of self disclosure by metaphorically articulating a collectively shared myth.

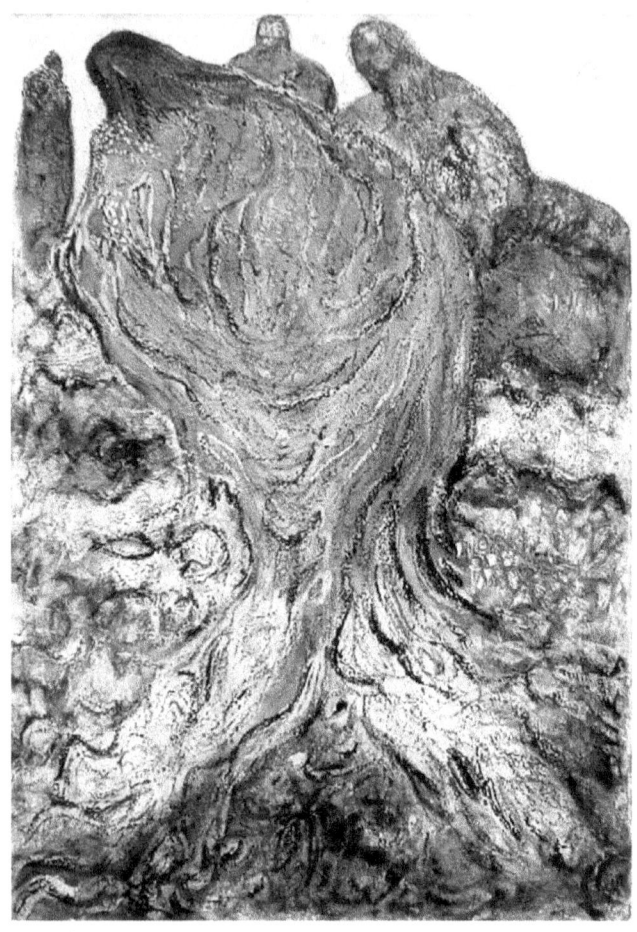

Mimesis (2004)

The goddess Mimesis who rescued Hephaestus from drowning, when as a baby, he was thrown from Mount Olympus into the sea. His mother Hera, when she saw that her son was deformed, rejected him. The story is that Mimesis happened to be swimming around one day, when she saw a new-born baby in distress and brought him home to her two sisters who lived deep below the sea. Together they raised him and taught him all they knew. When Hephaestus grew up, he became a gifted blacksmith and metal artist whose work was much in demand on Mount Olympus. Even by his mother Hera.

In this painting, Mimesis rises from the sea with her back to the viewer who is asked to imagine that she holds little Hephaestus in her arms. It's not hard, although the baby can't be seen. The clues are in her gesture and tilt of her head. She seems to be leaning towards a lone figure in the distance to her left. As if she is offering the child to his natural mother, but Hera has turned her back and is walking away. The two figures in the central right of the canvas depict her sisters, who look on with concern. Mimesis trails a garment of watery fish behind her, as she steps out of the primordial sea, bringing new life and regeneration with her.

Artists throughout the ages have expressed their all too poignant concern for the suffering of the disenfranchised in many different ways. Whether it is a painting, sculpture, or a tragic play, viewers are presented with an opportunity aesthetic understanding. Actively imagining the meaning of artistic form takes us out of ourselves and into the ancient mythologies or spiritual beliefs and historical record as viewed by another person. However, our understanding will always be to some extent culturally determined and limited by personal knowledge.

Sometimes grasping the complexity of aesthetic form goes beyond mere conceptualization. Therefore, making an aesthetic judgment, as Kant correctly points out, requires releasing the imagination to leap beyond personal and cultural limitations. A work of art may articulate an ineffable and mysterious vision. A brand new mythology might better explain reality for a new generation living in a globalized information age. This may require a fresh new language game to adequately express the truth of *Being* and being human for a new millennium. A new aesthetic language involves a sensitive awareness of the complexity of meaningful artistic form.

The more one is exposed to the possibility of a unique aesthetic experience, the better the imagination is able to reach beyond personal and cultural limitations. Artistic creativity and aesthetic appreciation cultivates the imagination, strengthening the mental ability to make the necessary connections between intuitive sensibility and the intellect. Building a broader aesthetic awareness is a valuable cognitive and affective tool that goes far beyond the practice of making or enjoying a work of art.

Making good aesthetic judgments is useful in other areas of life as well. Therefore we should be free to experiment with our chosen media. As the imagination plays between fleeting concepts, the creative act encourages us to trust our own way of doing things. We soon discover that artistic creativity has no standardized recipe that can be followed. It requires learning from our mistakes and delight in success when the image is a perfect fit. The practice of shaping aesthetically pleasing form shows that perseverance and discipline are a prerequisite to mastering the rules and skills of a particular medium.

It may take years to learn how to paint well for example, and a painter will always be learning to some extent. Without having a predetermined concept in mind, appropriate form materializes from a receptive and contemplative state of mind. Aesthetic form is capable of mysteriously going beyond mere words and text to express the ineffable, as in the painting *Sacred Marriage (2004)* where form tells the story.

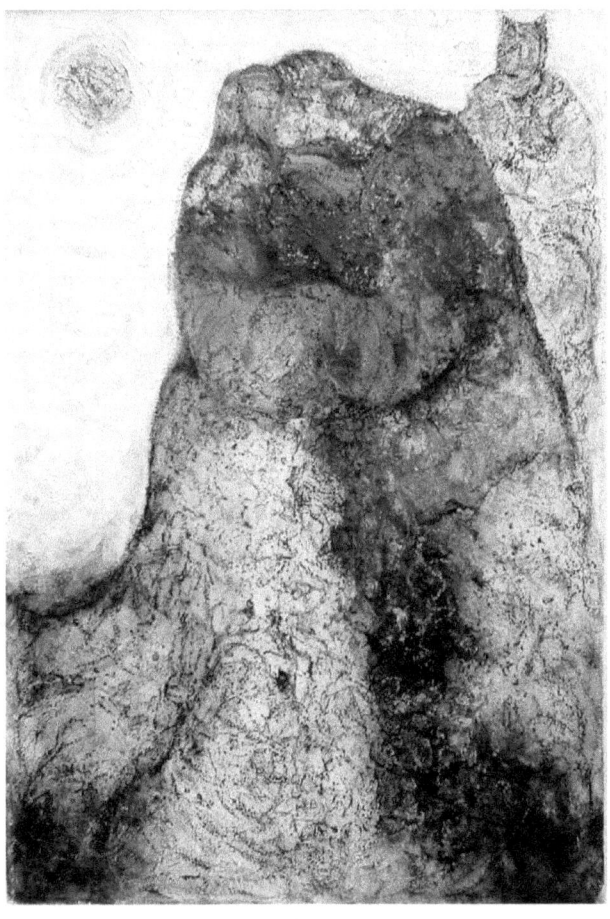

Sacred Marriage (2004)

A work of art seems capable of communicating inexpressible meaning in a visual language that goes beyond narrative that may only be alluded to through allegory and metaphor. The search for appropriate form requires following the imagination where it wanders so the mind can respond spontaneously to the aesthetic possibilities inherent in the art medium itself. Artistic creativity involves aesthetic judgments that extend beyond instrumental reason.

The object of artistic creativity is to be open-ended and flexible, yet set attainable limits within the collective framework of shaping form. This experience strengthens our mental and emotional power to respond appropriately to the often chaotic events in life. Art making also hones the ability to notice beauty in seemingly common place things, making us more aware of the pleasure of the moment. A greater awareness of the qualitative goodness of aesthetic form inspires profound appreciation, lifting the human spirit beyond everyday reality and personal concerns.

Artists know they have personal agency and self determination. They realize that they are not just products of consumerism. Each and every one has a unique point of view that needs to be expressed. Philosophical reflection and empathetic understanding of the often complex meaning inherent in a work of art may be the place where ethics and aesthetics meet. The ability to reason and comprehend the meaning of perception and experience requires activating the imagination to unify sensible intuitions and the intellect.

Although every generation sees things differently, each person has a part to play in the ongoing quest for enlightenment in the all too human struggle for personal and cultural transformation. Kant was correct when he proposed that the mind creates reality and not the other way around. It is true that perceptual understanding resides not so much in the world, but in the eye of the beholder. The complexity of the human mind embodies intentionality and will but also purposes, desires and wishes. It also encompasses memory, recollections and remembrances. The thinking, feeling mind is the seat or subject of human consciousness that together with the subconscious forms the psyche. The mind is where body, spirit, soul and the intellect meet. It is where the intuitive and the primordial find personal expression.

Seeing with an enlightened eye opens up a possibility of reconciling the public language of words and text with a 'subtler' articulation that originates deep within the discursive mind. Aesthetic form expresses a special kind of knowledge that is deeply emotional. Art's subtler language is capable of touching the heart as well as the mind. A work of art expresses how the artist felt about what they saw in the world and shares it in a way others can understand. An enlightened perception helps viewers make appropriate value judgments that expand both cognitive and affective perception. It seems that sharing aesthetic experience develops a sense of empathy and concern for others less fortunate in the world.

There are many benefits to artistic creativity when it involves playing with shape, texture and form. Manipulating the plasticity of the medium also develops cognitive and aesthetic sensibilities that carry over into pragmatic engagements with the real world. As people learn to express themselves in a new aesthetic language, they are able to visualize intellectual concepts in the materiality of a particular medium. Through trial and error, the artist learns the importance of authentic self expression, both in personal their art making as well as in appreciating the art of others. Most people in cultures across the globe honour the idea of passing on personal and cultural legacies to the next generation, as illustrated in the painting *Legacy (2004)*. This image depicts a shared human concern most everyone intuitively appreciates and understands.

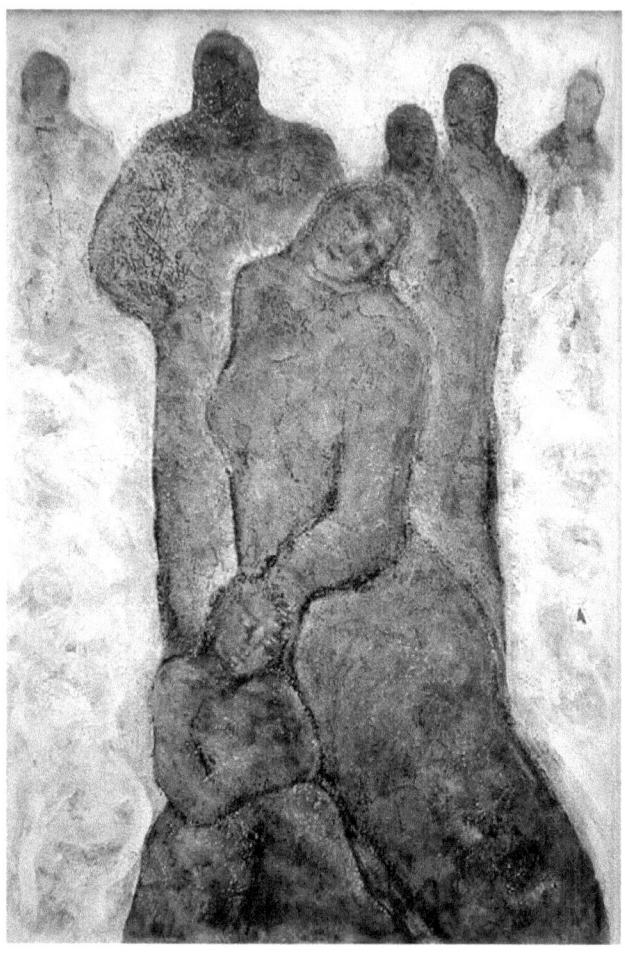

Legacy (2004)

The word *legacy* comes from the Latin word *legatum,* which means handing down something of value from an ancestor. Legacy can be material or immaterial, as in passing on a power or a duty. In the painting, a current seems to run from the seated child, through the mother's hand, to the figures in the background. Its triangular design implies a solid foundation, which is rooted in the child who becomes the heir to this legacy. The figures recede into the distance, suggestive of the passing of the generations into the mists of time. Form in this painting shows that genetics and cultural values have passed through from one generation to the next since time began. A biblical saying comes to mind, which states that the sins of the father will have to be paid by his heirs for seven generations. However this painting seems to exude a sense of peace and harmony, as the mother gently smiles and lovingly strokes the child's head.

Making good and innovative aesthetic judgments opens the window of perception. This allows the imagination to reach beyond personal and cultural limitations. Making sensible intuition visible in a complex and meaningful image others can enjoy. The language of art cultivates our finer sensibilities and speaks to the beauty of the moment. This aesthetic language often a rich and composite statement, who's meaning cannot be fully understood or expressed in any other way. But trying to understand an aesthetic utterance often provides insight in context with accepted codes of ethics and morality.

All too often, logic and instrumental reason offer only a limited explanation of things. It requires taking an imaginative leap to see the interconnectivity of all existence. Making our own unique connections between aesthetic ideas broadens our ability to see beauty in an increasingly complex world. Of course, aesthetic experience is satisfying for its own sake, but art also facilitates the ability to perceive the unity and connectivity of human experience; the common ground of existence as well as the beauty of diversity.

Understanding the subtle vernacular of a work of art requires making creative links between intellectual ideas and lived experience that goes far beyond any language rules. Aesthetic experience has been a crucial component of human evolution since time began. Aesthetic appreciation of goodness in a beautiful work of art elevates the human spirit and expands our awareness of quality and excellence. Artists and philosophers know that authentic self expression is vital for the well-being of the entire global community.

Art makes inner feelings public and invites viewers to share in the artist's search for the divine spark of *Being* that resides within the shadows of body memory. Inner truth exposes hidden archetypal images that are able to reveal philosophical concepts that may be difficult to articulate. By reaching beyond the horizons of an otherwise flat and nihilistic world, a work of art demonstrates that the imagination is an equal partner in the acquisition of knowledge. Therefore it is imperative that aesthetic sensibilities are cultivated early and art takes its rightful place in society.

The arts are an essential part of contemporary life. The subtle language of art has traditionally played a major role in the general well-being and cohesion of society. Since before the ancient Greeks, the arts in its many forms have been central to the seasonal celebrations and cycles of the year. In most places across the globe, art brings people together to share and enjoy the diversity as well as the unity of human self expression. The arts are the foundation of a culture and have value for contemporary society.

By showing a personal perspective of events in the context of a broader world view, a work of art articulates a deeper grasp of culturally significant philosophical ideas such as the unity of experience. The painting *Sisters (2005)* personifies the idea that aesthetic experience necessitates a reconciliation between different mental energies.

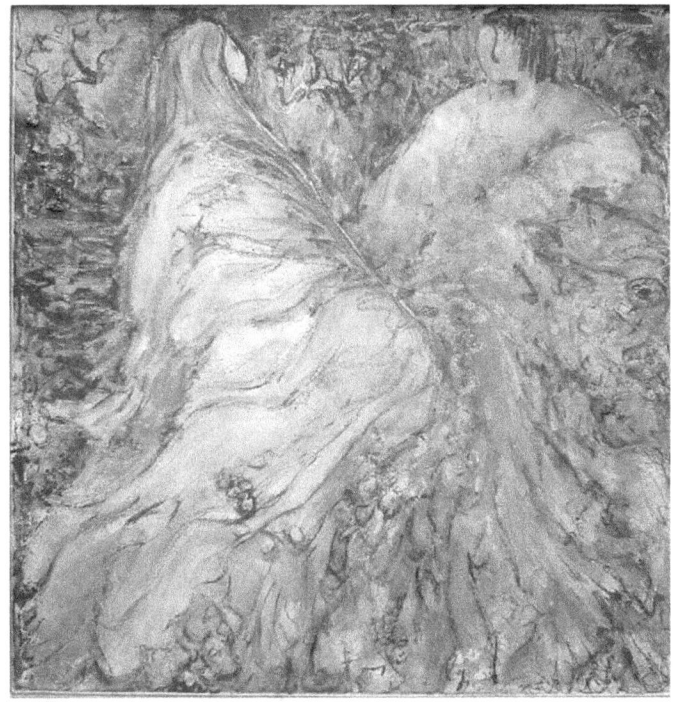

Sisters [2005

Difference is personified by a blonde shaking the hand of a brunette; with all that this implies. We are all sisters and brothers living on this tiny blue planet on the edge of our galaxy. Divided we fall – united we thrive. The time for opposition and division is over. Those are my feelings when I look at this image. Listening to the language the artwork speaks involves carefully exploring many possible options for interpretation. It requires taking the necessary time to grasp the significant meaning of a unique perspective of life.

Reflective attention to aesthetic detail is an affective and contemplative response to a unique artistic style and the formal qualities of the artist's self expression. This requires contemplative attention, which tends to slow the perceptual process down. Slowing down and paying attention to detail matters. It requires a conscious effort to discern the subtle nuances and variations of objects and ideas that are usually overlooked. This intentional act of reflective attention refines our ability to reason better.

Understanding what a work of art reveals requires trusting the imagination to make an intuitive value judgment to decide where the rules end or where there are no rules. Aesthetic judgment trains the eye to appreciate pattern, form and proportions while significant meaning of form is intuitively understood. Often a new language game opens up alternative ways of doing things that have value for the community as a whole. Aesthetic judgment may be contingent upon various unfamiliar perspectives that entail respectful consideration of new ideas and imagining a better world beyond the self.

Multiple layers of meaning may intersect and contribute to the viewer's aesthetic enjoyment and interpretation. This process of discovery at times shocks the sensibilities through an unexpected imaginative leap. There is always a gap between past and present experience that involves risking a cognitive plunge into the unknown. This mental shock reveals how little a person actually knows and how much there still is to learn. The delight of an aesthetic experience is sublime.

Grasping the inherent concept behind a work of art is both a cognitive and affective pleasure.. Aesthetic experience keeps the imagination flexible. Then the mind can discover significant form; whether it is in a play, painting or song. Then a work of art serves the greater good because the attempt to comprehend aesthetic form induces a reciprocal dialogue. Aesthetic understanding is a continuous process of evaluating and interpreting the complexity of interlaced formal relationships between composition and content.

In addition, a work of art asks viewers to attend to what it tries to say. Make an honest effort to respond with empathy to a new perspective. Aesthetic perception is relevant for society in general. It builds understanding of one self as well as of others. The arts across time confirm that aesthetic form speaks eloquently of enduring values and human accomplishment. The diversity of the arts shows each person interprets lived experience differently. It requires setting personal sensibilities aside, to imaginatively interpret its message.

However, it is true that many artists prefer to leave some details out of their work, suggesting form rather than making it explicit. It seems that simplifying form serves to draw viewers into a reciprocal process of mental creativity, which is a far richer aesthetic experience.Using the imagination decentres the mind from the confinement of private concerns, to see beyond our limited perception of reality. An expanded world view transcends individual and cultural frames of reference.

Aesthetic experience has effectively transmitted important cultural values as long as anyone can remember. Nothing can compare with the power of art to bind a community together and encode cultural norms. The arts have traditionally been the preferred means of sharing our sense of the divine. The painting *Eureka (2004)*, despite being a recurring image, depicts a broader perspective not limited to the planet earth.

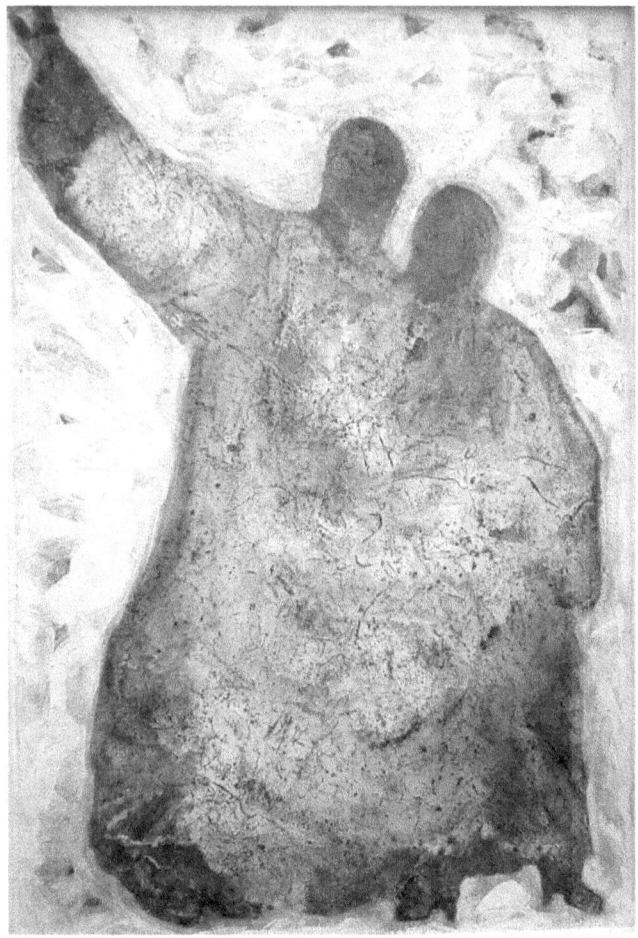

Eureka (2004)

Out there, what's out there, asks the male, as the woman tentatively looks over his shoulder. She perhaps more concerned about how to feed the family and keep them warm as winter approaches. Yet together, the masculine need to expand and the feminine need to feel safe can coexist. It's what has constituted the family unit for millennium.

By aesthetically engaging our feelings and emotions, perception and cognition work together to share values, which are deeply embedded into memory and preserves them for easy future retrieval. It is this complex engagement with aesthetic form on a cognitive, emotive and perceptual level that makes a work of art so valuable. Consequently the language of art is indissolubly intertwined with culture and human nature. For millennia, the arts functioned as a means of expressing interpersonal cohesiveness and fellow feeling.

Historically, the arts and philosophy have rich descriptive traditions of aesthetic appraisals of a particular world view. Be it in literature, dance, drama, poetry, music or the visual arts. Long before the tragic plays of ancient Greece, art helped shape and articulate personal thoughts and human experience. Engaging with a work of art has provided the social cement within society. In the rhythms of dance or a march to the beat of a drum, sharing cultural origins and common feelings and experience, every community has benefited from the cohesiveness inherent in art.

The arts are the cultural legacy our ancestors left behind to pass on how they experienced the world. Imaginative contemplation of the enduring value of art remains relevant today. Kant proposed that the human mind creates reality and not the other way around. It is true that aesthetic perception and understanding reside not so much in the world, but in the eye of the beholder. He also knew that make good aesthetic judgments required the imagination to unite two ways of knowing. The painting *Art and Philosophy (2007)* demonstrates this unifying principle.

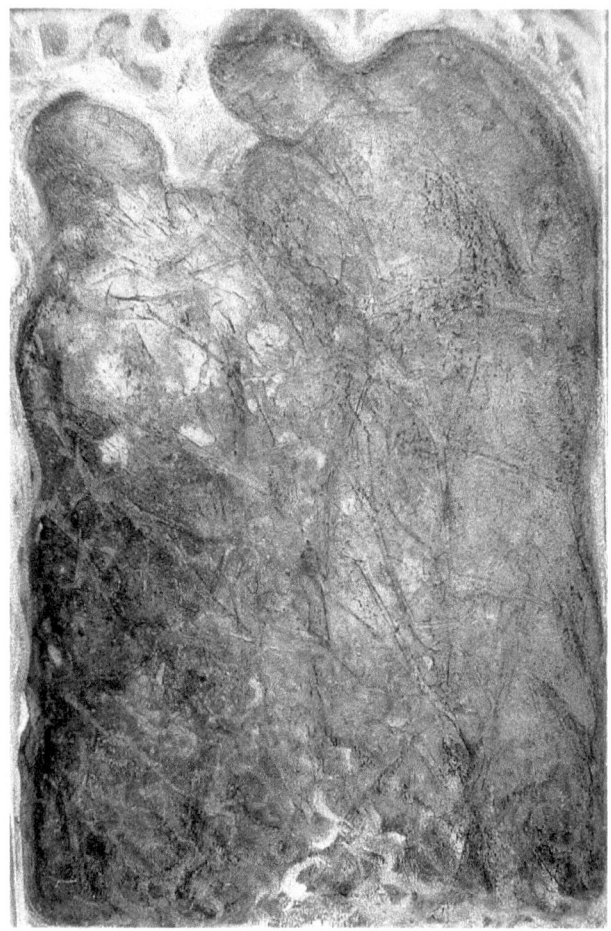

Art and Philosophy (2001-2007)

Whereas the meaning behind other paintings could be objectively discerned because I have had time to contemplate its aesthetic form, at the time of writing this image was still fresh in my mind, making it difficult to see it objectively. Although its meaning is still becoming clear, it is obvious to me that this painting contains many layered meanings, both personal as well as a more general cultural interpretation.

Its title provides a clue to an accurate perspective. This image depicts the possibility of reconciliation between two opposing disciplines that often vie for my attention. Although making art and studying philosophy do not necessarily preclude each other, one often takes precedence over the other. However, when these two energies meet, they seem to expand consciousness. Somehow, the struggle between art and philosophy seems to some extent resolved. Perhaps the implied harmony between these two figures shows the need for balance between masculine and feminine energies.

This unity demonstrates that art and philosophy are equal partners in my experience of life. But in the end, aesthetic judgment will require the viewer to use their own imagination to fully comprehend what this image attempts to articulate and more. Aesthetic judgment facilitates the necessary vision for creating a better future for our children and grandchildren. Artists and philosophers know that a work of art makes this possibility visible because it can articulate inner wisdom that cannot be spoken of in words alone.

BIBLIOGRAPHY

Abrams, David, The Spell of the Sensuous: Perception and Language in a More-than-Human World (New York; Vintage Press, 1997).

Albert, Robert S.(ed), Genius and Eminence (Oxford, New York, Seoul, Tokyo: Pergamon Press, 1992).

Allison, Henry, Kant's Theory of Taste: A Reading of the Critique of Aesthetic Judgment Cambridge, UK: Cambridge University Press, 2001.

Anderson, Richard L., Calliope's Sisters: a Comparative Study of Philosophies of Art (New Jersey: Prentice Hall, 1990).

Bal, Mieke, Reading "Rembrandt": Beyond the Word-Image Oppositions, The Northrop Frye Lectures in Literary Theory (New York: Cambridge University Press, 1991).

Ki-moon, Ban, "We should welcome the dawn of the migration age" Guardian (2007).

http://www.guardian.co.uk/commentisfree/story/0,,2122689,,00.html

Battersby, Christine, Gender and Genius: Towards a Feminist Aesthetics (London: The Women's Press, 1989).

Bayer, Thora Ilin, "Art as Symbolic Form: Cassirer on the Educational Value of Art" Journal of Aesthetic Education 40:4 (2006): 51-64.

Beardsley, Monroe C., The Aesthetic Point of View: Selected Essays. Wreen, Michael J. and Callen, Donald M. (editors). Ithaca, London: Cornell University Press, 1982.

Berger, John, Ways of Seeing. London, UK: British Broadcasting Corporation, 1982.

Berger, John, A Painter of our Time (London: Writers and Readers Publishing Cooperative, 1976).

Berger, John, The Shape of a Pocket (New York: Vintage International, a Division of Random House, Inc. 2001).

Berger, John, "Where are we?" Between the Eyes: Essays on Photography and Politics. David Levi Strauss (editor) New York: Aperture, 2003.

Biro, Matthew, Anselm Kiefer and the Philosophy of Martin Heidegger (UK: Cambridge University Press, 1998).

Bubner, Rudiger, Modern German Philosophy (Cambridge: Cambridge University Press, 1981).

Callow, Philip, Vincent van Gogh: a Life (London: Allison & Busby, 1990).

Caranfa, Angelo, "Lessons of Solitude: The Awakening of Aesthetic Sensibility" Journal of Philosophy of Education 41:1 (2007): 113-127.

Caranfa, Angelo, "Voices of Silence in Pedagogy, Art, Writing and Self Encounter" Journal of Philosophy of Education 40:1 (2006): 85-103.

Carroll, Noel, "Art and Human Nature" Journal of Aesthetics and Art Criticism 62:2 (2004): 95-107.

Carroll, Noel, "Art and the Domain of the Aesthetic" British Journal of Aesthetics 40:2 (2000):191-208.

Carson, Camin, "The Sublime and Education" Journal of Aesthetic Education 40:1 (2006):71-93.

Camhi, Leslie, "Dinner is Served: Judy Chicago: The Dinner Party" Brooklyn Museum of Art (2002).

http://www.villagevoice.com/art/0242,camhi,39170,13.html

Capaldi, Nicolas, Eugene Kelly and Luis E. Navia, An Invitation to Philosophy (New York: Prometheus, 1981).

Casey, Edward S., "How to Get from Space to Place in a Fairly Short Stretch of Time: Phenomenological Prolegomena", in Sense of Place, Steven Feld and Keith H Basso, ed. (Santa Fe, New Mexico: School of American Research Press, 1996).

Cheetham, Mark A., Kant, Art and Art History: Moments of Discipline. (UK: Cambridge University Press, 2001.

Chicago, Judy, The Dinner Party: A Symbol of our Heritage. NY: Anchor Press, 1979.

Chicago, Judy, "The Dinner Party" Layers of Meaning Journal (2007).

http://layersofmeaning.org/wp/?p=119

Clark, Kenneth, A Introduction to Rembrandt. (London: John Murray Publishers Inc. 1978).

Clegg, Jerry S., On Genius: Affirmation and Denial from Schopenhauer to Wittgenstein (New York: Peter Laing 1994).

Cohen, Ted and Guyer, Paul, (editors. and introduction) Essays in Kant's Aesthetics. (Chicago: The University of Chicago Press:1982).

Crowther, Paul, "Defining Art, Defending the Canon, Contesting Culture" British Journal of Aesthetics 44:4 (2004: 361-377).

Crowther, Paul, "The Containment of Memory: Duchamp, Fahrenholz, and the Box in Shave" The Contemporary Sublime: Sensibilities of Transcendence and Shock. Crowther, Paul (editor), UK: Art & Design VCH Publisher Ltd., 1995.

Crowther, Paul, The Kantian Sublime: From Morality to Art. Oxford, UK: Clarendon Press, 1989.

Crowther, Paul, The Language of Twentieth-Century Art: A Conceptual History. (New Haven: Yale University Press, 1997).

Crowther, Paul, "The Postmodern Sublime: Installation and Assemblage Art" The Contemporary Sublime: Sensibilities of Transcendence and Shock. (UK: Academy Group Ltd: 1995).

Eagleton, Terry, The Idea of Culture. (Oxford. UK: Blackwell Publishers Inc., 2000).

Eisner, Elliot W., "Evaluating the Teaching of Art" The Educational Imagination: On the Design and Evaluation of School Programs 3rd Edition. Boughton, Doug and Eisner, Elliot W. (editors) (New York: MacMillan College Publishing Company, 1994).

Eisner, Elliott W., The Enlightened Eye: Qualitative Inquiry and the Enhancement of Educational Practice. (New Jersey: Prentice-Hall Inc., 1998).

Eisner, Elliot W., "What Can Education Learn from the Arts about the Practice of Education?" International Journal of Education and the Arts 5:4 (2004): 1-12.

Elgar, Frank, Van Gogh: A Study of his Life and Work, trans. James Cleugh (New York: Frederick A. Praeger Publishers,1958).

Elliott, R. K., Aesthetics, Imagination and the Unity of Experience. Crowther, Paul (editor), (UK: Ashgate Publishing Limited, 2006)

Fish, Stanley, "Postmodern Warfare: The Ignorance of our Warrior Intellectuals" Harper's Magazine (2002).

Foucault, Michel, Aesthetics, Method, and Epistemology, Volume Two. (New York: The New Press, 1998).

Gardner, Louise, Gardner's Art through the Ages, seventh edition. (New York: Harcourt Brace Jonanovich, Inc. 1980).

Gilmour, John C., Fire on the earth: Anselm Kiefer and the Post-modern World. (Philadelphia; Temple University Press, 1990).

Greene, Maxine, "Art Works in Schools", in The Symbolic Order: A Contemporary Reader on the Arts Debate, ed. Peter Abbs (London, New York, Philadelphia: The Falmer Press, 1989).

Greene, Maxine, Releasing the Imagination: Essays on Education, The Arts and Social Change. (San Francisco, CA: Jossey-Bass Inc. Publishers, 2000).

Guyer, Paul, Kant and the Experience of Freedom: Essays on Aesthetics and Morality. (Cambridge, New York: Cambridge University Press: 1993).

Guyer, Paul, "Taste and autonomy" Routledge Encyclopedia of Philosophy (2007).

http://www.rep.routledge.com/article/DB047SECT12

Guyer, Paul, "The Difficulty of the Sublime" Histories of the Sublime. Brussels, (BE: Koninklijke Vlaamse Academie van Belgie voor Weten-schappen en Kunsten, 2005).

Harding, Rosamond E., An Anatomy of Inspiration (New York: Barnes & Noble, Inc. 1967).

Heidegger, Martin, Being and Time, trans. John Macquarrie and Edward Robinson (New York: Harper & Row, Publishers, 1961).

Heidegger, Martin, Existence and Being, intro. and analysis Werner Brock (Chicago: Henry Regnery Company, 1967).

Heidegger, Martin, Kant and the Problem of Metaphysics, 4th edition. Taft, Richard (translator) (Bloomington: Indiana University Press, 1973).

Heidegger, Martin, On Time and Being, intro. and trans. Joan Stambaugh (New York, Evanston, San Francisco, London: Harper & Row, Publishers, 1972).

Heidegger, Martin, Poetry, Language, Thought, intro. and trans. Albert Hofstadlter (New York, Evanston, San Francisco, London: Harper & Row, Publishers, 1971).

Heidegger, Martin, "The Original of the Work of Art" Poetry, Language, Thought Hofstadter, Albert (translator and introduction) New York: Harper & Row Publishers, 1971.

Heidegger, Martin, The Question of Being, intro. and trans. William Kluback and Jean T. Wilde (New York: Twayne Publishers, 1958).

Heinich, Nathalie, The Glory of van Gogh: An Anthropology of Admiration, Paul Leduc Browne (translator) (New Jersey, West Sussex: Princeton University Press , 1996).

Hinz, Renate, ed., Kathe Kollwitz: Graphics Posters Drawings_(New York: Pantheon Books,1981).

Hofstadlter, Albert, "Introduction", in Poetry, Language, Thought, Martin Heidegger (New York, Evanston, San Francisco, London: Harper & Row, Publishers, 1971).

Hooker, Richard, "Sublimity as Process: Hegel, Newman and Shave" The Contemporary Sublime: Sensibilities of Transcendence and Shock. Crowther, Paul (editor) (UK Art & Design, VCH Publisher Ltd., 1995).

Ishtar, Wikipedia, the free encyclopedia (2007).

http://en.wikipedia.org/wiki/Ishtar

Jaspers, Karl, Kant. Arendt, Hannah (editor) Manheim, Ralph (translator) (New York: Harcourt, Brace & World, Inc.: 1957).

Kandinsky, Wassily, Concerning the Spiritual in Art. Sadler, M. T. H. (editor and translator) (New York: Dover Publications, Inc., 1977).

Kant, Immanuel, Critique of Judgment. Bernard, J.H. (translator. and introduction) (New York Collier MacMillan Publishers: 1951, second edition 1974).

Kant, Immanuel, Critique of Pure Reason. Kemp Smith, Norman (translator) Caygill, Howard (introduction) (New York: Palgrave MacMillan, 2003).

Kant, Immanuel, Observations on the Feeling of the Beautiful and Sublime. Goldthwait, John T. (translator) (Berkeley, CA: University of California) Press, 1960.

Kant, Immanuel, Critique of the Power of Judgment. Guyer, Paul and Matthews, Eric (editors) (Cambridge, UK: Cambridge University Press: 2000).

Kearns, Martha, Kathe Kollwitz: Woman and Artist (New York: The Feminist Press, 1976).

Klee, Paul, The Diaries of Paul Klee, 1898-1918. Klee, Felix (editor and introduction) (Berkeley, CA: University of California Press, 1964).

Kockelmans, Joseph J., Heidegger on Art and Art Works_(Dordrecht, Boston, Lancaster: Martinus Nijhoff Publishers, 1985).

Koestler, Arthur, The Act of Creation (London: The Danube Edition, Hutchinson, 1976).

Kollwitz, Hans, ed., The Diary and Letters of Kaethe Kollwitz (Evanston, Illinois: Northwestern University Press, 1988).

Krauss, Andre, Vincent van Gogh: Studies in the Social Aspects of his Work (Goteborg, Sweden: Acta Universitatis Gothoburgensis, 1983).

Kunitz, Daniel, "The Art of the Familiar: Literalism and Relevance in Contemporary Art" Harper's Magazine (2002).

Kuspit, Donald, "Concerning the Spiritual in Contemporary Art" The Spiritual in Art Abstract Painting 1890-1985. Tuchman, Maurice and Freeman, Judi (editors and introduction) (New York: Abbeville Press Publishers 1986).

Langer, Susanne K., Feeling and Form: A Theory of Art (New York: Charles Scribner's Sons, 1953).

Lingis, Alphonso, "The Body Postured and Dissolute" in Merleau-Ponty: Difference, Materiality, Painting, ed. Veronique M. Foti (New Jersey: Humanities Press, 1996).

Lippard, Lucy R., "Kollwitz: Chiaroscuro", in Kathe Kollwitz: Graphics Posters Drawings, ed. Renate Hinz (New York: Pantheon Books, 1981).

Lopez-Pedraza, Rafael, Anselm Kiefer: The Psychology of "After the Catastrophe" (New York: George Braziller, 1996).

Lopez-Pedraza, Rafael, Kiefer: a Call to Memory (New York: Art News Vol. 86, No. 8. 1987)(.

Lyas, Colin, Aesthetics. (London, UK: University College London (UCL) Press, 1997).

Lyotard, Jean-Francois, "Answering the Question: What Is Postmodernism?"The Postmodern Condition: A Report on Knowledge. Bennington, Geoff and Massumi, Brian (translators) Jameson, Fredric (foreword) (Minneapolis: University of Minnesota Press, 2002).

McGrath, Melanie, "Something's Wrong" Tate Magazine (2002).

McMahon, Cliff, "The Sublime is How: Philip Taaf and Will Barnet" The Contemporary Sublime: Sensibilities of Transcendence and Shock, Crowther, Paul (editor) (UK: Art & Design, VCH Publisher Ltd., 1995).

Merleau-Ponty, Maurice, The Visible and Invisible, ed. Claude Lefort, trans. Alphonso Lingis, (Evanston: Northwestern University Press, 1968).

Moore, Leslie E., Beautiful Sublime: The Making of Paradise Lost, 1701-1734 (Stanford, CA: Stanford University Press, 1990).

Murdoch, Iris, The Fire & the Sun: Why Plato Banished the Artists (UK: Oxford University Press, 1977).

Nagel, Otto, Kathe Kollwitz_ (Greenwich, Connecticut: (New York Graphic Society Ltd., 1963).

Newman, Barnett, "The Sublime is Now" Tiger's Eye (December, 1948).

Oblak, Mojca, "Kant and Malevich: The Possibility of the Sublime Shave" The Contemporary Sublime: Sensibilities of Transcendence and Shock Crowther, Paul (editor) (UK: Art & Design, VCH Publisher Ltd., 1995).

Ochse, R., Before the Gates of Excellence: The Determinants of Creative Genius (New York: Cambridge University Press, 1990).

Olsen, Sanne Kofod, "Waiter, There's a Woman in my Soup! On Feminist Art and the History and Distribution of Art in Denmark".

http://www.artnode.dk/inserts/text/kofod/main.html

Pach, Walter, Vincent van Gogh 1853 - 1890: A Study of the Artist and his Work in Relation to his Times_(New York: Books for Li

Plato, The Republic 2nd ed. trans. and intro. Desmond Lee (Middlesex UK: Penguin Classics, 1974).

Pletsch, Carl, Young Nietzsche: Becoming a Genius_(New York: The Free Press, 1991).

Poiesis Wikipedia, the free encyclopedia.

http://en.wikipedia.org/wiki/Poiesis

Prelinger, Elizabeth, Kathe Kollwitz (New Haven, London: National Gallery of Art, Washington, Yale University Press, 1992).

Read, Herbert, "Pablo Picasso" The Philosophy of Modern Art. (New York: Meridian Books Inc.1953, eighth printing, 1960).

Richmond, Stuart, "Art Education as Aesthetic Education: A Response to Globalization" Canadian Review of Art Education 29:1 (2002.

Richmond, Stuart, "In Praise of Practice: A Defense of Art Making in Education" Journal of Aesthetic Education 32:2 (1998).

Richmond, Stuart, "Liberalism, Multiculturalism, and Art Education" Journal of Aesthetic Education 29:3 (1995).

Richmond, Stuart, "Once Again, Art Education, Politics, and the Aesthetic Perspective" Reason and Values: New Essays in Philosophy of Education. Portelli, John P. and Bailin, Sharon (editors) (Calgary: Detselig Enterprises Ltd., 1993).

Richmond, Stuart, "Remembering Beauty: Reflections on Kant and Cartier-Bresson for Aspiring Photographers" Journal of Aesthetic Education 38:1 (2004).

Rosenthal, Mark, Anselm Kiefer. (New York: Neues Publishing Company, 1987).

Pillow, Kirk, Sublime Understanding: Aesthetic Reflection in Kant and Hegel. (Cambridge, London: The MIT Press, 2000).

Schapiro, Meyer, Vincent van Gogh (New York: Harry N. Abrams, Inc. Publishers, 1952).

Sheiner, Marcy, Review Sexual Politics: Judy Chicago's Dinner Party in Feminist Art History. (CA: University of California Press, 1997).

http://marcysheiner.tripod.com/DinnerParty.htm

Silverman, Hugh J. (editor and introduction), Lyotard: Philosophy, Politics and the Sublime. (New York, London: Routledge, 2002).

Silverman, Hugh J., "Traces of the Sublime: Visibility, Expressivity, and Unconscious" Merleau-Ponty: Difference, Materiality, Painting.. Foti, Veronique M. (editor) (New Jersey: Humanities Press, 1996).

Schopenhauer, Arthur, The World as Will and Representation, Volume 1. Payne, E.F.J. (translator) (New York: Dover Publications, Inc., 1958).

Slatkin, Wendy, Women Artists in History: From Antiquity to the Present 3rd ed. (New Jersey: Prentice Hall, 1997).

Steiner, Wendy, Venus in Exile: The Rejection of Beauty in Twentieth-Century Art (New York: The Free Press, 2001).

Taylor, Charles, The Malaise of Modernity. (Toronto: House of Anansi Press, 1991).

Tuchman, Maurice and Freeman, Judi (editors), The Spiritual in Art: Abstract Painting 1890-1985. (LA: Abbeville Press Publishers, 1987).

The Dinner Party, Wikipedia, the free encyclopedia.

http://en.wikipedia.org/wiki/The_Dinner_Party

van de Val, Renee, "Silent Visions: Lyotard on the Sublime" The Contemporary Sublime: Sensibilities of Transcendence and Shock. Crowther, Paul (editor) (UK: Art & Design, VCH Publisher Ltd., 1995).

van de Windt, Gerda, Artistic Creativity: Transforming Sorrow into Beauty, Truth and Art_. (Vancouver: Simon Fraser University, 2004).

van de Windt, Gerda, Artistic Creativity: Is Originality Possible and Why is this Important to Education? (Vancouver: Simon Fraser University, 2002).

van de Windt, Gerda, "Imagination: The Essential Element in Creativity and Arts Education" Adventures in Creativity (2003).

http://www.adventuresincreativity.net/IMAGINATION%20van%20de%20%20Windt.html

van de Windt, Gerda, Kant's Theory of Imagination (Vancouver: Simon Fraser University, 2006).

Vandenabeele, Bart, "Schopenhauer, Nietzsche, and the Aesthetically Sublime" Journal of Aesthetic Education 37:1 (2003).

Vandenabeele, Bart, "The Feeling of the Sublime: Aesthetic not Ethical: Comment on Paul Guyer, The Difficulty of the Sublime" Histories of the Sublime (Brussels, BE: Koninklijke Vlaamse Academie van Belgie voor Wetenschappen Kunsten, 2005).

Vaughan, William, William Blake (New York: Park South Books 1985).

von Schiller, Friedrich, On the Sublime. Elias, Julius A. (translator and introduction) (New York: Frederick Ungar Publishing Co., 1966).

Wallace, Robert, The World of Rembrandt: 1606-1669 (Alexandria, Virginia: Time-Life Books, 1969).

Wallace, Robert, The World of van Gogh: 1853-1890 (New York: Time-Life Books, 1969).

Warnock, Mary, Imagination & Time (Oxford: Blackwell Publishers, 1994).

Weiskel, Thomas, The Romantic Sublime: Studies in the Structure and Psychology f Transcendence. (Baltimore: The Johns Hopkins University Press, 1976).

Whitehead, John W., "Women and Art: An interview with Judy Chicago" (1999).

http://www.gadflyonline.com/archive/NovDec99/archive-judychicago.html

Wilhelm, Richard, The I Ching or Book of Changes. Baynes, Cary F. (translator) Jung, C.G. (foreword) (New York: Princeton University Press, 1950).

Wittgenstein, Ludwig, Tractatus Logico-Philosophicus.. Pears, D.F. and McGuinness, B. F. (translators) Russell Bertrand (introduction) (London: Routledge Kegal Paul, 1974).

Wollheim, Richard, Art and It's Objects. (Middlesex, UK: Penguin Books Ltd., 1978).

Wollheim, Richard, "Hans Hofmann: The Final Years" Modern Painters 2:2 (1988).

Wright, Christopher, Rembrandt: Self-portraits (London: Gordon Fraser, 1982).

Young, Julian, Heidegger's Philosophy of Art (UK: Cambridge University Press,

Young, Julian, "Death and Transfiguration: Kant, Schopenhauer and Heidegger on the Sublime" Inquiry 48:2 (2005).